The Beaver Show

Jacqueline Frances

For Danielle

Names have been changed.
Everyone needs an alias sometimes.

Getting to know me

I love my hair, my dancing ability, and how I travel so often. I also like that I am Canadian. I also like that I have a dog to play with all the time

My dad dad says when I was a baby I was climbing and had a huge grin on my face.

My proudest moment was probably when I was 4 and I did my first dance recital and I had a nice costume and I danced infront of lots of people.

Grade 5, September 1998

9

The Nice Costume, 1990

I slide my credit card across the counter to pay for our two slices of pizza.

"Do you have another card, Miss? This one's been declined."

Fuck this. I'm going to be a stripper.

Flashing My Gash for Cash

"Just stand there for a minute, will ya, love? I just wanna *lookatcha*."

I'm in a hot pink g-string. A black pleather push-up bra squishes my boobs together, while a red elastic garter grips my thigh. My 'dress' is a two-panelled black tube of Lycra that hugs my ass while just barely clinging to my tits. This, I'm told by the salesgirl at High Heels, is a money-making outfit.

I feel cheap.

I'm standing on a black-tiled podium that's surrounded by mirrors. It is my stage. Jim sits across from me on a red vinyl couch. I told him my name is Iris.

I became Iris 20 minutes ago. Iris is my mask; Iris makes this all okay. Iris makes this not real. Iris is without doubt, hesitation, problems, cellulite or a boyfriend. She is your dream girl for hire, at increments of $90 every 15 minutes.

I chose Iris because I thought it sounded sophisticated. This will turn out to be a huge mistake in terms of fantasy girl marketing—apparently granny names aren't sexy. But I have nothing to lose and everything to gain in terms of learning how to appeal to the Every Man, Ever Horny. Plus, I've already introduced myself as Iris to this sturdy, middle-aged man. So let's just stick to the "Iris" alibi for the rest of this interaction, where I am expected to undress and exist in front a perfect stranger.

I grew up on Britney Spears and Christina Aguilera, so I feel like I have a pretty solid understanding of what is required of me as an entertainer. Hip undulations, panting rib isolations … hair flips. Lots of hair flips. Considering I have a pixie cut, I've planned to improvise by hiding my sultry eyes behind my wispy platinum bangs, and then flipping them away. You know, like Leonardo DiCaprio in his heyday. Or like the lesbian[1] I try really hard to be when I go to my least favourite place in the entire world: Ladies' Night at Sydney's local gay bar.

But all the planning I put into my stripper debut routine goes straight out the goddamn window when Jim asks me to *just stand here for a minute.*

So I'm standing. I shift my weight to the left, casually pointing my right foot toward my audience of one. I pinch my shoulder blades together, raising my chin high. I try to look comfortable, natural and sexy … until it becomes clear that I am standing like my Miss Teen Caledon[2] self in a Sears catalog.
In an effort to look less pageant-y and more fucky-fucky, I lower my chin. I don't know where to look. Scanning the couch, the maroon-shellacked walls, the transparent, metallic curtain, I settle my gaze on his splotchy red face—because he's not

---

[1] I hate the word 'lesbian.' In the English language, it's used as a noun, while 'gay' is a mere adjective. 'Gay' is an afterthought when describing a person: old, green, rich, blonde, bland ... GAY! *Lez...bi...an...* is a fucking designation, like a leper or a criminal or a pot roast. A type of person rather than a quality attributed to them. With each syllable, I feel like I'm being confined into a tiny triangle to be distinguished as something 'other,' to be observed from behind glass. In my research, the general consensus is that all women of the Sapphic persuasion hate the term 'lesbian,' and that most of us prefer just about ANY other designation. I've compiled a list of nouns that can stand in the place of 'lesbian' to which you are encouraged to refer if the word 'gay' is just not weighty enough for you: rug-muncher, bean-flicker, dyke, queer, gayelle, ladyfag, lady-lover, thoughtful-good-listener-but-crazy-ass-bitch, scissor-sister, U-Hauler, muff-diver, woman, sentient being.
[2] At the time of writing this, the only Google result when typing my full name into the search engine is that I held the title of Miss Teen Caledon in 2003. I wore a tiara, a sash, was interviewed by the Pennysaver and campaigned for 'global unity.'

looking at mine. His mouth is agape. I'm not sure whether to be flattered or if he's just one of those open-mouthed breathers I used to dread sitting beside in the library.

I try to quash my trembling fears with superficial, aesthetic judgments about the stranger in front of me, but my efforts are subverted by the fact that I'm trying really hard not to shit my g-string before I get paid for this absurd interaction. When I'm nervous, my bowels tend to empty themselves with remarkable ease. Usually this is a great solution to constipation: just do some public speaking, or smuggle some narcotics past men in uniforms, and unplug that colon! Right now, though, standing half naked in front of a man who has not confirmed himself a scat fetishist, is not a good time to shit myself.

Jim's eyes wander about my frame as though he were in an art gallery. A light year passes before he asks me to take off my dress. I pull at the tie behind my neck, and the panels of Lycra fall to my ankles. Now I'm wearing the bra, in addition to a pair of bikini bottoms, beneath which lies a g-string. My rationale behind wearing all of these layers was that the tease is the exciting part.

STRIPPER TIP #1: Less is always, ALWAYS MORE.

"Just take all of it off in one go, will ya?" Jim asks, his voice a flat and steady trance.

I'm about to show my fun bags and vagina to a total stranger. An old, fat Australian stranger.

I turn to face away from him, because that's what you do when you undress in front of just about anyone. I unhook my bra, and slip off both pairs of panties. While I'm bending over to slip them from around my ankles and over my brand new plastic platforms, Jim stops me before I can straighten up again.

"STAY THERE."

STRIPPER TIP #2: NEVER TURN YOUR BACK ON YOUR AUDIENCE.

I pause, folded in half, my bare ass a foot or two away from

Jim's unblinking eyes.

"Here?" I ask, incredulous.

He's staring at my vagina. Oh my god, he's staring at my vagina. I hope he can't smell anything. Oh my god, it probably looks so weird from this angle.

"Just there, yeah, love." His tone is a firm whisper. His Dungarees and dirty button-down have me pegging him as an agricultural engineer. You know, like a sheep herder or a horse whisperer. I settle on horse whisperer because I'm romantic but only when it comes to stories of human-animal companionship.

I'm worried I'm going to tumble over in my platforms. I latch a firm grip on my ankles to stabilize my frame, which is in an impressive jackknife. In an effort to keep my balance and calm the fuck down, I entertain the idea of what a gorgeous privilege it might be to whisper to wild horses on the plains of Mongolia. Or on Walkabout. I consider peeking through my knees at his face, but I'm too embarrassed. Instead, I look at his studious expression in the mirror.

"It's the most beautiful thing in the wooooooorld," Jim says with a sigh. He leans in closer. I contemplate snapping up from this precarious forward bend, shielding my bits from these predatory eyes, but I just can't. I need to get paid; I must tell this story, and I also admittedly wouldn't mind hearing more about why my vagina is the most beautiful thing in the entire world.

Breathe in, "Iris."
Breathe out.

I consider the possibility that my vag is the most beautiful thing in the world. I have personally found it rather funny looking, perpetually petrified that it smelled 'off.' But Jim here says it's the most beautiful thing in the world, and my vanity likes to give people the benefit of the doubt.

"Will ya get on your knees? And stay bent over?"

I can see from my reflection that Jim is staring at my cunt with the concentration of a boat-in-a-bottle builder.

Oh god. Now I'm going to have to bend so he'll have a clear view of my asshole, too.

I've never been particularly asshole-confident. Is anyone? I may or may not have perused several online dating profiles and no one has made clear that their most favourite feature (eyes? smile? collarbone? tramp stamp?) is their anus.

But now is not the time to weigh out who would be better suited for Jim's most recent request. I am here because he chose me, and he wants to see me on all fours. I must now serve up my asshole—and accompanying mole—with confidence, panache, and maybe a bit of passivity.

I get onto my knees and bend over, my forearms pressing onto the freezing tiles, which send goosebumps down my arms and probably over my ass too. I am frozen.

Please don't fart. Please don't fart. Oh please god, don't let me fart in this guy's face.

In the months to come, I will become highly skilled at refraining from farting when putting my body into positions that are emotionally harrowing and also biologically conducive to relieving flatulence.

"Whoooooaaaaaaaa" he says, leaning in, six inches from my cornhole.

At this point I am focusing on harnessing all of the energy of the universe to keep myself from blowing gas in the face of a man who whispers to horses and has deemed my vagina the eighth wonder of world.

"I can see a little bit of moisture," he observes.

At this point, the WASP in me reaches to clutch her proverbial pearls. Blood rushes to my quickly reddening face, confirming that I am most definitely embarrassed. I certainly don't have the composure to identify whether I am turned on—as Jim suggests—or just sweating bullets of vagina anxiety.

I look into the mirror in front of me to see if Jim has suddenly pulled a magnifying glass from his pocket. He hasn't. He is just very intent on looking very closely at every single one of my feminine folds.

I was blessed with a very sweet and very dumb First Boyfriend who was generous enough to go down on me twice in our two-year relationship. I, on the other hand, blew the shit out of his teenaged dick. You could say I've always been an explorer. It's not that his reluctance to go downtown was mean-spirited; he was probably just scared and clueless. At first, second, and maybe even third glance, the vagina can seem like pretty daunting terrain for a boy who's been tugging on his junk for the past five years. Basically, what I'm saying is that no amount of money could ever make me jump into a time machine that would transport me back to my 16th year—a boy scared and a girl forever scarred. Perhaps this can help explain why one might think their vagina smells like a six-month-old Wonderbread, mustard and bologna sandwich, when someone with whom you're retardedly in love doesn't want to go near it. Little did I know eating pussy is a fucking TREAT compared with even the most loving and valiant efforts at deep-throating.

So I don't really give blowjobs anymore.

But First Boyfriend liked snowboarding, never pressured me into anything, and his totally sweet and fashionable mom may or may not have gifted me my first and only pair of vintage Versace lace pants that I still wear every now and again. We take the good with the bad. And thank fuck my teenage years are over and that my new friend Jim thinks my pussy is the neatest thing since sliced bread.

Years of pussy-shame conditioning are beginning to unravel as I kowtow on this cheesy podium, ass up, trying to understand if I'm actually enjoying myself or not. I may or may not be losing feeling in my feet, but the adrenaline of being "wrong," being sexy, making money, and just fucking existing makes it hard to connect whatever physical sensations I might actually be feeling in relation to my mind being blown to the goddamn milky way of pussy power.

I decide to not say anything regarding the alleged moisture down there, because really what the fuck does anyone ever say in a situation like this? I'm not yet seasoned enough yet to say, "Yeah, baby … I'm a goddamn Slip 'N Slide for your colossal wiener … how bout a little pre$ent for being such a wet girl?" (this will happen later).

My gaze is still fixed on Jim's reflection. His nose is a few inches away from everything Teddy Ruxpin[3] told me specifically not to show to strange old men. He closes his eyes, swaying his head to and fro as if he's smelling a pot of his mother's homemade secret-recipe spaghetti sauce.

A sturdy woman with fake tits and business-casual attire parts the curtain, poking her head into our booth.

"I'm sorry, sir, but your time with Iris is up. Would you care to extend?"

"No, thank you," he replies, standing up.

"Thank you so much Iris," Jim says, nodding his head and leaving the room.

I slip onto my side, butt cheeks kissing the cold tile. My knees are white. My thighs tingle.

I just made $50 for flashing my gash.

*

I slip my kit back on in a hurry. Years of backstage quick-changes at dance competitions and recitals have gifted me with a remarkable competency to put on tiny and sequined costumes in a very short amount of time. Strutting through a maze of booths,

---

[3] Teddy Ruxpin: an animatronic children's toy, in the form of a talking bear. The bear would move his mouth and eyes while "reading" stories that were played on an audiotape cassette deck built into his back. A TV series was later created where Ruxpin would go on adventures. At the end of every episode, Teddy would make a PSA. The one I most vividly remember was when Shannen Doherty guest-starred and accompanied Teddy in telling viewers not to let people you don't know touch parts of your body that are covered by your bathing suit.

gossamer curtains, and mystery girls, I tie the bow of my halter behind my neck. My stride is wide as I make for the main room. Is this what heroin addicts feel after their first high? Empowered? Hooked? Hungry?

Determined.

I'm ready for my next 50 bucks.
But the main room is practically empty. Jim is nowhere to be seen. Was he even real? The only people in the room are an old man and another dancer, sitting in the corner. They nibble at what appears to be a cheese plate. She smiles, carefully scraping a sliver of blue cheese onto a cracker. From across the room I can see the precision with which she holds the knife and cracker using her hot pink, acrylic nails. Beautiful and effortless. As though dancing Swan Lake in slow motion, the dancer lifts the cracker to his open and smiling mouth. He looks like a baby: fat, happily coddled, and pink in the cheeks.
In spite of the fact that I was raised to understand that it is rude to stare, especially at an intimate moment between two strangers, it's impossible to look away. Everything anyone does in this space is performance art.

I look down at my watch. It's 10 minutes before 7 o'clock. It being my first day, I arrived 45 minutes early for my 'orientation and tour,' which consisted of a very small man telling me, "Don't get too drunk; don't get too high. Got it?"

So I hopped on the tail end of the day-girl shift, I've already had the most insane experience of my life, and my shift hasn't even officially started yet.

Perhaps Jim was just my luck: My fairy-godmother-in-bogan[4]'s-clothing, offering up a quiet and quick initiation into the world of vagina dollars in the calm before the storm. It's Saturday night and I'm pumped to make more money. But this is show business: hurry up and wait.

I try to push through a door marked "Employees Only," only the

---

[4] Bogan: An Australian redneck.

door won't open all the way. I peek my head in to discover there is a bare ass in the way. The ass is in the process of being slathered with tinted moisturizer by a small pair of nimble hands with a French manicure. The ass moves just enough so that I can slide myself through the jamb.

I whisper "sorry, excuse me," to no one in particular as I weave between bodies. Try as I might, my Canadian politeness and unrelenting apologies cannot be shaken.

The dressing room is a place to hide, to gossip, to dry-shave and apply concealer to your butt cheeks, face, and any other place on your person where you can develop a bruise, pimple, or ingrown hair. It is perpetually overcrowded with hair straighteners, designer handbags, and women in all phases of undress.

Showtime is in T minus ten minutes. If you're late, it will cost you. This is the dressing room's frenzied peak hour.

A dozen women crowd in front of the mirror lining the longest wall in this room that I can only assume by its size and narrowness is a repurposed broom closet. No one is talking. Everyone is just staring at themselves in the mirror, brushing on war paint or wrapping their hair around a steaming curling iron. Quickly and calmly, they transform themselves into fantasy girls.

They all just seem so... normal. And young. Fresh-faced. Bored, but composed. I was anticipating a herd of Playboy Bunnies, but in front of me are just a bunch of girls like me, putting on costumes and getting into character. At first I feel I should be disappointed, but instead I just feel like I am more at home than I've ever been.

Never in my life have I ever known a stripper. Strippers are ubiquitous in pop culture, but only ever in this tragic, two-dimensional way. So the act of becoming one is surreal. Growing up in the upper-middle class, going to university to become a journalist or some shit, you just don't ever imagine any of your peers doing anything but working for a fortysomething boss with an 'innovative business model' where there is a Nerf basketball hoop in the lunch room. Sex work wasn't an option outlined in my guidance counsellor's office wall of career pamphlets.

It's a class thing. Middle-class girls with degrees don't become strippers. If anything, they take on a safety career as a dental hygienist, and marry up to the dentist.

But I am here, doing something that I only thought less-fortunate, single moms with no college education were doing because it was all they could do to support their families without working 80-hour work weeks. I want to be here, because I've always been a shameless exhibitionist[5], but also because I can't pay my rent or afford to eat anything but oatmeal in this new city I thought I'd try living in, on the other side of the goddamn world.

Where are the crack whores? Where are the cesarean scars? Where are the triple-D boob jobs? All of these chicks are here to work. Unless you're a Middleton, everybody works.

I'm just sort of staring at everyone. I reach for my bag, which is now buried under several other bags. I plunge into an abyss of backpacks, leathers, and gym bags and fish out my trusty Jansport. I start rummaging through it, looking for nothing in particular. I'm just trying to look busy. Always look busy, I'll learn. No one wants what's readily available. What a thrill to learn that high-school economics lessons of supply and demand are finally proving themselves useful.

"Are you American?"

I look up, and see a poster woman for the curvy-and-impeccably-toned brunette looking at me through an eyelash curler. She's wearing what appear to have once been a pair of Abercrombie jeans, and a raggedy t-shirt.

"Canadian."

---

[5] My brand of exhibitionism: getting changed with the blinds deliberately drawn open, electing to not wear pants to class, pranking friends by getting naked when they weren't looking, and subsequently asking them "Is this yours?" They would then look over, see my bare ass, tits, or both, and squint uncomfortably.

"Cool! I'm from Hawaii," she says as she slips out of her tattered jeans and into a pair of pink and black polka-dot panties and a black bustier. "You new?"

"First day ever."

"No shit!" She assesses her artistry: mascara on the top lashes, and a hint of bronzer (not that she needs it; her tan is perfect and mystifyingly authentic). She presses her lips together to even out a wine-tinted lip gloss. She, too, does not at all look like what I thought a stripper would. She looks like a pretty girl. A Real Girl. She pulls her hair out of its ponytail and gives it a flip. Perfect waves. "You'll be fine," she says, as she drops her mascara into a pencil case.

She slips on a garter and into her heels. Walking past me, she's out the door. I hesitate, and end up following her into the main room, where she takes a seat at one of the tables by the stage.

I want to ask her what she's doing here. I want to know what EVERYONE is doing here. But I'm already realizing that asking that question makes you kind of an asshole, so instead I ask, "How long have you been here?"

"A year?" She sounds unsure of her answer.

Over time I will learn that answering a question with a question is common parlance for strippers. Is it because it's a lie? Because we lie so often we forget what the truth is? Or because every day or night sort of looks the same when the lighting suggests that it's always 11 p.m. on a Saturday night? After all, being perpetually elusive about oneself is a main tenant of the archetype of the Beautiful Young Mystery Girl. Plus, no one really likes to admit that they are anything but fresh meat. Especially in this business.

Her name is Tommie. Tommie loves to surf and thinks other jobs just don't pay enough for the amount of time it takes away from her wave-riding. She is the most beautiful, hilarious, and feminine tomboy I have ever met in my life.

"Ugh, I just hated college in Michigan. Everyone there wears Ugg boots, but for the wrong fucking reasons. Ugg boots are for surfers. They don't actually keep your feet warm when it's below freezing … Anyway, this is the good life."

Tommie's eyes fix upon something behind me. Immediately, they sparkle. She gets up quickly, walking over to an old yet strikingly handsome man in a custom-tailored suit. Her hips sway, her arms are outstretched. When a stripper sees gold, her eyes shine like diamonds and nothing can get in her way of claiming it.

Gradually, the seats fill with customers. A good-looking thirtysomething with a smug grin wants to go for a dance, but "not just yet." A white-haired man in a sweater vest is keen to tip the girls on stage, "but no private shows for me, love … a pensioner's gotta enjoy the simple pleasures." A team of accounting colleagues just wants to buy me a drink. Contrary to a common assumption about establishments like this, girls don't make any money off liquor sales at this club. There doesn't seem to be much else going on, so I oblige.

"So where ya from, love?" the suit beside me asks. He smiles like a jerk: goofy and entitled.

"Canada," I say with a smile.

"Oh, it's cold there!" This is all anyone in Australia will ever have to say about Canada. They will follow up with an embarrassing misuse of "eh," and then they will ask how I like " 'Straya."

But this is day one. These questions are lame, and I'm not yet rehearsed enough with quippy comebacks to entice them to open their wallets at every turn of phrase. I'm nervous, but smiling through it.

My drink arrives and I down the vodka soda with unprecedented ease.

"Slow, down, Sheila! We wanna hang out with ya for more than 40 seconds!"

Before I can make up an excuse for why I'm "just so *parched*," there's a tap on my shoulder, followed by a firm whisper: "IRIS,

I've been calling you on stage."

Iris, right, Iris. You're *Iris.* I remind myself.

I excuse myself from the fraternizing suits and make for the stage. I bring my nearly empty drink with me. It feels rude, but I'd rather be rude than dumb enough to leave a drink unattended.

I've danced on stage before. Hundreds of times. Leisurely, competitively, and professionally. Throughout middle school and high school, I was an overachieving bun-head—the stage is where I've always felt comfortable. I figured out from an early age that an attention-seeking person is really fucking annoying unless she channels her insatiable need for love and accolades in creative, entertaining, and hilarious ways. If we were to forget the money part (but who can, really?), the performative aspect of stripping is why I considered shaking my tits for strangers in the first place. A few years ago, while I was a broke-ass university student, I was seriously considering this same job. Instead, I chickened out and opted to pursue the career of a penniless burlesque diva.

What's different now from my dance-troupe days of flight suits and trophies is that I am wearing obscenely high platforms that are made of plastic. And—assuming I make it through the first two songs without toppling over, shitting my pants, dying of embarrassment, or all of the above—I'm supposed to flaunt my vagina for the entirety of my third three-minute song.

I climb the three steps to the stage and reach for the nearest pole. Clutching it for stability, I smile nervously at my hot-pink-manicured colleague, who has been waiting for me to relieve her of her nudity duty for nearly an entire song. The smile I saw earlier has vanished. STRIPPER TIP #3: NEVER MAKE A STRIPPER WAIT. HER TIME IS MONEY.

Alas, the stage is mine. A techno remix of a shitty top-40 pop song plays. Repressing my Mouseketeer training, I try to look seductive (read: no smiling, ever) as I sway back and forth. I'm at a loss for what to do with my upper extremities. If my hands can't be jazzy, what the hell am I supposed to do with them? I look to the stage opposite me for an answer, which is clearly illustrated by another colleague: fondle your tits.

27

So I fondle them through my bra and dress. My sweaty palms rub the Lycra against the lace of my bra. I realize this move is better done topless.

Clasping my only free hand to the same pole, I make an attempt at a spin. My knees clunk into the pole. Loosening my grip with the pulse of a very inexperienced driver, I slide down in a few jerky motions.
But all these nerves and lack of rehearsed routine don't seem to matter. The men sitting at the tipping rail are waving five- and 10-dollar notes in my direction.

I slowly make my way toward the edge of the stage where a $10 bill has IRIS stamped all over it. A guy happily slips it into my garter belt, nodding in appreciation. And then another one does the same thing!

The shitty song morphs into another shitty song by the volume of track A being lowered as the DJ announces in a voice you might hear at a monster truck rally, or a Chuck E Cheez: "And hello everybody! This is song number two for the sexy Iris."

Song number two? Shit. I'd better start peeling off these six separate articles of 'clothing' if I need to be completely naked for the next one.

I'm trying to shimmy my hips all the while pulling at the various strings, clips, hooks and elastic bands that hold my hoochie ensemble together.

The alternating red and orange lights illuminating the stage and us dancers, are hot. A drop of perspiration slides from my temple, streaking through my rouged cheekbones. It leaves a dark, tear-like trail.

I look back across the room where the other dancer is effortlessly grinding her pelvis a few inches from the pole-phallus. A keen observer continuously slips crisp bills into her garter belt. She isn't at all sweaty. Did she spray her entire body with deodorant?
At a glacier's pace, she moves her hips in a figure eight. She appears to be moving in slow motion. It looks like I'm watching

28

a soft-core sex scene.

STRIPPER TIP #4: However slow you think you're dancing, move SLOWER. You don't have to do much to impress a man at a strip club. You've already done the hardest part: You showed up. A naked woman—in heels, no less—can really do no wrong. Knowing this, and knowing that you have to dance for the next six or seven hours, AND that you have to look good doing it, do not waste one iota of energy trying to dance with reckless abandon. EVERYONE is watching. You can't look like a maniac; you have to look like an expensive and sanctimonious goddess. And dancing in a strip club is nothing like ACTUAL dancing, whether it's ballet, jazz, hip-hop, or that weird and amazing ravey shit you do when you're rolling on MDMA and listening to dubstep. "Dancing" from here on out is to be understood as moving your naked body from one flattering and slutty pose to the next. Like vogue-ing, only S L O W E R, and less creative.

Once again, I remind myself to breathe. I stand still as my dress falls to my ankles. Gripping the pole for stability, I step out of the dress, bend over, and pick it up. This chore is in fact a signature 'dance' move in the business. Bend like Reese Witherspoon in *Legally Blonde*, pick up that g-string or $50 bill, and snap back up.

By some grace of god, I am naked by the time the third song starts pumping and scratching over the speakers.

I take small steps, pressing together my thighs and knees for fear of my heart dropping out of my vagina.

A pinkish, snivelly man comes up to the edge of the stage. He waves a neon piece of laminated paper in my general direction. What he's holding is a Dancer Dollar, or what strippers callously refer to as Funny Money. Each Dancer Dollar is about the size of a $20 note, but worth only $2. They can be purchased using a credit card. The ones who use the Funny Money as a means of tipping are the men who go to the club on their company's expense account. Or if they are too stingy to part with fives or tens. Rather than use their own cash, they can buy Funny Money and on their monthly bill it shows up as "ABC Restaurant," the registered business name of the club. "When did you spend $500 at ABC Restaurant, honey?" oblivious wives everywhere ask. "Oh, just took a few clients out for dinner." On the other hand, accountants of large corporations needn't ask; if you don't use the company card to keep up client relations, then why did we hire you?

I wedge over toward the glowing slip of laminate, smiling, lifting my garter belt.

Pinky is about to slip it beneath the elastic before he snatches it back towards his chest, lifting his chin.

"Come on, now, I wanna see you do a trick!"

It's my first day. Isn't getting up here naked and bopping about enough of a 'trick'? Especially for what amounts to two whole dollars?

I don't get it. I smile, because that's what you do when someone tells you a joke and you don't get it.

I'm embarrassed because I don't know any tricks. I feel unprepared. I feel like I owe him a trick. I feel all of these things because I'm a rookie stripper and it won't take long to learn that entitled assholes abound and they are yearning to be put in their place.

But for now, I have to undergo this humiliating feeling of not being enough for a man; to feel like I have to go above and beyond the call of duty to earn his attention, approval, and laminated money. I haven't been with a man in a long time, or felt this way for one, but it's kind of like riding a bike. It comes back, and it comes back strong.

Fortunately Tommie walks up to Pinky, plucks the dollar out of his hand, and slips it into my garter as she leans her weight into his shoulder.

"Isn't she just *beautiful*?"

Pinky nods. Tommie rests a hand on the back of his neck, which brings Pinky's shoulders to an immediate drop. His shit-eating grin melts into a resplendently longing gaze.

30

Men are that easy. They just need some encouragement and direction.

"This is Iris. She's Canadian!" Tommie uses her other arm to reach for Pinky's forearm. She inches her glossy lips closer to his ear: *"Would you like to watch us take a shower together?"*

A shower show is a special show where a client sits on a couch and stares at a girl through plated glass. She gets sudsy and giggles and wastes water while taking the least effective rinse of her life. She will not get to wash her ass crack, exfoliate her face, scrub under her arms, or shave the tops of her feet. A double shower show is the same, only two girls will be rubbing their sudsy tits together.

I step down from my stage to see that Tommie and Pinky are waiting for me at the bar.

Tommie takes Pinky in one hand, me in the other, and guides us to the front desk.

The business casual woman stands like an ox. She has total dominion over her Funny Money booth and security cameras. She doesn't seem to give a fuck about anything else.

"How long would you like to go with Tommie and Iris?"

Tommie inches between the Ox and Pinky: "It's $280 per girl for a half hour," she says with the biggest salesman smile I have ever seen.

Oh my god. She didn't even offer him the 15-minute option. This girl is a genius.

"And we're so *dirty*... I don't even know that half an hour will even be enough time for us to get clean, right, Canada?"

Tommie raises her eyebrows, glaring at me. *Play along, already. Don't be a dead weight.*

"Yeah, I'm just so dirty and sweaty and gr-"

Subtly, Tommie shakes her head in a panic.

You're not gross, Iris. You're SEXY. Horny. You're a nymphomaniac who will certainly die if she doesn't rub up against any and every body and/or surface in this establishment. Come on.

"I mean, I just really need to get wet already!"

Tommie smiles and nods encouragingly.

Thank fuck, yes. I am not a dead weight.

"Half an hour it is," Pinky says as he slides his American Express over to the Ox.

Pinky takes a seat on the couch while Tommie and I slip out of our shoes. A tiled wall separates the voyeurs and the exhibitionists. We hang our dresses up on the hooks. I am about to take a shower with a hot girl I just met a few hours ago, for which we will each be paid $200.

Tommie reaches into a small bag, pulling out a loofah and miniature shampoo bottle. "Don't worry about getting a yeast infection; it's unscented."

I don't really know what she's talking about, nor do I want to try to figure it out right now. I'm about to perform, and this girl is beautiful, smart and Hawaiian, so, naturally, I trust her.

Tommie lifts the detachable showerhead from its cradle, cranking on the pressure. She waves for me to step in with her. On the opposite side of the glass, Pinky sits in the middle of a couch, knees apart, arms outstretched to his sides. Expectant.

Tommie gives me a wink and shouts through the glass: "Hey, Pinky! Oooh—it's chilly in here!" She sprays me with the showerhead. "Look how hard Canada's nipples are!"

Alright, it's show time. I can do this.

"Ohhhh... Hawaii... I'm just so filthy! It feels sooo good to be... wet!"

32

I feel like an idiot. But the lesson my dance teacher taught me when I was eight is ringing true: If you feel stupid, you're doing it right.

"Look at her TITS, Pinky—don't you just wish you could squeeze them?"

Tommie grabs my tit in her hand and gives it a jiggle. "Damn girl, you have nice tits!" I think she just said that in earnest. It's been hard to tell what is sincere and what isn't since I walked into this place.

"Oh, it's all that maple syrup we drink in Canada that keeps us soooo perky and … sweet?"

Pinky has the stupidest grin on his face. I think I'm getting the hang of this.

"Bend over," Tommie whispers. "Face the wall and show him your ass."

I oblige.

"And would you LOOK at this Canadian bacon, Pinky! I just want to take a bite out of it and have it with my eggs in the morning!"

I feel something cool dripping on the small of my back. I look over my shoulder to see that Tommie is drizzling white goo— the body wash—all over my booty. I can barely see Pinky through the mist, but I can hear an encouraging "yeahhhh," so I'm assuming he is enjoying this trompe l'oeil of cumming all over a girl's ass.

Tommie slathers the loofah over the 'cum' and gets the suds in the relevant places: tits and ass. We repeat the same act again, only now Tommie is the one bent over and we replace the words 'maple syrup' and 'bacon' with 'pineapple' and 'coconut.'

"It looks like Iris is enjoying this more than I am," Pinky offers with a grin.

I blush.

Facing the wall, rump still in the appropriate position for Pinky's viewing pleasure, Tommie yells over her shoulder, "Oh, Canada and Hawaii have always been great allies, baby!"

There is not one comment for which Tommie does not have a clever retort. She is queen of improvisational comedy.

The Ox thrusts her head past the curtain.

"Time's up." It appears the moderate politeness she displayed earlier in the evening has worn thin.

"Oh no! But we were just getting to the naughtier part of the show, Pinky!"

"Yeah," I chime in. "I'm still a dirty girl and need a sudsy spanking from Hawaii!"

Pinky pulls at his slacks, gets up, and lowers his head. "I really shouldn't, girls. But thank you."

Tommie shrugs. "The water was getting cold anyway."

The Ox leaves. Pinky follows.

"You did great," Tommie offers as we dry off and slip back into our g-strings for the umpteenth time this evening. "Always try to nab a shower show," she advises. "You get paid twice as much and you don't have to reprimand them for pawing at you. Everybody wins!"

Tommie is out the door before I am even halfway dressed. It's becoming apparent that, no matter how quick I am at getting dressed, the more pieces of clothing I wear are only costing me time, and therefore money: Less is More.

I walk, I chat, I accept a few more drinks, and before I know it another man wants another moment of my time in private to stare at my bits. By the third private show, the I'm-naked-and-he's-a-stranger factor is completely underwhelming. It's a job. The exciting part is that I'm told it's high-paying and, well, it's naughty and secret.

By the time the DJ's worn-out vocal chords announce last call, I look down to my feet to notice the plastic strap has lacerated the top of my foot. Now that I see the bruising, chafing, and blood, I can finally sense the pain signals shooting to my brain.

The dressing room is once again chock-full of girls, only now they're moving with lethargy rather than grace. I slip into my Real Girl clothes and sling my backpack over my shoulder.

House lights up, we slink into the chairs and wait our turns to get paid. Tommie slumps into a chair beside me.

"How was your night?" she asks.

"It was alright. I did five rooms."

Tommie raises her eyebrows, tired but encouraging. "That's good!" As my career goes on, I will learn that, for a Saturday night, that is not good. Not good at all. But tonight I feel like a champ.

"When are you working next?" I ask her.

"Oh, this is my last night. I start training to be a flight attendant back in the States next week."

The potential for a friend vanishes; she's gone before I can even get her real name. This is how it will almost always be in this business.

The Ox pays me. After a bunch of house fees that don't seem to make sense, including a towel rental and DJ tip-out, I end up with $324.

Slumping into a cab, I watch the drunk kids on the sidewalk flail for taxis, tripping over their own feet. *They probably just spent $324 tonight.*

I go home and recount my earnings. Then I count them again. Suddenly, I'm not at all tired anymore. I'm buzzing.

SOMETIMES I REALLY
CAN'T BELIEVE MY
ENTIRE LIFE IS
FUNDED BY
OPTIMISTIC
PENISES.

Beginner's Luck

At the club, it doesn't take long before I'm no longer the new girl. Another sheepish-looking twentysomething has already showed up to claim my former title. A week passes, and all I can do when I'm not working, eating fancy lunches alone, or sleeping, is plot and plan on what am I going to do with all this money that is suddenly mine for the taking. The only person I know in this city is Maxine, or Max, who I met on a gaydargirls.com. We've been dating for 10 days. In lesbian, that's about six months.[6]

Max is sexy, frail, and nostalgic about everything she never experienced but saw in a movie once. She always looks hungry, but like she's also afraid to eat. She is a perfectly square-shouldered, scared stray kitten and no matter where I am or what I do, she's quietly enthusiastic to tag along.

Hand in hand, we explore every inch of Sydney's Eastern Suburbs on foot. It's the first time I've ever experienced the month of May as a time where temperatures plummet. As Aussies gear up for 'winter,' Max and I fuck the afternoon away

---

[6] Lesbian Time Continuum: When two women enter a romantic relationship, the word 'casual' immediately vanishes from our lexicon. Something about an 'attachment' hormone that gets released... whatever it is, us dykes are *committed*. The math is: 1 hetero day = 18 fingerbanger days.

in my sublet, pausing only to drink espresso after espresso in quick succession. We become cafe groupies, bopping from one independent establishmcnt to another, because really, what the fuck else does anyone do purposefully these days but drink pretentiously roasted coffee that's allegedly been purchased 'fairly' from somewhere seriously far from this bucolic street in Surry Hills?

"These are Jacaranda," Max offers, in her soft English-Aussie whisper. She flashes her cobalt eyes up toward the canopy of leaves as it throws its wet and recently deceased members down at us. I sneeze. "And you're sneezing from the London Planes, or *Platanus × acerifolia* … just dreadful for hay fever."

I wonder if all Australians know the Latin names for its indigenous plants. Ignorance toward wildlife on this continent doesn't seem particularly trendy, as every creature that roams the island can kill you. "Did you know that kangaroos can disembowel humans by leaning on their tails, securing you with their arms, while clawing out the intestines of their opponent with the claws of their hind legs?" I did not know kangaroos were such dirty fighters.

Maxine spent her first 15 years in the inner suburbs of Sydney. She moved to Southampton, England, at 16, a place she haughtily describes as 'a shithole.' I'm amused hearing her talk about the dreary industrial city, as the only time she speaks confidently is with disdain about something she has since left behind. She's only back in Sydney by the good graces of a childhood friend who flew her home on his tax return money. I see in her what I see in myself: a beautiful young woman who gets what she needs from the people who will do anything for her, just to keep them around.

One morning, I wake up in a state of near asphyxia. Wordlessly, Max slips on her dirty black jeans and makes for the door with my wallet. She returns with drugs and potions to quell my itchy eyes and congested sinuses. Resting a hand on my back, a whisper: "You'll feel better soon, baby." By afternoon's end, I'm spritely as a court jester and ready to get back to my charade as Iris: Naked Goddess.

Max doesn't seem to mind that I strip. I told her about it the day after my first shift. One of the most satisfying privileges my new money affords me is the ability to intentionally overspend at the grocery store. I buy organic everything: heirloom tomatoes, fresh basil, and a two-figured-sum bottle of olive oil. Passing the plastic can of pre-grated sawdust Parmesan, I go straight for a rock of the good shit. I pick out a bottle of wine that cost more than $10—also a first—and invite Max over for dinner. It's our third date.

Pausing only to pour Max a glass of wine, I buzz about the kitchen as I try to figure out where my flatmate keeps the cheese grater.

"So I started my new job yesterday," I begin, turning on the faucet. As a pot fills with water, I reach for a colander, waving it about for no other reason than to calm my skittish hands.

"What's your new job?" she asks.

I'm nervous to tell her. I consider making the big reveal like it's no big deal, as a sort of side note when asking her how well-cooked she prefers her linguine. To me, stripping doesn't really feel like that big of a deal. I dance. And I'm naked. I'm cool with it; I just don't want anyone to know about it. But I worry that perhaps for her it will be a big deal, and I don't want to be a jerk.
Meditating on the rising water line, I exhale, turn around, and tell her, "Stripping," and turn back to the sink. I turn off the faucet.

That was good. Breezy; off-the-cuff. You sounded like it was no big deal. This increases my chances of being met with a no-big-deal reaction.

Max is silent for a moment, then asks me where, have I stripped before, if I *like* it.

"Yeah, I do. It's kind of funny, really, what happens to men when a beautiful woman gets naked in front of them. They kind of turn into babies, or ... grunting cavemen."

Max takes a minute to process it all. I refill her glass, then mine. This wine is delicious. Or maybe it's just not shitty. So far I'm really into this job and the trips to the fancy grocery store, so I think there's possibility to become quite the connoisseuse in my future. I take a greedy sip.

"I'm cool with it," Max says with a slow nod.

"I'd rather you don't tell anyone about it, though," I say. "It's not a profession that people understand or respect, so I don't want anyone to know. I can't really put this on my resume, if you know what I mean." I swirl the oxblood truth-serum in my glass. "I need you to keep it a secret."

"Okay," she says. "But if anyone asks, what do you want me to say that you do?"

"Tell them I work for … a catering company."

If Maxine is bothered by the fact that I'm secretly a stripper, it is eclipsed by the fact that I pour most of my winnings into our activity fund. I'm too busy with my head up my naked and profit-turning ass to see that this dynamic is probably not the best foundation upon which to build a healthy and lasting relationship. Hot-girl goggles can do this to a person, and my recently elevated status from penniless vagabond to nouveau-riche megababe has me doubly intoxicated. I feel like Jane Fonda in *9 to 5* when she's mastered her phone-answering-"please-hold" skills, smiling to herself at her newly discovered competence and aptitude.

I got this.

Show up, get naked, smile, chat, and never take no for an answer. Get rich quick.

The following week, at the club, I watch a middle-aged man waddle to a seat in the middle of the room. He orders a drink from the waitress, and by the time it's on a cocktail napkin in front of him, I plunk down in a chair beside him.

"Hi!" I smile, as broadly as possible. His name is Donald. Donald likes the way I look, does not seem to be much of a chatterbox, and appears to be in a hurry, so we get straight down to business. I lead him by the hand to the private booth, riffing about life, love, and my recent beach walk from Bondi to Coogee and back, and how much I'm just "*loving* my time in Australia!" In most cases, Australians love to hear this.

I step up onto the podium while he takes a seat on the couch.

I stand, effortlessly sexy, on my little stage. This is the 15 minutes of adoration that I get to experience a dozen or so times a night—at least, every night that I decide to work. Lately I've decided to work a lot. Beginner's luck has me hooked on a great fortune that I have every intention of claiming as mine.

"I'm just loving the sun and the easy-going attitude of everyone here," I go on, reaching for the string at the nape of my neck. I pause, reflecting on this moment in which I'm sharing an epiphany with a complete stranger. I love these interactions.

"I just feel like I really like who I'm beco—"

"Yeah, yeah, just show me your Wendy, Donald blurts, impatiently.

My Wendy?

This guy wants me to shut up and get naked. How rude. But he just referred to my beaver as my "Wendy" which I find highly entertaining, so I am going to forgive this misstep and shall heretofore refer to my vagina as My Wendy. Offensive behaviour is often forgivable in the name of hilarity.

This moment is a learning opportunity for the aspiring self-made millionaire. STRIPPER TIP #5: Even though the job, the act, the risqué nature of it all becomes commonplace in a matter of days, it does not mean that I can talk about my grocery list and big-picture dreams to my current vagina spectator. Each one is excited and excitable and you need to treat him as if he is special, and that this is special for you. Because the single most unifying characteristic of every man who walks into a strip club is that he feels he is *unlike* every other man in a strip club. STRIPPER TIP #6 To make money in this business, a woman must honour this golden rule and always act shocked by the uniqueness of the man who stands before her.

Since slapping myself in the forehead with the heel of my hand would be a total mood-killer, I flutter my eyes to bring myself back to money-making reality.

Using my eyes, hips and demeanour, I offer up my best silent-actress rendition of the following monologue:

My Wendy is especially excited to say hello to this fascinating *gentleman. It's making me* hot. *I* never *get hot. This man is* different.

Donald gazes at my Wendy for the remaining 13 minutes and then leaves.

An old man in a sweater vest drags a chair near the stage and takes a seat. Legs crossed, he fans out his Funny Money and gazes up at me, adjusting his spectacles. His name is Nielsen. Nielsen will be my first regular customer. He shows up at the crack of 5 p.m., buys $30 worth of Funny Money, and requests that I go on stage first. Like all the keeners[7], he is old and likes to stare at my young pussy while his devoted wife of 40 years waits for him to come home and share a glass of sherry as the clock strikes half past 6. He and the other half-dozen Golden Boy Gawkers file daily complaints that the lights are too dim.

Nielsen is tedious but sweet. We sit together beneath a speaker in the corner of the club, where it's the most quiet. He tells me about his favourite authors, pausing only to barely take a sip of the cranberry juice he is obliged to buy upon entering the establishment. He knows I have nothing better to do than listen to him, and for the most part I don't mind. I enjoy his soft-spoken conversation and find his respectful enthusiasm for strip clubs a little endearing. Nielsen is also great because he lets you know when you need to apply some concealer to your ass: "Are those mosquito bites?" he asks with a schoolboy grin, his bushy grey eyebrows raised. "Yes," I lie. I finish my stage, fold my

---

[7] Keeners: Canadian informal. an enthusiastic person; one who is keen.

thirty laminated dollars into my garter belt, and make for the dressing room to dab some concealer onto the zit on my ass.

I'm beginning to see the emergence of an Iris Fan Club.

Other eventual members of The Iris Fan Club are Warren, the 71-year-old accountant who is so round he has suspenders keeping his pants up. He tips me for holding his hand while listening to him spout about his grandchildren. Michael, a boring middle-aged lawyer who thinks we have a lot in common, but really we don't. And then there is The Gynaecologist—who is in fact a computer science genius of sorts and not a gynaecologist at all. He has a high-pitched yet remarkably quiet bumbling voice with which he requests me to 'come closer,' while I'm dancing on stage. He proceeds to lean in, getting a generous whiff of my feminine scent with his massive nose.

Contrary to what I thought a 'regular' would be, the men are not typically big spenders. The ones who can afford to blow thousands of dollars are usually working around the clock, and the globe. The ones you can count on to be waiting at the door for the club to open are devoted, consistent and on a budget.

The fourth member to join the Iris Fan Club is Greg.

The first time I ever meet Greg, he shows up in ironed jeans, crisp Converse sneakers and a black cashmere sweater. He wears glasses that I don't know how to describe in any other way than "Weezer Glasses." Greg is a reformed punk-rocker-turned-stockbroker. Unlike most of my regulars, he is obviously very successful. My trained money-making eye can tell because a) successful men always wear cashmere, and b) you can't be a stockbroker and wear Converse unless you have some sort of impressive seniority. His weekly visits are always at happy hour, during which he orders a Jack and Coke and buys one private dance.

One evening we are enjoying each other's conversation so much that we lose track of time, missing the 9 o'clock cut-off for the $25 discount. Checking his Rolex to make certain that the hostess is not merely trying to rip him off, he condescends with a squint, "Oooh, that's too much." He leaves without tipping or apologizing for wasting my time.

45

Greg, like a lot of rich men, is a cheap bastard. This dichotomous breed of motherfucker is a common fixture at strip clubs.

The following week I make sure to lead Greg to the hostess booth well before happy hour comes to a close.

"Leave your dress on, just take off your knickers," he says. Greg makes this request every time. I happily oblige. It's less work for me. The fewer times I have to undress are fewer times I have to get dressed again. Successful strippers are big fans of efficiency. I sit with my legs parted just enough for a sneaky glimpse of my money shot. He gazes longingly at my Wendy and we talk about rock 'n' roll. This makes Greg feel more like he's on a naughty date and less like a paid peep show.

"You know," he starts. I already know what he's going to ask. He asks every time. "We could go to a hotel, and pleasure ourselves without ever *actually ... touching* each other … just ... *watching...*"

He licks his lips, adjusts his junk through his starched jeans and brings his pointer finger to his temple: "I would make it worth your while."

Somehow, with his reticence to dish out an extra $25 for a private dance, I find this hard to believe.

"Well, as tempting as your offer is, I will have to politely decline. You can always come back and see me here." STRIPPER TIP #7: Always act like you wish you could, but just can't. Especially when they are wearing Converse.

Another night, Greg shows up visibly plastered.

"Iris!" Greg bobs and nods his head toward the back room. "Let's go." No pleasantries, no talk of the Billboard Hot 100 … He wants to go for a dance, immediately.

I follow his hasty initiative, and in moments we are in the booth resuming our usual program. I slip off my g-string; dress stays on. As the ditty progresses, I bring my legs into a spread eagle, as per my routine at the 10-minute mark. Greg takes out his wallet, extracts a fifty, and slips it into my garter belt. *A tip from Greg? How wondrously unusual! I* don't think much of his sudden burst of generosity, as even the cheapest of men, when hypnotized by a vagina, can bring forth the unexpected. When a client hands a dancer money, extra money—a TIP—she takes it. Tips are appreciated, but not required. I accept it with a smile.

But one should always question sudden bursts of generosity, particularly from men. Because in this business, there is no free lunch.

I'm learning back on my forearms, legs apart before him. Before I can utter a "thank you," Greg's hand reaches for what is a distinctly a NO GO zone—my vagina. In this passive, trusting position, I've resigned myself to be defenceless. He grazes a finger along a lip before I can jolt back, my body pulsing with adrenaline. Greg has broken a cardinal rule. He has crossed a line and broken my trust.

I scramble to stand up, yelling and pointing to the door.

"GET THE FUCK OUT."

When something like this happens I've been instructed to hit the security button. It's on the ceiling in the corner of the room, easily accessible from the podium. But when you feel violated and in danger, you're not going to press a fucking button. You're going to get yourself out of that situation, as soon as humanly fucking possible.

I storm out of the room naked, clutching my dress, calling for security.

The brick house bouncer, Charles, comes rushing to me with the widest stride I've ever seen.

"He touched my vagina. Get him the fuck out of here." My voice is hurried and shaky and I wish it was a strong, domineering bellow, but it's just not. I feel small. The only way this naked dancing gig works is having strict boundaries. When these boundaries are crossed, it is extremely shitty and debilitating.

The pendant around my neck jumps with the quickened pulse of my heartbeat. The other bouncer, Devon, puts his arm around my bare shoulders as I watch Charles grab Greg by his upper arm, escorting him out the door. "You know what happens when you touch her, mate ..."

"Are you okay, sweetheart?" Devon asks.

"I'll be fine." I will be fine. But now, this just fucking sucks.

Shortly afterward, I'm called on stage. The show must go on.

When I get home that night, I decide against telling Max about my spoiled night. Because everyone always worries that I'm in danger when I go to work, I am always reticent to share the stories that don't end up with me coming out on top. There aren't many, but they do exist. I want to appear strong and unflinching in the face of danger. The truth is, I didn't feel unsafe when Greg decided to have absolutely no respect for the boundaries I have always kept clearly established and firm—the bouncers were right there to take care of him when I summoned their forces. I feel safer in my club than I do just about anywhere else. I don't have a bouncer when I'm out with my friends, taking the bus home late at night. I don't have a bouncer when I'm reading on the beach, getting hassled by men, and being photographed without my consent. I will always feel safe in the club, but these brief brushes of violation make my stomach churn.

I crawl into bed and welcome Max's warm, soft, and reassuring embrace.

"How was work?" she asks, half awake. It's 4 a.m.

"It was alright. Not the best night, but you can't win them all." A common turn of phrase I'll grow to use whenever I close the book on a shitty night.

The next morning, Max and I wake up and take our regular morning coffees and breakfast at a cafe beside my apartment. I don't work until 7 p.m. that night, and Max has, in the past three weeks since we broke up and made up, once again lost or quit her job. She doesn't specify which.

I settle the bill.

Seated across from her, I am tired, unamused and frustrated with her complacency. She's so fucking beautiful but right now I can't look at her.

We have a brief conversation about Max getting her shit together. This has become a constant topic of conversation. I suggest that she takes some time to herself to sort it out without having me as a distraction (read: I am trying to break up with her).

*

Spending so much time in the company of rock-hard tits and perfectly liposuctioned asses, I start to have plastic surgery nightmares.

My chest feels as though there is a medicine ball pressing down on my lungs. I flutter my eyes open. Looking down, I discover Pamela Anderson's plastic surgeon has done a routine inflation job on my precious tits. Two mounds of silicone stand lifelessly atop my ribcage. Hard, cold nipples reach for the heavens. I am mortified, and filled with regret. I don't remember making the decision go under the knife. But it's too late. My soft, natural fun bags are gone and I didn't even get to say goodbye.

Body-modification dreams creep in and out of my consciousness more and more frequently as I immerse myself more into this fascinating and mind-fucking career. It doesn't take long to understand that that which is fake sells more than that which is natural. This is a fantasy world where all the dudes who watch too much porn come looking for a girl who looks like that girl from *Backdoor Babes 6*.

I'm always curious to conduct the following experiment: put a set of twins stood side by side, one with real tits and the other with some basketball tits. Same long, flowing, blonde hair, same toned bod, same spray tan. The hypothesis? Basketball Tits will make more money, and faster. Maybe it's because they look more like pros and less like amateurs. Maybe it's because no one watches seventies porn anymore and every man under the age of forty wants a hairless vagina and silicone jugs to titty fuck. I grew up in the sticks with the cast of *Dawson's Creek* setting the archetypal bar where only the virtuous are truly beautiful; only the sluts got highlights and wore mascara. The pristine, natural beauty of Joey Potter always won out over sexy, campy Jen Lindley.

But in the stripper world, my *Dawson's Creek* paradigm is continually turned on its head. Despite my willpower and hourly affirmations, fake girls just get paid more than the natural ones. Among my colleagues, even the strongest of character, with the most symmetrical tits, will at some point cup her breasts while looking in the mirror, lifting them toward her chin, thinking *it's really too bad that they don't defy gravity*. No one is safe—as the old venture capitalist saying goes: *You gotta spend money to make money.*

It's a paradox: In most ways, this job has made me infinitely more confident. I look at myself on stage and think, "DAMN, YOU FINE GIRL." Smouldering red and orange light flatters my every angle, and I can't help but swoon over the magically slenderizing effect of stilettos. I love my curves, my moves and my swagger. I'm finally liking —nay, LOVING—what I see, and at every turn. This is a big fucking deal for me because I spent the bulk of my high school and university years throwing up everything I could muster when my roommates were out of retching earshot. All of this self-love is being validated with more money than I ever fathomed earning with my highly marketable degree in Russian literature.

But when I watch the surgically-enhanced girls claiming extra winnings, I cannot help but feel the need to conform to this fucked up ideal of plastic hair, plastic tits, and plastic lips for which these porn-schooled men come dawdling in.

"Not all blokes prefer this sort of woman, Sheila." I'm reassured by Robbo, the manager, as I watch Destiny saunter back with a client for the fifth time since I started my shift an hour and a half ago.

Destiny always stands out, because she's like a cyborg from the galaxy of Pornopolis. She is crafted using misogynist technology! Can I blame a guy for wanting to see what this looks like up close? Hell, even I want to squeeze those tits! It's unlikely that Destiny is the kind of woman clients have waiting for them at home, so why not go full-tilt fantasy girl when you're paying by the minute to stare at her?

Maybe it's the Joey-Potter-idolizing days of yore, but I still maintain that fake is kind of gross. But that's a personal preference, and for the time being I'm not shopping for a wife, but rather sussing out what it is that makes you the top-earning titty shaker in the pussy patch.

To avoid dealing with the relationship woes that come along with dating someone with a profoundly frail sense of self-worth, I take on extra shifts at work. Sunday? SURE, I'LL WORK SUNDAY. Everyone needs a little vagic viewing after mass to restore their sense of guilt.

Sundays are days where the music is quieter and the men are slightly more sober than on Saturday, unless, of course, they are still drunk from the night before, in which case they are likely snorting cocaine off the urinal to keep their eyes open and uncrossed.

The general demographic of Sunday strip club clientele are:
34 percent regulars
50 percent international businessmen who just landed in Sydney for a Monday morning meeting
15 percent under-25 party people coming down from shitty drugs
1 percent rock stars

This Sunday is particularly quiet, so I send out a few text messages to my fan club and within an hour Michael shows up. Michael is a lawyer who sorts out the estates of people who have been assassinated. He likes to read books of the non-fictional variety that are of absolutely no interest to me. But since he caught wind of my formal education, he assumes that the pleasure I derive from literature paired with my penchant for glittery eyeliner means that I like to read about the physics of paint drying and which Macedonian leaders preferred

51

hermaphrodites. (Actually, both of those subjects sound more interesting than what he usually likes to discuss).

This particular Sunday, Michael shows up with *Studies in Greek Colour Terminology.* "This one is out of print," he tells me, as he inspects the spine through his bifocals. I leaf through it, and insist that he keeps it "since it's so special." It's a heavy motherfucking book. I appreciate that these strangers want to share their passions with me; I find it charming and infinitely more fascinating than discussing whether or not I'm shaved and how much I enjoy anal sex. Still, I don't want to tote this tome around with me for the rest of my time in Australia.

Michael appreciates that I see how important the book is to him and thanks me for letting him keep it. "I was just really excited to show it to you," he says with a giggly sneer as he heaves it back into his canvas laptop bag.

With a maternal warmth, I reach for his wrist: "Shall we go for a private show?"

Michael nods.

During our half-hour together, Michael sputters useless knowledge. I half-listen and ask erroneous questions to entertain myself.

"WERE THERE MERMAIDS THAT SANG TO THE SLAVE WORKERS IN MESOPOTAMIA?"

Or, "Do you think the hermaphrodites were really just mystical gods who understood all the secrets of the universe?" Unamused, he answers, flatly, "No," and resumes with his monologue. I think I'm being hilarious and he thinks he's being brilliant. I'm also getting paid, and he's also staring at my snatch. Everybody wins.

The receptionist comes in to tell Michael and I that our 30-minute fantasy has come to an end. Back on the floor, there remain only three clients, sitting in a far corner, clearly no older than 19, drunk and coming down off some speedy drugs that peaked no less than six hours ago. Certainly not tipping or going for dances.

52

I spin around on my heels and go back to reception. With a quick exhale, I announce, "I'm going to go home now." I've started to feel pretty confident about the way I run my own business. My time is valuable and if there is no one here to pay for it, I may as well leave.

Quickly fanning through my stage tips, I breeze into the dressing room.

"You seem to do quite well," a girl says to me in an accent I can only guess as very English and very northern. I look up. It's the girl with the most fantastic, natural bod in the whole club. She is always booked on end for private dances, so I've never really had a moment to talk to her. Plus, when you can smell the success of someone you're working with, spiteful feelings tend to arise. And lest we forget: hot girls are intimidating, even to other hot girls.

I don't want to be disappointed by hanging out with her for too long, only to find out that she makes twice as much as I do. This will happen, time and again, as I get deeper in to my stripping career. It happens to everyone. No one is always on top. A stripper cannot make the most money she's ever made, every night.

And I never think of the money in my hand being 'a lot.' I always assume that it's not enough, that there is more to be had. Simply, it's what I earn and I could always be earning more. This hot girl, then, a Top Earner, is acknowledging me as one of her kind.

"I guess so…" I reply, looking at the bills fanned out in my hand.

"You seem to do very well in that dress," she adds, pointing with her French manicure at my stripper-starter-dress: black, tiny, simple, and extremely revealing. "They like you here," she says, smiling.

I'm taken aback by her warmth. She's smiling at me, introducing herself as Tiffany and telling me about how she moved to Australia a year ago, and started dancing a few months ago, and how she just LOVES it.

Beautiful, buxom, bubbly, and nice. *Weird.*

It soon becomes apparent that most of the girls in the dressing room are nice, too. They are asking after one another's kids, studies, travels, and man problems as they share bronzer and bags of chips.

Tiffany is also wrapping up her night, counting her money and slipping her plastic shoes into her duffel bag.

"It was really nice to meet you," she adds.

"Likewise," I say back. "You don't live in Bondi, do you?" I assume she does, because she's an English transplant with a healthy tan. Anyone who transplants from the London fog always stations themselves by the beach. And only hot strippers can afford the real estate in Bondi.

"I do! Do you? Oh my gosh, we absolutely must do lunch sometime!"

"I don't live on the beach, but I'm not far. I would love to lunch," I reply.

I cannot imagine seeing any of these girls in daylight, without make-up, and in Real Girl clothes. But they're all real. I've just refused to acknowledge this. I keep my life as Iris separate from my life as a lady-loving hobo.
"Do you want to share a taxi home?" I ask. I'm taking a step.

"I'd love to, but I'm going to my boyfriend's tonight." Tiffany and I swap numbers and decide to meet for a seaside weekday brunch later in the week.

I slip on my Real Girl jeans, t-shirt, and jacket, hauling my knapsack over my shoulder. At reception, I wait for the Ox to finish her conversation on the phone to collect my nightly winnings. She hangs up. "Iris, Slash is coming in a half-hour. Will you stay?"

"Which one is Slash again?"

"He's the lead guitarist for Guns 'n Roses."

"Oh, you mean the guy with the top hat!" All of my rock star knowledge is based on aesthetic signifiers. Names, songs, bands, genres … forget it. But if he wears a top hat and/or leather pants, I'll buy whatever magazine he's on the cover of.

Strippers and rock stars go together like cocaine and champagne. This is an opportunity to be the most authentic stripper goddess I can be, so I drag my ass back to the dressing room, take off my cozy briefs, and slip the piece of rectal floss back in my ass and wait for Slash to arrive. Peeking out from the dressing room, I notice that Michael the Lit Freak is still sitting there, alone, heavy books in tow. The club kids are there too, but there seem to be more of them now. It's not worth a strut around the room, only to be lassoed in by the most uninteresting literary enthusiast known to humanity, so I stay in the dressing room and study the ingredients in my foundation.

"And now we have, coming up next on stage, the lovely Iris!"

I pull myself together and walk out on stage. At the tipping rail sits a man in a trucker hat and mirrored aviator sunglasses, with a lot of cronies and even more hair: Slash.
I dance up to where he is sitting and smile like I'm a six-year-old. Even though I don't really know that much about him or his music, he's a living legend and therefore I am nervous. Celebrity culture makes people act like buffoons. It's embarrassing.

"Hi," I say, getting on my knees and sliding onto my stomach, ass high in the air. "How are you?"

"I'm good," he replies with a sneer. Noticing my lack of Australian accent, he asks, "Are you American?"

"Canadian," I assure him, sliding back up onto my knees and arching my back, offering up the perkiest angle of my tits.

"You know, I've got a couple Can-ooks in my band."

"You mean *Canucks*?"

"Yeah! You're good people. Really friendly."

I turn my knees to face the rock star, and flash Slash my gash.

"You know you're the only person I've ever seen come in here who was allowed to keep his hat and glasses on? I can see a perfect view of my box in the reflection of your shades!" I exclaim.

And I do. I see it in all its pink and red glorious folds. The more I do this job, the more I realize how beautiful and awesome vaginas are. Like fingerprints, no two are the same.

Slash smiles, and reaches behind to one of his cronies, rubbing his thumb and fingers together, giving the universal, 'cash, please' sign.

He slips me a $20 bill.

My song ends, and that is the end of my interaction with Slash. Twenty lousy dollars. Any stripper pipe dreams I had of having rock stars shower me with hundies[8] have officially been crushed.

*

If you're a stripper and you feel shitty about anything regarding your physical appearance, you are guaranteed not to make any money. STRIPPER TIP #8: Insecurity is something you have to leave at the door if you're going to make a living off of your tits and ass.

The night is slow. I look at the other girls, men fawning over them, going crazy, some drooling. Pangs of jealousy wipe the smile off my face and take the bounce out of my step. I know that sometimes I'm that girl but lately it feels less so. My trademark messy pixie-cut, which is always dishevelled (the essence of its charm), is starting to look scraggly. My rock-and-

---

[8] Hundies: hundred dollar bills

roll roots are looking less trendy and more dumpy. I observe that it's not really selling as much as it used to. Also, I'm getting sick. *Is this the end of my beginner's luck?*

I'm about to throw my hands up in the air when a man waves me over to his table. I take a seat in a hot cloud of whiskey-breath.

"I noticed you are not having fun," he professes in a thick Russian accent.

"I'm losing my voice," I whisper, touching my neck.

The Whiskey Man pulls a pen from his pocket, and starts scribbling on a napkin. In practically illegible chicken scratch penmanship, it reads: "3 oz. of Johnny Walker Black for your sore throat."

"Trust me, I'm a doctor," he says, without any conviction.

He waves over the waitress and has her bring three ounces of the firewater that I've sworn off since that time I didn't remember how I got home and woke up with scratches on my knees and shoes that weren't mine.

Well, fuck it: I oblige. In one gulp, I follow the Whiskey Man's careful prescription, and wince.

*

The clock strikes 4 and our fake smiles drop.

I concede that these days, the only man to whom I am genuinely nice is my cab driver. He is my transporter from the Palace of Skanks where I work to my sanctuary—only he is privy to my 10-minute decompression from sassy bitch to the tired, normal girl who wants a glass of soy milk and to crawl into my unmade bed.

Outside the club, I queue up for a taxi. Tiffany is already in line, alongside Satine. Satine is an aspiring costume designer with the weirdest outfits I've ever seen. She always wears black lipstick, but her hair colour is always changing. Today, it's fire-truck red.

Rolling suitcase in tow, Satine sucks back a Virginia Slim bitch stick[9]. Tiffany smiles at nothing in particular.

We discuss where the money is at the moment (read: in which cities we've heard through the vagabond stripper grapevine the girls seem to be making the most cash). "I hear Perth is good," she says. Perth is the most isolated city in the world. The weather is nice and there are a tonne of miners with a lot of money and not enough pussy to throw it at.

Satine inhales, pauses, and says, "They're cunts in Perth." Exhale. "But they're all cunts. So I guess it doesn't really matter."

A drunk girl in a short metallic skirt has cut the line and hailed the latest cab. Everyone groans.

Satine goes on. "I'm surprised I haven't become a lesbian, having put up with all this shit for a year. At the end of the day, men are all the same: simple-minded, self-entitled cunts." She throws a butt to the pavement and finally hops in a cab. Tiffany and I shuffle up the line.

"I'm heading up to the Gold Coast for the weekend," Tiffany says. "Do you want to come, Iris?"

"They can touch your boobs there, right?"

"Yeah," she says with a shrug.

"Ugh. I hate that." But I hate the slump of mediocrity I'm in right now even more.

After waiting 45 minutes and brushing off two clients whom I had seen earlier that night in the club (who try to make me share a cab with them in a dual effort to take me home and skip the taxi queue), my cabbie saviour arrives and I hop in.

---

[9] Bitch Stick: a very skinny cigarette, smoked mostly by frowning Eastern European women with acrylic nails.

Cabbies always ask how my night has been. We swap notes on whether it has been slow or not, and both posit that it must be because of the weather or the lack of tourism given the ridiculous increase in the value of the Australian dollar. In my experience, never has a cabbie made a sexual innuendo. The only time any of my cabbies has mentioned sex was when one told me that he was to be married in Bangladesh next month. "Yes, you see," he said, "In the west you make the sex before marriage, so many people do not marry so soon. But in Bangladesh, we do not make the sex before marriage. So we marry."

I consider having my boobs groped by strange men, and weigh it against the sad relationship mess I'm in now. I text Tiffany: "I'm in."

Greener Grass

Because I am an asshole, I break up with Maxine via email.

It's really hard to break up with someone so beautiful and needy. I tried to do it in person, at my favourite sunny breakfast spot, the previous morning. But it felt like I was slowly breaking each leg of Bambi, just after he came in from the thunderstorm, scared and soaking wet. Max's eyes flickered, confused, as she stared at her Vegemite on toast. My valiant effort to subtly communicate "it's not me, it's you" in person came out as "I want you to focus on yourself for a while." And Bambi just didn't quite read through the lines of my pussified version of "let's take a break." Max left the cafe while I was still working through my pile of smoked salmon, egg, avocado, and sprouts. On the plate across from me, her lonely slice of toast sat cold, a single semicircle of a bite missing from it. I exhaled, a little sad, but relieved.

Several hours later, a text:

"I don't feel good about the way we left things this morning. I'm confused."

Jesus Christ—is she in denial? Am I completely incapable of effectively communicating with hot girls, or is my Canadian accent sometimes indecipherable? Because this is horseshit.

I type out a blutter of what I perceive to be kind—but will likely be perceived as condescending—words:

My Dearest Max,
I feel like you're investing too much thought and worry into our relationship, rather than taking that energy and focusing it toward feeling stronger, happier, and more confident in your own life. Yesterday we talked about you getting your life into gear; that what I need from you, if we are going to be together, is for you to be an inspiring, supportive, and challenging force in my life. However, first you must be that kind of person to yourself.

Jacq

SEND.

The next morning, Tiffany and I hop on a plane headed north to the Gold Coast. There is nothing in the universe to assure you that you've made the right decision to break it off than a beach vacation. We sip chardonnay as the discount aircraft bumps us up the coast. Stripping has taken me to embracing my inner lush. These perpetually and perfectly manicured nails are not for drinking glasses of tap water in public.

"Let's change our names," offers Tiffany, eyebrows raised and eyes flashing. "I've always thought 'Jessica' was a sexy name."

I decide against disagreeing with her. All the Jessicas I've known in my lifetime have been annoying six-year-olds. Acknowledging my bias, I nod encouragingly and riff off a handful of potential names for my new alias:

"Violet?"

"That sounds Vile. Vile Violet."

"Chelsea?"

"That sounds cheap."

"Chloe?"

"You're definitely not a Chloe. What about Roxy? Your cute little hairstyle would most definitely suit a Roxy. I mean, of course, I'll still probably call you Iris, because that's what I'm used to calling you."

And so Iris is rechristened by the sandy shores of Queensland to become Roxy.

The Gold Coast is to Australia what Miami Beach is to America: pristine, with white sandy beaches and year-round sunshine, populated by leatherettes with bobble boobs, retirees, and golden-girl vacationers gussied up in wedge heels, visors, and pastel jumpsuits. STRIPPER TIP #9: If you don't like tacky things, don't become a fucking stripper. Throw away that tanning oil, buy some edgy eyeglasses, open a bitchy art gallery, and be bored for the rest of your life.

Tiffany got the idea to come here from our colleague, Jessie-Lee. A native Aussie, Jessie-Lee has her own set of saline-filled bobbles, which she sports with an amazing sense of humour and a concentrated dose of self-awareness. She trots around the globe, getting naked for any and every nationality (as long as the chance of being trafficked is low-risk). Jessie-Lee is my latest role model.

"My goodness, Jessie, your waist is significantly slimmer," Tiffany noticed in the dressing room last week. "What have you been *doing*?"

Jessie-Lee leaned in to the mirror to inspect her lip gloss, "I've been up on the Gold Coast … they've got a pole all the way up to the ceiling of the second floor … let me tell ya, climbing that thing is *work*."

"And you're just … glowing!" Tiffany had yet to manage to scrape her jaw off the floor.

"Yeah, ya tan all day, work all night … and it's good money up there. I made $4,000 in three days."

With dollar signs in her eyes, Tiffany flashed me a plotting glance. We decided then and there that we, too, would get rich while trimming our waists and bronzing our butt cheeks.

When she's up here on the Gold Coast, Jessie-Lee works at the most coveted club in town. Tiffany's done a bit of research, and gives me the lowdown.

"It has *a waterfall*, Iris. It's three stories of red velvet couches and loads of rich customers."

Apparently, contrary to what I've led myself to believe the past few months, Sydney is not big or easy money, but the Gold Coast *is*. I've been really happy with the money I've been earning, but since catching wind of the fact that there is more to be earned—somewhere new, hot, and exotic!—my Sydney hustle has instantly stopped making the cut. I want more. I'm excited to meet some fat tourists who are in dire need my affections and doubly eager to pay for it.

Tiffany and I deplane, get in a cab, and beeline it straight for The Coveted Club. We want to audition this afternoon so that we can work tonight.

A red carpet is being rolled out as we exit the cab in microscopic minidresses. A linebacker-sized man we will learn to call Hamish takes a vacuum to it.

"Hi," we say, smiling in unison.

Hamish smiles weakly and nods toward the door. It's unclear as to whether he thinks he knows us or he just doesn't give a fuck. Time will teach me that this is how all bouncers greet all dancers: like they know you, and don't really give a fuck, but that they do care *just enough* to merit a tip at the end of the night.

Walking past the cleaning crew, we reach a windowless office where a petite brunette with braces looks up at us blankly. Her eyes scan us both up and down, although it doesn't seem as if she's actually looking at us.

"Hello!" Tiffany beams. "We're here to audition!"

"When do you want to audition?" she asks with a slow blink.

"We want to audition now, that's why we're here," Tiffany responds, in her bubbliest of tones, pretending to ignore the fact that she's now had to repeat herself twice.

"You can come in tomorrow to audition at 7 p.m."

"So we can't work tonight?"

"No."

"But it's only 3:30. Surely you have auditions tonight at 7?"

"Tomorrow."

Deflated, Tiffany and I roll our suitcases back along the red carpet. We pause at the curb to observe a parade of twentysomethings swarming by. Through a haze of neon singlets and knock-off Ray Bans, I notice a flashing sign across the street: 'GIRLS.' A few bulbs have gone out, and there isn't any sort of regal carpeting beckoning us in, but this is clearly the place that has haphazardly opened up to cater to the overflow of The Coveted Club. Silk stockings beget nylons and cocaine begets crack, just as high-end strip clubs spawn dank titty bars. And the world keeps on spinning.

Drawing a deep breath, Tiffany brushes a perfectly highlighted lock of hair from her face. "We came here to work, so let's work. How bad can it be?"

The place is wall-to-wall carpet, and resembles a house that just hosted a high-school house party. Everything is damp and smells like drink. A mousey-haired, naked-faced woman in a beige maxi dress approaches us. Before we can introduce ourselves, the Madam begins:
"Ladies, would you like to work tonight?"

We are caught off-guard by her straightforwardness, which is made even more confusing by the fact that she looks like a Mormon sister-wife. In most cases, anyone who runs the front end of any strip club gives off the impression that they'd rather be filing off their grandfather's corns than speaking to a new recruit. I've come to assume that 'general lack of interest in potential cash-cows' is in their job description. In their defence, receptionists and managers probably see a dozen starry-eyed hopefuls like us on a nightly basis. But this place is different. With a quick glance around the room, management seems to be entirely female, and remarkably polite. What a delight! From where Tiffany and I are standing, the only shortcoming is the fact that the venue is a total dump. I choose to overlook this minor setback and respond affirmatively: "Yes. We would absolutely love to work tonight."

"No audition?" Tiffany whispers in disbelief.

We are wearing profoundly small and extremely tight dresses, but still, auditioning is part of every club's hiring process. What if I had a Nazi tattoo on my stomach? What if I can't dance? What if there's a red, bumpy, and highly contagious rash covering a significant portion of my body?

None of this seems to concern Madam, as she is already leading us past the main stage, which features a rotating platform. On the platform is an upholstered stiletto. It is the size of a pony. A very skinny dancer with slumping shoulders and an impossibly fresh-looking cesarean scar straddles the arch of the shoe and bobs her head, offbeat. Her eyes appear to be closed.

Breezing through a saloon door, Madam orders us to sit down on a bench in the middle of the dressing room.

"The only rule we have here is no lace. Lace makes men want to break the rules, so you're not allowed to wear any."

I'm tempted to tell her that her fugly Maxi dress will make a "certain man" want to break the rules. All men ever want to do is break the rules. That's why we have bouncers, and pepper spray, and why so many women live in fear every time they leave the house. Instead, I worry about what the fuck I'm going to wear tonight, since all I wear is lace. I brought with me several g-strings in an assortment of colours and fabrics. Every single panty has a lace waistband. On my figure, it's the most flattering and comfortable of stripper rectal-floss options, and so I buy them, much like my mother buys her Hanes, in bulk.

I plough through my bag, pulling out a black pair in desperation: "this one is barely lace," I plead.

"No lace," she responds, stone-faced.

Not a single one of my g-strings is acceptable. I lift up my dress to show her the thong I've been wearing all day. The elastic in it is dead, frayed and curly. "Is this okay?" I ask, half serious. Without blinking, Madam approves.

The no-lace rule extends to dresses, too, which means I'm stuck once again with nothing to wear.

"I love lace," I tell Tiffany, pouting while I stare at my rainbow-explosion suitcase.

"Oh, darling, please just take one of mine. This should fit you," she says, holding up a black, frilly, strapless bra.

I am blessed with a great rack but I swear to fucking god I have a missing vertebra, because my torso is really short. Babes with biggish boobs and short torsos should never be seen in high-waisted pants, monokinis, thick waist belts, or… strapless bras. But this is my last resort. It's either wear this black frilly bra and these dirty panties, or mope in the hotel room alone by myself.

The bra is too big, so it sags as the rubber along the inseam fails to properly cling to my ribcage. It makes my torso look even shorter than it already so fucking blessedly is. I look chunky, and not in a sexy way.

I'm too busy overthinking the shortcomings of my wardrobe situation to remember that this club is a club that offers lap dances. Neither Tiffany nor myself have ever given a lap dance before. We both got our start in Sydney, where you just sit on your little podium, dance, squat, and listen to grown men's sorrows without ever having to get on top of them and simulate some sort of a high-school session of dry humping. Fortunately, this club has the ambiance right, with the room smelling like a dank basement.

"So we just sort of get on top of them and wiggle around, is that it?" Tiffany asks. We stare into a room that is rimmed with shin-level benches, which seem to have once been upholstered in cheetah print. Two men are receiving lap dances. Immediately, I understand the reasoning behind the low seating: a dancer is on the floor, propping herself up with her forearms, offering up an impressively flexible rendition of a spread eagle. Out of the corner of my eye, Tiffany's expression changes from confused to mortified in a single curl of her lower lip. In a panicked whisper, she brings her trembling lips to my ear: "Oh my goodness, Iris, when do you think was the last time this carpet's been cleaned?"

"Lap dances involve floor work? Does everyone do that?" I ask Madam.

Madam points to a sign at the entrance of the room:

THERE MUST BE 30 CENTIMETRES BETWEEN THE CROTCH OF THE PATRON AND DANCER

For anyone unfamiliar with the metric system, a ruler has been taped beneath the text for reference.

My first dance is with an Indian man whose eyes are perfectly level with my nipples when I shake his limp hand and ask him if he'd like a dance. Wordlessly, he agrees by starting to walk toward the ruler on the wall. I sit him down, taking a seat beside him to collect the $30. The bench is damp. I try not to notice.
For the entire song, he plants his hands on my breasts and fondles them using the same hand motion one would use to hold and subsequently squish a ham sandwich to ensure the mayonnaise and mustard oozes out in every direction.

This is the most uncomfortable, awkward, and embarrassing thing to which I have ever willingly subjected myself.

I would like to ask this guy, who is at least 40, "Is this how you think a woman likes to have her breasts touched?"

I say nothing. He's a paying customer, so he gets what he wants—right?

WRONG.

It will take me at least two more years to realize that you can tell any motherfucker, paying or not, what you like, and what you don't. Because you're doing them a fucking favour by giving them a goddamn clue when it comes to knowing how to please a woman. If anything, a dancer should charge a premium for the tutorial.

For the next two and a half minutes, however, I won't be saying anything clever or empowering. For the next two and a half minutes, this is going to suck.

His eyes dart to the ceiling, the carpet, and to other dancers and patrons. Never does he look directly at me. His hands, however, are all about testing the plumpness of my tits as though testing for the freshness and sponginess of this ham sandwich he seems not to be looking at. I am too nervous and repulsed to say, YOU HAVE A GORGEOUS SET OF TITS IN YOUR HANDS, BUDDY, AND YOU'RE FUCKING IT ALL UP. He doesn't even seem to be enjoying it! It feels clinical, as if he's a doctor looking for a lump, but he is obviously a clown doctor and there is absolutely no indication that either of us are aroused.

Why am I here? Because he's already paid, and he hasn't broken any of the rules, which are: No licking no kissing no touching the pussy.

A minute passes. He is still doing the same thing: testing the firmness of my rack.

Across the room another lap dance is going on. The dancer is using her ass like a barrier. Leaning forward, she shoves her booty in the guy's face. While he's mesmerized by the figure eight she makes with her badonkadonk, she takes a moment to roll her eyes and yawn.
How innovative!

I attempt the same move. I lean forward, stand up, and thrust my ass a few inches from his face, which I can only assume is still inspecting the ceiling tiles. He takes hold of my hips, and turns me around so I am facing him once again. I didn't even get to squeeze in a quick eye-roll. He resumes his position of mitts-on-tits and eyes to the sky. The confident, bitchy, take-no-prisoners attitude I see in other dancers has yet to rise up within me. I'm too insecure to get in his face and assert my authority: *Don't tell me how to dance, fucker.* STRIPPER TIP #10: No one says or does the right thing on their first day as a titty shaker. Go easy on yourself, rookie.

Defeated, I stay put, wiggling around like a dying fish, my tits fixed in the grip of his clueless hands. I feel disgusting and unappreciated and I decline to ask if he'd like to continue when the song finally ends.

My first full-contact lap dance has left me with the assumption that most men who come in to a club to pay 30 bucks for a few minutes of boobie groping are a lost cause.

As I refasten the clasp on my borrowed bra, I look over my shoulder to see Tiffany settling into the lap of a man who looks like a Swiss Olympian: tall, lean, sensibly dressed and correct in demeanour. She will remain on his lap for the next two hours. He's not squeezing her tits like a hand puppet or ignoring her personhood. He looks like he's enjoying her company and she appears to reciprocate. My chest grows hot with jealousy. But Tiffany is always overflowing with kindness, and she is also my friend, so I negotiate with my emotions and settle on a healthy envy for her sweet success. I return to the main room to hunt for a second attempt at a lap dance. Surely they cannot all be as terrible as Mr. Handsy McDoesn'tHaveaClue.

I exhale, spin on my heels and stride up to the first man I see in my new line of sight. As I come within a metre of his personal space, I can taste the cloud of Johnnie Walker oozing from his pores. He is radiating stink. Before I can make a U-turn to avoid my inevitable ill-fatedness with this hot mess, he ropes me in.

"Hey you you are so beautiful oh come here come closer I need someone to lift my spirits. I just lost my job because of that fucking Wikileaks guy."

I reel back, trying to gasp some fresher air, but would really like to hear more about what sort of scandal he's about to divulge.

"No one died," he reassures me. "But now I've lost my job and my life is ruined."

I love gossip. I will trade a few minutes with a pervert for a juicy chunk of hearsay almost any day. Sadly, tonight is just not my night for extracting secrets or making money. Instead of learning gory details about government corruption, I'll swat away his probing hand. In between indecipherable laments about his crumbling career, this guy was fixated on caressing my ass—for free! Surely if your life was ruined by Wikileaks, you could understand that nothing is ever free, especially in a strip club. Alas, most men who walk into joints like this leave logic and decorum at the door.

Being groped by a man for the first time in over two years is completely unexciting. If anything, I find it slightly tragic. All the men for whom I dance on this dank and depressing night are clumsy, aggressive, and completely uninterested in mutual pleasure or satisfaction.

The night wraps up with me making a very small amount of money, and Tiffany not earning much more.

"What a shitty night of being groped," I whine during the cab ride back to our hotel.

"At least I didn't make anyone cry tonight," Tiffany offers.

My ears perk up: "You make men cry?"

"Well, one of my regulars in Sydney comes in quite often— he's an opera singer—and he sings to me, and, more often than not, subsequently bursts into tears. It's quite uncomfortable when you're sitting there naked and he's crying."

I gaze out the window, shielded from the drunk kids stumbling home. "I want to make men cry."

71

The next day, as Tiffany and I are sunning ourselves poolside, the following conversation occurs:

"Who knows that you dance?" I ask.

"My parents."

"REALLY? That just seems so… counterintuitive."

Rolling over, we check each other's ass cheeks to ensure we're setting ourselves up for perfectly wedgied tan lines.

"I asked them both if they'd be alright with it before I started. My mum and I came and checked out the club together when she came to visit from the UK."

"I could never tell my mom. She nearly shat her pants when I told her I hitchhiked."

Two details I probably should have spared my worrying mother were: 1. That it was on the autoroute in France, and 2. That I was wearing booty shorts. Since that misstep in oversharing, I've decided that it's probably best not to tell her that I'm getting completely naked for strange men on the other side of the world.

"So then your friends know, too?"

"Oh heavens, no," she says, shaking her head and then carefully adjusting her sunglasses. "They just wouldn't understand."

I find it bizarre that we share inverted feelings about who would high-five us for our recent career choices, and who would immediately start praying for us.

"I've told one or two of my friends back home," I say, "but I couldn't imagine asking my family for their approval before I even went through with it."

"I'd like to be able to tell them. But my boyfriend is ashamed. I mean, he would never say that he was, since we met at the club, but I know that he is."

*

The night we have both been waiting for—the night where we will have the opportunity to undress beneath a waterfall, climb a 20-foot pole, and give dance upon dance to cavalier billionaires on leather-quilted couches—is nigh.

Striding confidently past the doors of yesterday's horror show, up the red carpet, and past Hamish, Tiffany and I reintroduce ourselves to the still-absent-minded manager. I audition first. As I dance through a Rihanna remix, my judge and potential employer rifles through what must be some very important paperwork. She checks her phone, and giggles. When it's Tiffany's turn, the manager offers her the same respect. She waves her offstage midway through the song, getting up to make a phone call.

We are handed a stack of photocopied paper that must be the entire Old and New Testament. It is held together with a handful of staples.

SHOWGIRL CONTRACT for THE COVETED CLUB

Every club has one of these to save their asses from lawsuits. So, every time a club has a lawsuit—and they're usually being sued from three different directions at any given moment—the contract gets amended to avoid a repeat in offences. Hence the tome we have just been wordlessly handed and are expected to study.

Essentially, it reads:
Thou shalt not solicit the fornication of patron and dancer.
Thou shalt not text nor tweet whilst strutting around the magenta carpeting of the club.
Thou shall give 10 percent of thy earnings to thine Father.

We sign the contracts and hand them over to another manager, a tall and moderately handsome man who seems pleasant enough. He is on a stepladder, fixing the security camera that surveys the cashier.

"Thanks, girls. Just so you know, though, we're going to be taking 20 percent, and not 10."

"But we just signed a contract that says the club will only take 10 percent." My voice drops an entire octave. "That's the contract that you wrote and we just signed."

"Yeah, well, we changed it. This isn't a democracy. If you don't want to work here, I understand." Turning back to his work, our choice is clear: stay and be robbed for an additional 10 percent, go back to the dump across the street, or tap out and watch cable at the hotel.

In the business of sexy entertainment, you're damned if you do and damned if you don't. Every club exploits its entertainers in different ways. This ethicless prick on a stepladder is the direct beneficiary of this particular horseshit business practice: At the end of the night, my extra 10 percent will go straight into his pocket. If a stripper wants to get out of paying taxes and union dues, she is still going to be forced into giving 30 percent of her hard-earned dry-humping dollars to some sort of managerial pimp. If I put too much thought into it, my stomach aches.

The petite manager pooh-poohs all of our dress options and orders us to go down the street to buy new ones that adhere to The Coveted Club's dress code (floor-length; no cutouts; side slit or front slit ONLY; no zippers or lace). By the time we return to the dressing room, the girls are already out the gate. Tiffany and I slap on our lip gloss, stretch out our hamstrings, and embark on a game of catch-up.

The Coveted Club is no place for rookies like us. The waterfall is nice, but the pole is impossibly high, and the winding hallways and hard-to-find lap-dance room makes me feel as if I'm wandering around a brothel and not a strip club. The other dancers are shellacked from head to toe. They look like wax figures, sitting with old fat dudes while engaging in what I can only imagine to be less-than-thrilling conversations about golf. There is money to be made, but Tiffany and I are not making any of it. I eye a woman who passes by me on the way to the dressing room. Without a care in the world, she leafs through a wad of fifties. She wears a dirty blonde wig that hasn't seen a comb in months. *What it is that she has that I don't?* My eyes scan down her haphazard boob job and narrow hips. A belly of taut skin protrudes: this woman is at least four months pregnant. But her irreverently fake tits are so distracting that the baby bump kind of disappears.

How the fuck is it that preggerz Plain Jane is killing it and I'm sitting here twiddling my goddamn thumbs?

Even if the tit-grabbing feels shitty, it doesn't feel nearly as shitty as going for broke when you specifically came all the way up to this goddamn place to make bank.

My tits are awesome! And natural! Why doesn't anyone want to play with them?

For a moment I convince myself that if I had introduced myself as 'Cherish' instead of Roxy I'd be totally killing it. It will be a while before I understand the highly lucrative sit-and-bullshit business model. Tonight is the night the universe has designated for me to learn humility.

Tiffany and I go back to our hotel, pack our bags, and book the next available flight back to Sydney. The hotel refuses to refund the five days we will not be staying, and the discount airline's flight-change fee is more expensive than the flight itself. My first stripper trip is a complete fail. And I barely even got a tan.

The plane lifts into the sky, transporting our weary souls and over-fondled breasts nearer to safety.

"Iris," Tiffany begins, "What made you choose 'Iris' as your stage name? Of course, I think it suits you, and yet at the same time I find that the only other Irises I know of are practically senile. Of course, you're not senile. It's unique. Anyway, I was just wondering what prompted you to choose that particular name …"

I am often asked why I chose 'Iris' as my sexy stripper name. If you can believe it, some people don't find it to be the most fuckable designation out of the Baby Names iPhone App.

"It just happened. On the day I decided I would become a stripper, I also decided that my name would be Iris."

Although I do have an unhealthy affinity for nineties alt-rock jams, I didn't name it after the Goo Goo Dolls song, nor the flower, or the part of the eye that seems to inspire so many other sappy love songs. Like most of my creative endeavours, I just pulled it out of my ass. And it works, or at least I think it does.

It just so happens that Iris is also a descriptor for a rainbow or 'rainbow-like appearance,' so maybe it's some gay-pride subtext I'm using to lezzify my identity unbeknownst to my string of male suitors. Yet by some stroke of fate, I did not consider any of this upon picking the name.
When I decided to become a stripper, there were a lot of other palm-sweating factors that ranked higher on my list of concerns: Am I too fat? Can I dance? Will I get raped? What if my roommate happens to be a frequent strip-club goer?

Something else I did not bother considering was what could rhyme with my potential alias. Fortunately, a team of UFC fighters came in one night to clue me in:

"What's your name, sweetheart?"

"Iris."

"IRIS! That rhymes with VIRUS!"

"What drew you to Tiffany?"

"Well, I just always loved the movie *Breakfast at Tiffany's*." Flipping through a dog-eared copy of SkyMall, my flight companion stops to inspect a chip in her French manicure, visible only under a microscope. Tiffany is always meticulously put together. "I don't know that I like it that much, but I tried to change it and my favourite regular just didn't want to adjust. It's like I was sabotaging his fantasy of me. Of course, I like the money more than I mind what they call me when I'm bent over and stroking my own arse."

"Why is he your favourite?"

"He's reliable. He always comes in and spends lots of money, without demanding that I comply to his mind games. He talks to me like a human being. He doesn't make me feel like I'm a stripper. Sometimes they just direct you like you're a puppet, you know…. 'Stand like this, bend over, spread your lips'… *he* talks me to like I'm a real person. He's just a very lonely man. He's not very handsome, though, which is a shame, because I would much rather dance for a hot guy."

"I hate dancing for hot guys! They think they don't have to pay. And the handsome ones are so arrogant. I much prefer the oldies and fatties."

"I guess you're right. But it feels less like work and more like fun with a hot guy." Tiffany closes SkyMall, slips it carefully back into the pouch, and looks at me, confused: "If you're a lesbian, Iris, can you tell if a man's attractive?"

"Can you tell if a woman's attractive?"

"You're right. Sorry. You're just the first lesbian I've ever met."

"I'm sure you've met a few, you just weren't aware of it. We're everywhere, you know. And we're not all carpenters."

We touch down in Sydney. It's a relief to know that this trip is over. I can't wait to get back to my sublet, my bed, and the corner in the dressing room that I've designated as mine. My shoulders slump at the thought of not having a warm and sexy body crawling into bed with me. A part of me doesn't trust myself to resist the temptation to call Max. She was my only touchstone in the entire southern hemisphere who I didn't meet under the guise of getting paid for being cute. Suddenly, Sydney feels pretty empty.

As we roll our suitcases across the tarmac, I notice two girls waiting to board the plane Tiffany and I just got off. They have matching platinum, waist-length extensions, hot pink acrylic manicures, and oversized sunglasses that someone from outer space would know are DIOR. Fact: Strippers love rhinestone lettering.

"You know," I offer, "I've heard good things about Melbourne ..."

So the Gold Coast was a bust. I probably should have learned not to give too much credence to the rumour mill of bedazzled vagabond money-sniffers. But I also learned this valuable lesson: STRIPPER TIP #11: When trying out a new club, a) Do your research, and b) Allow for a very, very wide margin for error and disappointment.

I just can't seem to help myself; I'm an adventuress. Nowhere in any definition of 'adventure' does the term 'money back guaranteed' appear.

The Fish Bowl

"Melbourne's like, the cultural capital of the country. Compared with the rest of 'Straya, Melbourne's got crap weather," Jessie-Lee—my latest role model and international cash cow—tells me when going through a list of all the cities she works in. Melbourne is one of her favourites. "And because the weather sucks, the city makes up for it with art galleries, cafes, casinos … and strip clubs!" Melbourne is also home to a raging clan of sports fans. At any given moment. there is some sort of momentous game happening: "There is footie, soccer, rugby, and then football again, and then cricket. And then there are The Races—that's what they say when they're talking about horses."

Jessie-Lee seems to understand everything about strip clubs everywhere. Yet in spite of her openness and easy-going attitude, she is reticent to divulge more when I press her. She would rather dish about the really hot young guy she's going to fuck when she finishes work. She stares at her phone, looking at videos of llamas grunting like humans. She giggles to herself. "…and then there are The Other Races—that's when they talk about cars."

Being aloof is her competitive edge. She's been at this game a long while, and she's not about to spill all her tricks to a rookie. Jessie-Lee is as sweet and smart as they come, but she's not my fairy godmother, either. If you want to find out what every single city is like for its working conditions and earning potential, go see for yourself.

*

So I book a ticket to Melbourne.

I have a reservation at a hostel. When I started stripping, I vowed never to sleep in a hostel again. Sharing a dorm room is for college students. I do not spread my labia for strange men so I can listen to the snores and farts of other strange men on my down time; it's not my kink. But although I can smell the money as I wait in the taxi line at the airport, I have yet to personally pocket any of it. I refuse to commit to anything remotely expensive until I confirm these money-making rumours to be true: I'm not about to repeat another Gold Coast misadventure.

I make straight for King Street, which Jessie-Lee told me is commonly referred to as The Golden Mile. Hostel second; hustle first.

At the bottom of the strip—as King Street is commonly called—I spot a Starbucks. I don't like Starbucks. They give people an unrealistic expectation of coffee. Coffee is supposed to be cheap and shitty, or expensive and decadently delicious. Starbucks fucks with everyone's understanding of the universe by making shitty, burnt coffee that's also expensive. There was a time when I would give the Establishment second, third, and 47th chances to not fuck up my Long Black[10], but those days are long gone. However, I don't see any other stores or cafes with a private area where I can freshen up, so lugging my heavy suitcase, I sneak into the washroom.

Once inside, I slip into a pair of patent plastic eggshell heels. They're so cheap that when I stand still in them, they wobble. I stole the shoes from the set of the last photo shoot of my peaking career as a stock photography model in Thailand[11]. They are my walk-into-the-club-and-make-an-impression shoes.

---

[10] Long Black: The Australian version of the American 'Americano,' or the French-Canadian 'Allongee.'

[11] Thailand: Before I moved to Australia, I was making a living as a 'Lifestyle' model, where I would smile while appearing to do activities like yoga, getting massages, or attending business meetings. At one point I got in a motorcycle accident, which, after five otherwise hard-partying months in Bangkok, I took as a sign from the Universe to move to wherever the sun is still shining in February: Australia.

STRIPPER TIP #12: If a stripper wants to be taken seriously as a potential hire, she needs a pair of these. They are the only Real Girl pair of heels I have. The nomadic life I've been living for the past year or so means I wear the same pair of black leather boots every single day, alternating only to slip on a pair of dollar-store sandals for a beach walk. Giving my best professional slut-gaze into the grey-spattered mirror, I puff on some extra blush, line my eyes with a dulling pencil, and slop on my for-auditions-only lip gloss. (Once I get hired, I wear lipstick. But I've discovered that blood-red lips are too intimidating for most managers, so I stick with a slippery Porn-Star Pink for meet-and-greets.) On my way out, I bypass the barista without purchasing anything and strut up the sidewalk to the first club.

Each club is derivative of the previous one. The walls are red, black, or some sort of muted mahogany plywood, and the receptionists are always busy doing nothing while you press them for serious information like, "Are you hiring?" or "What is the house fee?"

The final club at the top of King Street is the dodgiest. It's a massive, velvet-foyered, multiple-storey monstrosity that I cannot even begin to comprehend. It smells like steak and perfume that's marketed to pre-teens. As usual, I fill out the necessary paperwork asking where I've danced, how old I am, whether my breasts are real or fake ("circle R or F"), and my top three preferred stage names. (The bigger the club, the higher the number of entertainers, and lesser is the likelihood that a new recruit will get the name she wants.)

I hand over the completed application to a receptionist who is busy reading an Aussie gossip rag.

"Can I work tonight?" I ask her.

Without looking up, she drones, "The manager has to go over your paperwork and call you in for an interview."

My dorm at the hostel is already occupied by a party mom and her son; a Scotsman who seems to really like buying oversized posters; an English woman who sprawls her belongings—which

83

at first I confused with trash—across half the room; and some other quiet non-English-speaking dude who plays a lot of Sega Genesis (or whatever its current equivalent is). Bedsprings squeak and the Scotsman farts while the drunk mom whispers to her son about how much fun she had that night; how he "really should have come." He nods, although he's not listening. He's streaming *Skins* on his laptop. Somehow, I manage to fall asleep.

I wake up to my phone buzzing beneath my pillow. I can't tell if it's morning or afternoon, because the English chick has used a tie-dyed sarong accented with a marijuana leaf to cover the windows. My mouth feels like it's filled with unused tampons. I struggle to lick my lips and press 'call answer.'

"Hello?" I whisper. Most of my co-eds are still sleeping.

"Hi, is this Iris?"

"Yes."

"Would you like to come in to work tonight?"

"Which club is this?"

"The Fish Bowl."

"The one with the velvet staircase?"

"Yes."

"Okay, yeah, sure, I'll be there. What time?"

"Show up at 6:30. It's Thursday, so it's costume night. You have to wear a costume."

The Fish Bowl was that club that smelt like red meat and Bonne Bell. Without bothering to say a prayer so that another—and slightly less dodgy—club calls me back, I throw my phone down and flop my head back on the pillow.

When my roommates seem to be stirring enough that I don't feel like a total jackass by milling about the room, I rifle through my bag of lace and Lycra. Nothing could possibly be considered a 'costume' unless it were Halloween and I wasn't a stripper and I was dressing up as a sexy cat, skanky hipster, or slutty doorknob. I know that by the end of the night I'll have at least something to shove in *The Corrections*,[12] but after a sleepless night of snore-fart symphonies, I am in no mood to visit a sex shop and buy a $50 pair of red vinyl underwear with matching devil horns.

I consult the nearest dollar store instead. Angel wings, witch hats (in March?), Aussie paraphernalia of all sorts—boxers, lighters, chain wallets. Strolling the shop, aisle by aisle, every single dollar-priced item fails to inspire. Defeated, I drag my feet toward the door, where I'm stopped by a rack of plastic-wrapped sunglasses. Perfect.

Leaving a one-dollar coin on the unattended counter, I leave with a pair of black-rimmed shades. Tossing a blazer into my bag, I head to work.

Night falls and the girls trickle in to the largest dressing room I have ever seen in my life. Each entertainer has her own personal space at the sprawling vanity to make herself up. Every wall has a mirror and counter, and is lined with a string of glowing yellow bulbs. Everywhere I look I see an endless repetition of my own reflection. There are showers, complimentary fresh towels, and lockers that appear to have a fully functional locking mechanism! There is a kitchen with a fridge, sink, and kettle offering tea and coffee! There are couches everywhere—and judging by the sleeping angel with her halo and wings resting on her hip—they look comfortable.

The house madam shouts at me from a panopticon at the centre of the room.

"HEY NEW GIRL. COME INTO MY OFFICE."

---

[12] I keep my money stashed in books. I picked up this life hack from my friend Emma who I met in my Russian class. We both worked in night clubs, and also enjoyed counting our cash more than depositing it in the bank. Being able to count it all the time made me better at saving it. Enterprising sluts can learn a lot from Mr. Scrooge.

I walk into the office, dreading that I'm being fired before I can actually enjoy the privilege of using this dressing room of my dreams.

"You can't be Scarlett. We already have a Scarlett."

"Okay, well, what about Roxie?"

"We already have a Roxie."

"Zoe?"

"No."

I scan the office, trying to draw inspiration from the faded tear-outs of eighties-era playmates on the walls. I don't relate to any of these women; I'm 20 years too young to idolize Christie Brinkley. I think of strong, sexy women from my cultural vernacular and the only person who comes to mind is that character in the white dress who forgot her panties[13]... I can't remember her name in the movie, so I say: "What about 'Sharon?'"

"Alright, Sharon, your first podium is at 7:45. If you're late, it's a $50 fine. Do you have a costume?"

I nod.

Without any conviction, she wishes me good luck.

Sharon? I love Sharon Stone. But 'Sharon' was not the name I had in mind. I know a sexy Sharon in real life, too, but it's just ... All of my mom's friends are named Sharon. Or Linda. Or Gayle. They are pretty, matronly names. But I'm a stripper. I'm not old enough to try to pass as a MILF. I would like to think that I look more like a girl who makes weird mockumentaries using her vagina and claymation prosthetics. I want to turn around and tell the manager that my name is "Zelda," but the

---

[13] *Basic Instinct,* 1992

clock is telling me that I need to get a move on applying my base if I want it to set in time for contouring perfectly assertive cheekbones.

Mousey girls, homely girls, haggard students, and mothers-of-two transform into vampire vixens, French maids, bumble bees and cheerleaders. I step into my g-string, punch out the lenses of my new glasses, and slip on my blazer.

My first target, average in every way, including his choice of brown suit and matching tie, asks me, "Are you my secretary?"

"I'm your boss," I reply, unflinching. "Shut up and step into my fucking office."

He obliges and I drag him by the arm into the lap-dance room.

It takes a little less than an hour for me to understand that this club is a free-for-all. I can't seem to find any security guards, and I'm not sure if it's because they are nowhere to be found, or because I'm too busy stuffing my wallet with 50- and 100-dollar notes. The Fish Bowl opens at noon and closes at 6 in the morning. All a girl has to do is show up, pay $65, and hustle until her legs fall off.

At this particular club, the hustle works like this: one dance for 20 bucks, or three for 50. Almost everyone goes straight for the three-song set. There are five or six rooms with benches, chairs, and security cameras, where most of the lap dances take place. A dancer can also give a lap dance at the tipping rail during one of her 15-minute stage shows. She can give a lap dance at the bar, on one of the massage chairs, or at any place anywhere in the club that doesn't obstruct a safety exit. Pay upfront; no contact.

In spite of my efforts, I don't have the stamina to last until sunrise. I get back to the hostel at 5 in the morning. I'm too tired to even count my money, but I can feel through the thickness of my wallet that there is a lot of it. Paying no heed to the snoring, bleeding headphones, and cougar-son gossip, I stash my winnings inside my pillowcase and sleep like a kitten.

Early the next morning, way before my roommates stir, I gleefully drag my suitcase across the floor of the room and out the door, never to return. I roll up to a bar in an almost-hip-but-mostly-just-conveniently-close-to-the-hospital neighbourhood. Upstairs are half a dozen rooms. I request an east-facing room at the end of the hall. My reasoning for this is that I've found that most strippers sleep until 2 or 3 o'clock in the afternoon. As stoked as I am about pretty much everything in this new lifestyle (Cash! Free booze! Butt muscles! Social stigma!) I would like to avoid this particular habit. If it's a beautiful day outside, I want to know about it, and I want to be sitting in it, sipping on sangria and dipping into a pool at random intervals. I've endured too many Canadian winters to know that sleeping in is for rainy days and the cocaine blues. I'm counting on the sun to disturb me from my slumber so I can enjoy the daytime hours.

The room rates here are twice the price of a hostel. But after a successful first night in this new city, I'm feeling confident and worthy of a comfortable and quiet place to rest my head. I hand over enough cash to keep me shacked up for the rest of the week.

A purple-haired barmaid shows me to my room. It has a television, bar fridge, and I can still smell the fresh lick of stark white paint on the walls. "There is a shared bathroom down the hall," the barmaid says. "But no one else is here tonight, so you'll have it to yourself." The bed is white, too, and looks hard. An iron rod juts out from the wall, and four wire coat hangers dangle, clinking together as the door clicks to a close behind me.

Have I just admitted myself to a psych ward? I reason that maybe it's just so the guests feel simpatico with the sickly loved ones they are visiting down the road.

I am finally alone.

The next day I arrive at The Fish Bowl with a bag of carrots, raw almonds, and two industrial-strength, sugar-free energy drinks. I don't think I've ever taken any job as seriously as I'm taking this one. I've come to Melbourne, alone this time, with the sole purpose of making money. There is just too much potential to make so much cash and it has me AMPED.

I walk into the dressing room 30 minutes early so I can get my Sharon on without being surrounded by mayhem. I still hate this name, Sharon, for my stripper alias, but everything moves so fast that no one—including myself—seems to give a shit. I'm pretty sure most of my clients remember my name as Short Blonde Hair 34C Big Smile, anyway.

I set up my makeup at the vanity and pour myself a cup of tea. A tall woman with a mane of brown crimpy waves storms into the dressing room, smacking her gum and tousling her hair. She sets a duffel bag down on the vanity, next to my spread of concealer, rouge, and eye shadows. Raising one eyebrow, her eyes narrow as she analyzes my reflection:

"You're new." Her voice is low and husky.

"Yeah, I'm … Sharon."

"Where are you from?" she inquires, in an indecipherable accent.

This woman is intimidating as fuck. There is something outlandishly domineering about her eyebrows. They are so … archy.

"I just arrived here from Sydney, but I'm Canadian."

Pouting her lips, she lifts her chin and sweeps a dark brown eye shadow across her almond-shaped eyelid. She does all of this without breaking eye contact with me. She is a lion and I am an antelope, frozen.

"Is tonight your first night?"

"No, I started last night."

"And how did you do?"

"I am pretty happy with it."

"No, *how much did you make*."

This is not kosher. Every dancer is accustomed to making different amounts of money. Strip clubs are highly competitive environments, and it is only professional to respect that each entertainer has a different expectation, and not to boast, complain, or talk numbers. It's rude, just like it's rude to talk money in any other professional environment. "The only place that's appropriate to talk money is at the bank," I recall. Apparently this Lioness didn't get the memo. And she's so fucking intimidating that I can't not answer her. I feel like if I lie she might strike me down with a single swipe of her paw.

"I made seven hundred."

The Lioness raises her eyebrows, "You can do better. I made two thousand."

Two thousand fucking dollars on a Thursday night?!

She goes on: "I've been in this industry for 11 years. I only work in Melbourne, London, and in New York. I own three properties, I'm just finishing my law degree and I never leave without making two thousand dollars. I'm very good because I can spot the whales." Her eyes scan my hair, my chest, and my fresh coat of Mango Get-Em on my fingertips. "You'll do very well here. You have an accent, and you look … interesting. You will learn."

I'm pretty sure she's being condescending, but I don't care because all I can think of is walking out of the club tonight with two thousand fucking dollars.

Throughout the night, I search for The Lioness, hoping to glean some money-making strategies. She's hard to spot, because she always seems to be in cahoots with some fat cat in the lap-dance room. I see her leaving the powder room: she pauses, standing with her back against the wall. She scans the room, smacking her gum like it's a fucking callisthenic exercise for her jaw, and picks her target. She weaves through the crowd, whips her chestnut mop over her left shoulder and leans in, right arm around his neck. It's 9:42 p.m.

He smiles. They chat. She whispers into his ear: 9:43.

90

Using the weight of her matronly hips, she leans in a little closer. He shakes his head; she nods and walks away. It's 9:43 and she's on to her next target.

The vibe of The Fish Bowl is playful and busy, so selling dances is easy and fun. Every man I talk to is either celebrating a team win or lamenting a loss; either way they're Stoked! About! Titties! The club's sprawling layout has everyone in constant motion. People are always moving to another room for another activity, stage, or seating arrangement. Money moves in quickly, and in all directions. Apart from the habitual drunken douchery and occasional ass-grabbing, the only serious shortcoming I can find about the general demographic of Melbourne strip-club goers is that their breath is—more often than not—fucking putrid. It smells as if years of alcohol and cigarettes have killed any potential cells or nerves that could alert a man to his own personal fetor. One kindhearted man opens his mouth to ask me my name, and I nearly faint at the rotten stench emanating from his whiskered and yellowing pucker.

"Sharon," I tell him with a squint. My eyes are burning.

"Shaaaaazaaaaaaaa!" he replies, jubilant. Australians have nicknames for everyone, and oftentimes they end in a string of superfluous z's and a's.

STRIPPER TIP #13: In situations like this, the best course of action is to pretend that the music is too loud, which is often the case. Turning her head, a dancer can offer up an ear. Moist beer breath sputtering into an ear is marginally less worse than having it spray into one's eyes, up nostrils, or onto a carefully painted-on and perfectly set face. If I'm smiling—and an entertainer should be, always—I also risk having this cloud of rotting meat pies waft into my mouth. All options suck, and there are times when it's just so foul and unbearable that I have to walk away. But none of these men is exactly Prince Charming, so it's best to either overlook their imperfections, or muster the ingenuity to manoeuvre around it. When I get around to taking them for a dance, I pray that they're ass men, because that's the asset I'll be thrusting inches from their face to keep my face as far from their breath. Yet—as fate would have it— these stinkers most often identify as pussy men. I don't usually like to disappoint, so I tend to compromise by standing a few

91

feet away and offer up the more explicit rendition of Hey-Look-No-Panties! meets Look-at-How-Flexible-I-Am!

Two middle-aged Indian men are hunched close together in silence. They sport matching bushy moustaches.

"Hi!" I beam, shouldering up to the one who I estimate to be closer to his golden years than the other. STRIPPER TIP #14: When given a choice between two potential clients, always approach the older, less attractive, or chubbier one. He never gets chosen first and will feel special that you did, and will therefore probably want to hang out with you. And, unless he has a weird I-like-to-be-mean-to-pretty-girls-because-HIGH SCHOOL complex (and this breed is rampant in this sort of establishment), he will probably be sweet, appreciative, and happy to pay you for your time and loveliness.

"Won't you join me for a special, private, *sexy* dance?" I ask, eyes aflutter. The reality is the dance I'm selling is not special, nor is it—in my opinion—'sexy,' and it can only be considered 'private' if a simulated orgy of five girls and five guys in a room with security cameras is what one might consider private.

"If I take you," he begins in his rolling accent, "you must co-operate."

It's Friday night and I immediately consider moving onto the next gent. At peak hour, it's not usually worth lingering to negotiate. When a guy has the gall to insist that I do something as absurd as 'co-operate' with their Jessie Jane-inspired fantasies, I pass. And although I do aim to please, in this particular job I am generally galaxies away from being cooperative, submissive, or acquiescent. My performance gives the illusion that I am co-operative, but I find the explicit request crass and also intimidating. Whenever someone uses the word 'co-operation,' my mind immediately thinks HOSTAGE NEGOTIATIONS.

But my toes are poking through my fishnets, lacerating my already blistering feet. I need a break. I reason that since he will be paying upfront, he risks not getting a refund if he gets too particular with his demands.

He goes on. "I want you to sit on my lap."

I'm not sure what kind of dances this man has had before. The vast majority of lap dances involve some degree of sitting on laps. I'm curious as to what sort of deviant lap-dancing divas have levitated or done handstands in front of this guy, and I wonder where on Earth this club might be so I can go there soon. But this is no time for daydreaming. I shoo away my drifting thoughts of contortionists in hot pink baby dolls and magicians in crotchless panties, and lean in closer with my perky ears, keen eyes, and rapturous cleavage.

"I want you to sit on my lap, and lay against me." He demonstrates by crossing his arms against his chest, and gives himself a hug.

This seems simple enough. Should any of his requests become problematic in the following 10 minutes, I'll work it out with the heel of my shoe. Before he can go on to further illustrate his fantasy, I grab him by the wrist and weave through the throngs of drunken bachelors, sports fans and the steadfast crew of unathletic, drunk, and lonely chaps.

I start dancing and slowly begin to unhook my bra when this Indian Golden Boy reaches out to me, like a child. Beckoning me in, he brings me to his lap. He wraps his arms around me, pulling me close to his chest, just like he demonstrated not 30 seconds ago. My cheek squishes, pressing hard against his sternum.

We stay this way for all three songs. My breath whistles through my puckered lips. While I inspect the fabric of his poly-cotton blend sweater, I make a mental note to redo my blush and lipstick once I escape this clutch of deprived affection.

'Hugs' aren't really in my job description. Hugs are for feeling vulnerable and for having someone meet you halfway to tell you that you're safe. Strange men are incapable of providing that sense of security, and it is entirely of their own doing. A strange man cannot ask a woman to 'smile' while she's walking down the street carrying groceries and then ask for a goddamn hug. Nineteen-year-old customers with a crumpled up twenty ask for a hug all the goddamn time. It makes me roll my eyes SO

HARD. I just gave you a lap dance—you didn't say anything except "Whoa," and now you want a hug? Are you serious? WE ARE NOT IN HIGH SCHOOL AND THIS IS NOT THE CAFETERIA AND I AM NOT ABOUT TO GO TO FIFTH PERIOD CALCULUS AND I ALSO DO NOT, COINCIDENTALLY, HAVE A CRUSH ON YOU, SO NO, I WILL NOT HUG YOU.

The sanctity of the hug is exploited by creeps and douchebags all the fucking time, and I motion to start a petition to ban the 'request' for a hug. Because when a girl says "no" to a creep she barely knows, she's slapped with the moniker "cold-hearted bitch." Or maybe I should just start a petition to implore girls everywhere to embrace that very title.

Hugs are warm, wondrous experiences when they are shared between friends, family, and lovers. But this guy is at least 40, and he's looking for a hug like he hasn't nestled his head into the Pantene-scented hair of a woman in a really, really long time. Risking a complete smudge of my lip liner, compassion takes over and I slump deeper into his chest. The thump of the bass gets muffled by the lub-dub of his beating human heart.

This job has changed me. I'm either a raging volatile bitch, or I just want to touch the back of every lonely-looking man's neck and tell him, "If only you weren't already spoken for…" Even if it's a total lie, I'll say it with this calm, loving tone … just to make him feel good. This shift in attitude occurs within a millisecond.

None of my colleagues care to dish about moments of compassion. It seems defeatist to discuss enjoying an aspect of the job that extends beyond the pride we take in extortion. We all 'like the money,' but for some reason it's just not socially acceptable to talk about what else we like about it. The predominant ethos of the working girl is Hate Men/Love Money. And sometimes I sincerely share this feeling, I really do. Most men are fucking pigs—snorting, drooling, stinky, stupid, aggressive fucking pigs. And sometimes they are sad, lonely, and shy.

As the cymbal crashes to denote the end of the third song, I strain to tilt my head up, asking Indian Golden Boy if he would like to continue.

"Yes, I would."

Exhaling, Golden Boy releases me from his grip just enough to reach for his wallet. He peels out another fifty, hands it to me, and resumes exactly where he left off: squeezing. With what feels like a juvenile wiggle, I rotate my ankles, loosening the grip of my shoes around my ailing toes. Touch-ups will have to wait.

The second round of hugs ends, and I excuse myself for my scheduled midnight podium on the main stage. I step into the spotlight, stretching out of my hug-cramp by taking a quick climb up the pole. Clenching my thighs around the brass phallic symbol, I drop upside down, take off my bra, and shake out my hair. Twenty minutes off my feet has done wonders for my mood! I'm reinvigorated with a refreshed desire to provoke these inebriated gawkers for attention, money, and my own personal entertainment. Suddenly I'm really into high kicks, fan kicks, and dropping into the splits at random intervals. Could it be that I, too, may have also benefitted from the healing powers of a stranger's hug? I rack my brain for the last time I received a hug from anyone, and my mind draws a blank. Must have been from Maxine. It feels like a lifetime ago.

After my 15 minutes of flirting with my own reflection, and coaxing 20-dollar notes out of a squealing bachelorette party, I gather my scattered skivvies and step out of the limelight. I start for the powder room when I am tapped on the shoulder. It's Indian Golden Boy's younger sidekick, Raj.

"You made my friend a very happy man," he says, grinning, hands in his pockets.

"Good!" I respond, slightly out of breath, but smiling ear to ear. "I aim to please."

I wonder what Golden Boy said I did to him; like fishermen and joggers, strip-club patrons are prone to embellishment.

"Could you make me happy too? More happy than my friend?"

Why are men so competitive in the PURSUIT OF HAPPINESS?

I have no idea what's in store for me, but I'm on autopilot: grab the wrist, make for the back—hurry! Time is money.

Before I can even catch up to the beat with my hip-sway, Raj outstretches his arms and asks me to sit down. He hugs me. I am sweaty and he is wearing polyester. We embrace for three … six … nine … *nine songs*. Then it's done and I'm back on the floor, hunting for my next prey.

The next guy I go up to introduces himself by asking, "Do you like being turkey slapped[14]?"
The one after that "would absolutely love a dance, please," and tips me with a lollipop. As I peel back the wrapper for a quick sugar fix, I see The Lioness assessing me from the corner.
The Lioness doesn't talk to the other girls. She only talks to me. This could be for a number of reasons. 1. She's talked to them and sees nothing in them, or 2. They see nothing in her and no point of making an attempt at any sort of cordiality, given the fact that she is SO FULL of herself. But her confidence is amazing to watch. I feel like her unofficial protégé.
She tells me about hustling. She talks about how to get a lot of money out of individual clients. I want this. I see her and think, *yeah, I could do this a little while longer*. I could dance the decade away and have a law degree (or an MFA, more my style… more frivolous), three properties in New York, London and Copenhagen with a cushy flat in Melbourne and stacks of cash to stow away in a safety deposit box. She is so successful because she is relentless as much as she is ruthless. *Oh, Lioness, you fascinate me beyond comprehension and intimidate the shit out of me. It's sexy. I wish I were attracted to you. But my god, your head is so far up your ass.* My only critique of her business practice is that never have I seen her without a wad of gum in her mouth, smack, smack, smacking away. But she has two symmetrical tits, a gorgeous, old Hollywood face and a husky

---

[14] Turkey slap: When a man slaps his penis on a person's cheek, or pretty much anywhere on the face area.

Danish accent, so the boys never seem to mind. Like Donald Trump, The Lioness is a wonder to watch. She has the power, the success, and the respect, yet she's a fucking twat. Every time you see a hustler in action, it's magic. Especially if her tricks are hitherto undiscovered by you.

The Lioness joins me for no more than 4 minutes and 59 seconds to try to lure two young, broke men into her 'Boobie Sandwich.' Deflecting her invitation, one of the boys asks "How much do you earn, on average[15]?"

Without hesitation, The Lioness sparks up, flipping her mane of crimped curls from left to right. "TWO THOUSAND." She resumes smacking her gum.

They glance over to me, repeating the question.

Casually and matter-of-factly, I tell them: "I earn just enough to support my crack addiction." This is the story I stick to. STRIPPER TIP #15: How much money I make is nobody's fucking business.

I look at my approach to selling and then I look at hers, and I don't know which one is best. She makes more money than I do. But in 10 years' time, If I'm still stripping, I'd hope to have a salary increase.

Besides The Lioness, who I've only really hung out with between moments of getting ready and during sporadic run-ins throughout the shift, I haven't made any friends in Melbourne. I have nothing else to do with my time, so I throw "Sharon" onto the roster six times in the upcoming week. That's what The Lioness does. So that's what I'll do. Eat, sleep, work, repeat.

Eventually, The Lioness divulges more personal details after I introduce her to a Danish client who claimed he was 'homesick.' STRIPPER TIP #16: Connecting clients and dancers hailing from the same hometown, (or tiny Scandinavian country, it's basically the same thing) is a bad idea. "I have quite a face in

---

[15] By saying "on average," this does not make you any less of a nosey fucker.

Denmark, so I do my best to dodge the Danish clients. So if you ever meet a really shy customer with a sheepish accent, don't send him my way. I was on a TV show there and was quite famous. I keep my life in Copenhagen separate from my life here."

I tried to help out my sensei and totally bombed.

"I've been fired *three* times from Bar 20," she continues.

"Why?"

"For making too much money. You see, in Australia, they don't want you making too much money. In America, they congratulate you for milking the clients. But here, they protect their clients and not their dancers."

I would like to get fired for making too much money.

This woman knows nothing of me because she's never asked. It's refreshing to just sit and listen to her talk at me. On paper, she's enormously successful: A law degree, three properties, some watches, a thoroughly-stamped passport … but in the flesh, she hasn't an ounce of grace. Never have I seen her with her mouth shut.

After spending a sunny afternoon spending over $20 on macarons at four different French pastry shops across the city, I make my way to work on a decadent sugar-high. Pouring myself a cup of tea, a dancer comes up to me, asking, "Are you English?"

"No, I'm Canadian."

"Oh, I joost saw you pourin' yourself a cuppa when everyone else is drinkin' Red Bull and just assumed you were from the U.K. I'm Martine." Sheepishly, she reaches out to shake my hand.

"I joost started dancin' last week. It's foon, boot I joost don't know wha I'm doin,' like. I saw ya workin' last noight. You're so good at makin' moon-eh. How do ya do it?"

I've been so preoccupied with attempting to match The Lioness' quota that I never even considered myself 'good' at what I do. But I see Martine's nervous smile, her fresh platforms with the price tags still stuck to the soles, her awkward gait, and I see myself less than a year ago.

"Well," I start, "always match the body language of whoever you're talking to. If a guy is sitting down, sit down. If he's leaning against the bar, do the same. If his arms are crossed and he's looking away from you while you're talking to him, don't fucking bother, because that's rude."

Martine's eyes widen as she searches for a pen.

"Flirt by touching his shoulder or forearm. Never ask 'Do you want a dance?' but ask 'Can I dance for you?' Make it sound like you really want to dance for him. Make it about your desire more than just about haplessly catering to his. Always be touching him when you ask this question. But you don't need to be crass. I see a lot of girls grabbing at a guy's balls while they pitch. It's unnecessary.

"Don't just smile the entire time you're on stage … it's not a pageant. It's about making your target believe that you actually like him; that he's the only one in the room who has your undivided, horny-as-all-hell attention. So, yes, smile, but only after making eye contact with someone. Always dance slowly— you save energy and it draws out the dance. And, when in doubt, flip your hair."

I'm shocked at how I just riffed all this off while covering up my blemishes. I guess I am pretty okay at what I do.

***

A Colombian guy takes a shine to me—he's handsome like a primetime drama firefighter. His name is Carlos and he smiles a lot. I am charmed as I sit on his lap, half dancing but mostly just drinking in his beauty. His English is terrible, but he's so confident that I stop noticing.

"I've always wanted to go to Colombia!" I beam, leaving out HOW GOOD IS THE BLOW THERE? My first girlfriend was

Colombian and told me never to ask a Colombian person about cocaine; they'll be insulted and subsequently put a hit on you. Instead, I say, "I want to see Mexico, too."

"I live dere when I was jounger—six jears old. I get lost in Mehico City for five days. I stay with other family who find me. I'm lucky," he says with the most pearly white smile. "... Many missing children in Mehico."

Carlos is beautiful and cute and nice. He makes me requestion my sexuality. I take his money, kiss him on the cheek, and decide that labels are stupid.

Later that night, I see Martine walking out of the lap-dance room: her scrunched-up face leads me to believe that she's trying really hard to hold in a fart. I have confidence that she's succeeding, because heels do that to a person. They make everything tight. Behind her is a man I've noticed at the club every single night since I started working here. He looks like he just strutted off the set of *Miami Vice*. He wears white jeans, a brown belt with some sort of bedazzling on it, and a shirt with a dragon on it. He appears to have a perm.

I've never approached him; there's something about white jeans and a spray tan on a man that makes me feel like I might get skin cancer just by being in his vicinity. Plus I've already learned that guys like that that usually like to get dances from girls who also have spray tans, bedazzled navels, and complementary dragon accessories.

As he smoothes out his jeans and thumbs down his boner, he looks past Martine and directly at me.

Mirroring my lean-and-survey position, Martine rests her elbow against the bar and scans the crowd.

"He said I didn't give'm a dirty enough dance. Fook'm."

"Yeah, fuck him. There are always guys like that. And even if you did give him the dirty dance he wanted, he probably wouldn't tip accordingly. Guys like that watch too much porn." I slip a fresh straw into my vodka soda and slide the glass across the bar. "Want a sip?"

I like taking this girl under my wing. Everyone needs a friend to console them when something shitty happens. When the baseline is that you dry hump strangers for money, shitty things tend to happen more often than if one was working at, say, a call centre.

The next day, I see Martine on the main stage in a brilliant purple lingerie set and a gorgeous mane of black shiny curls that she's flipping like she's been at this gig for years. An Asian tourist sits alone at the stage. He is wearing khakis, a red windbreaker, and fisherman's hat. Around his neck, a large camera with an even larger lens swings and bobs as he smiles and nods. Martine gestures toward her g-string, and this guy keeps on smiling, giving her a thumbs-up. Non-English-speaking customers do this all the time. They know what it means when a stripper pulls at her panties, lifting the elastic band, invitingly, but they pretend they don't by nodding, smiling, laughing, and instead showing their appreciation by giving one, or, if they really want to communicate 'fuck you,' a DOUBLE thumbs-up. They sit right up front in pervert row and act as if it's their first fucking rodeo. As I've grinded away on different laps over the past year, I've racked my brain for something that could be more cliché than the way tourists behave in strip clubs. Maybe it's because they're so uncomfortable and—in order to save face—they try to reduce their personhood to a stereotype.

I want to grab this guy by the collar of his windbreaker and tell him, squarely in the face: *You are in a strip club. You walked in here of your own free will. The concept of strip clubs are the same everywhere: if a girl is dancing for you, and she is naked, and unless you're in Cancun and it's Spring Fucking Break, you tip her. Even if you truly have never been to a strip club before, and accidentally stumbled inside and up the velvet staircase, you can at least take a quick look around to see that the custom in places like this is to show your appreciation for the show you are clearly enjoying in the front fucking row.*

Lecturing an ingrate can be really satisfying. But sometimes lecturing someone is just not as satisfying as getting paid. And my girl Martine is up there, giving him everything. She is

101

flawlessly masking her nerves with brilliant hair flips, and this asshole is just sitting there, giving her nothing in return.

Whatever, I can fix this without wasting a single breath.

I plop into the seat next to him, with a comical grin plastered across my face. I giggle and touch his arm, smiling to Martine, then turning to smile back at him. I nod my head, rubbing my thumb and index finger together. He starts to shake his head, waving his hands in front of his face. Before I can chastise him for such rude behaviour, a woman in khakis, a red windbreaker, fishing hat, and smaller camera necklace sits down beside me. She points at me, looks at her male doppelgänger, and nods.

She takes my wrist, leading me to the lap-dance room. The male doppelgänger follows. Before I can apologize to Martine for not succeeding in helping her earn a well-deserved tip, I am dragged away for what I am hoping is not an evil twin dance but a husband-and-wife dance.
As soon as I start with my routine ass-sway/bra-unhinge, the wife's hands are reaching for my panties, fingers outstretched. I smirk, waving my finger "no," and place her soft hands back down by her side. She looks to her partner with this plotting grin on her face. As I trace a finger over my breast, I see this woman's hands slide over to his crotch. Her eyebrows dance as she tickles her husband's balls over his khakis.

I love seeing couples who look like virgins get freaky in front of me. It's the best reassurance in the world to know that even the unlikely are getting laid.

But the husband isn't such an exhibitionist and pushes his wife's hand away, embarrassed. I sit on his lap, about to lean over the wife's lap so it looks like I'm eating her out through an imaginary pair of crotchless khakis. But before I can perform this brilliant move, wifey takes a full grope of my tit. I sit up, nearly knocking the camera off the husband's neck. I am shocked that it is the wife who is the perpetrator. I stand up, making an X with my forearms: the universal sign for GAME OVER.

It makes me so sad and angry when female customers don't respect the boundaries of dancers. It happens more than it

102

should. I expect it from men. But not from women. I expect women to be respectful and compassionate. But because there is so little entertainment that is created to cater to the pleasures and the fantasies of women, we have to improvise with what is on offer. Strip clubs are certainly designed for male entertainment; even if you're a woman who is attracted to women, there is something completely hetero and downright intimidating about strip clubs for anyone who isn't a straight man. Although it's very rare, whenever I pause and take a moment to consider my own desires that extend beyond making money, I ask, *is this how I'm supposed to think women are sexy? Dawdling around in all these ridiculous outfits, looking spaced out and pouty?* When women walk into these places, they assume the role of male chauvinist pig in order to fit in and get the entertainment they think they want. Strip clubs, I love you, but you're killing my lady boner.

Before I can take a moment to process my feelings about this most recent assault, I am scooped up by a guy who could easily pass for my grandfather.

He chooses the quietest lap-dance room, with round-back chairs instead of benches. We sit opposite each other, he fully clothed and I wearing only my shoes. My knees flop open, and my pussy takes centre stage. He leans in, but I stop him. "You know the rules," I start. "No touching."

"Oh, I know, I know. I just wanna *lookatcha*." He adjusts his glasses, peeling a fifty from his money clip. He hands it to me, gazing into my eyes over his spectacles. "I mean really, sweetheart, I just wanna lick it."

With a sheepish smile, I shake my head. "I don't do that."

Gramps goes on staring.

Had I known that this guy was so intent on staring so closely at my vagina for hours on end, I probably would have chosen a different day to get naked for him. I'm on day two of surfing the crimson wave and—in spite of my meticulous efforts to cut off the tampon string and make sure there isn't any visible or noxious evidence of the fact—I find it inconceivable that he hasn't noticed. I acknowledge that it is very possible that he has

103

noticed and that is precisely why he is still sitting there, peeling another fifty and handing it over to me. Men are into all sorts of weird shit—especially the silver foxes.

Maybe Gramps is a vampire, I ponder. They do, after all, have a lot of money.

"How much would it be, just to lick it?"

I shake my head again. He peels another fifty.

"A thousand?"

I shake my head.

"Five thousand?" He hands me two fifties this time.

At this point I am getting paid a lot of money to shake my head.

"Ten thousand? Come on, ten thousand just to eat that precious little box o' yours, sweetheart." He licks his lips.

"No, sweetie. I'm just a dancer."
If I weren't bleeding, I would consider it. *Ten thousand dollars to get something that I begged my first boyfriend of two years to do, to which he only obliged twice? Why the hell not?* Of course, there are lots of logistics to consider: location; security; is this guy diseased? Then I must also consider whether or not this would turn me on and/or crush my soul. Torturing random guys by waving my pussy in their face taps into my kink and turns me on a hell of a lot more than the idea of actually being eaten out by one of them.

I count 16 fifties from Gramps—way more than anything I ever got in any birthday card—stuff them in my purse, and go home. Maybe one day I'll do it. Stripper, whore; they are quite similar in a lot of ways, and I'm starting to think I'm comfortable being judged for either or both of these unorthodox and scorn-worthy career choices. The main incentive behind all work is the validation (read: cash) we get for doing it. I imagine $10,000 would feel pretty validating. But if I don't draw a line somewhere, no number will ever be enough. I'm happy with getting 800 bucks to sit with my legs open for a geriatric peep show. The Lioness leads me to believe that I'm capable of making two thousand a night, every night. Is this even true? Is she bullshitting me? I wonder: do I value myself less than she does? Is that why I'm not as rich as she is? But if I want to stay sane in this business, I cannot simply adopt someone else's idea of success as my own. For me—right now—$800 is a lot of money and I'm thrilled not to be paying any taxes on it.

A few more nights pass and Miami Vice is back, making a handful of increasingly obvious attempts to make eye contact with me. He stares at me from the corners, watching me while I consort with management, other girls, and other clients. Acutely remembering him as the type who wants a girl to pierce her cunt on his belt buckle for 20 measly dollars, I avoid him by busying myself with anyone else in sight. Since he's always at the club, I feel as if I've developed an incredibly disciplined work ethic since arriving here just two weeks ago.

On one particular occasion of stealth avoidance, I lean into the lap of a handsome man seated on a barstool. His beard is perfectly manicured and smells like Bloomingdale's. Before I can properly wiggle into a comfortable lean-sit, he recoils. "Hold on, I just don't want you to crush my cigarettes."

"You know," I begin, "smoking is bad for you." I'm one glass of extremely shitty champagne into my night. It tastes like sweetened paint thinner, and I'm feeling cheeky.

GQ removes his cigarettes from his slim-fitting jeans and places them on the bar.

"It's a filthy habit," I insist.

We go on to chat about where I'm from, the weather, and where I've been in Australia. Like all young and moderately good-looking men of his age, appearance, demeanour, and empty wallet, he doesn't "really want to be here;" a friend merely insisted that he come along to reluctantly gaze at a sea of naked breasts.

"You poor thing!" I exclaim with emphatic sarcasm, picking a piece of lint of his lapel. STRIPPER TIP #17: when you peel lint off a man's lapel, it shows him that you care for him. He will

105

appreciate this. If he's not a total dumbass, he will show his appreciation with money.

Without offering me his seat, GQ buys me a drink.

Now that I'm on my first sip of my second glass of champers[16], I've fewer inhibitions. I reach for his cigarettes. "Now, GQ, to truly make your experience here at The Fish Bowl as authentic as possible, I'm going to leave lipstick marks on your cigarettes."

"By all means, go ahead."

One by one, I take out a Stuyvesant cancer stick and gently place my Russian Red lips around the filters so they look like my grandma's ashtray. On the third of what would be 16 smokes, he interjects apprehensively. "You don't have herpes, do you?"

GQ doesn't buy a lap dance, nor does he tip me. I finally get up and leave his perch, mildly entertained and a little bit drunk, but ultimately spiteful for the time I spent with him and his complete lack of monetary compensation for my candidly coy entertainment.

I walk over to The Lioness, who is scanning the room with eyes like lasers. "That arrogant asshole totally wasted my time," I begin, throwing a fist up into the air and in GQ's general direction.

"No, he didn't. He didn't do anything." The Lioness pauses from her recon and points to my chest with the tip of her finger, the nail the colour of oxblood: "*You* wasted *your* time."

I drop my head in shame. I can't wait until I'm 30, and say all the right things at the right time.
I knew I wasn't going to get anything out of that boy the moment I sat on his smokes. But sometimes you need to use one

---

[16] Champers: Aussie slang for Champagne

man to hide from another. And sometimes a girl just needs to flirt.

Sometime well after 1 o'clock, I climb onto my last stage of the night. Pervert Row is packed with a horde of keen eyes. They are wearing matching tracksuits.

"ATHLETES!" I scream, squatting down to greet the runt of the litter. I rub my hands through his brush cut and squeeze his bicep. He blushes. His buddies bounce their buzzed heads and roar, nudging him in the shoulder.

"What do you boys play?" I ask, looking over at the rest of them. I inch my ass toward the stage. Lifting my legs high, I lower my knees onto this cute boy's shoulders. I squeeze his face with my thighs.

"SOCCER!" They beam back, some raising their arms in pride, but the rest fanning their bills, eagerly waiting their turn.

"Oooooooh!" I squeal, wiggling my fingers in delight.

"And what country do I need to travel to to meet such hot, sexy men?"

"HUNGARY!" They bellow in unison. One guy opens his zip-down to reveal a Hungarian flag on his t-shirt, taut against his pectorals.

In one move, I rise to my feet, tug at the knot of my bikini top, and rip it off, yelling, "I'M MOVING TO HUNGARY!"

Cheering, roaring, laughter and beer bottles raised; I am electric. These are my favourite moments: flirting with a sea of adoring fans who may not have a ton of money, but are celebratory, playful, and responsive to my performance. It's giggly, innocent, and flirtatious. I feel as if I'm Marilyn Monroe entertaining troops of soldiers—respected, adored, and professional. No one is asking me if I like having a dick slapped in my face.

The show's over when I look over my shoulder to the entrance of the stage, where another dancer is waiting to replace me. By the tapping of her foot, I realize I have gone over my allotted 15 minutes. Miami Vice stands beside her. Although he is not tapping his feet, his raised eyebrows tell me that he, too, is impatient. I sweep up the scattered five-dollar bills that litter the stage, blow a few kisses to my Hungarian fan club, and make for the stairs. At this point there is no avoiding Miami Vice. He is blocking my only exit.

"Are you busy?" he asks, shaking his head, irate. He has an accent that sounds like he could be from the same region as my adoring athletes.

"Uh…. no?" I reply, too short of breath to improvise with a fib.

"Let's go," he says, beelining for the private dance rooms.

We settle onto a bench. "Would you like to do a three-song dance?" I ask.

Miami Vice rolls his eyes. He has been leering about this club for god knows how long and yet acts offended by money talk, which I am certain he understands is routine procedure. He slips out a $50 bill from what is very obviously a hefty stack of fifties and hundreds in his wallet. He throws it at me.

"Vy you ignore me?" he starts. "Every other girl in dis place come up to me and vant dance. But not you. Vy?"

STRIPPER TIP #16: Ignore him, and he will come bearing gifts. It's just like high school. His name is not Miami Vice, but "Jiggy." Jiggy is from Croatia, and talks a lot of bullshit about how he's his own man. "I am different," he says to me. I roll my eyes, yet he persists: "Ven I go to da toilet, I vash my hands *before* I touch my dick."

Jiggy will keep paying me to sit on his lap and listen to self-aggrandizing tales of ex-wives and lawsuits. He doesn't want a dirty dance, nor does he want to know anything about me. He just wants me to sit there so he can talk at me. But every time I ask him for more money—"That's three songs, darling, do you want me to stay?" —he gets annoyed and throws another fifty or hundred at me. He never seems happy to pay, yet never wants me to leave his lap. After an hour or so of just sitting there in my skivvies, he offers me his white blazer to keep warm.

He goes on: "And even if I am here every night, I don't vant any membership card. I pay every day to get in dis place. I am not a member of any club. *I am no von's beetch.*"

Jiggy shows up to see me every night. We sit—he talks, I listen—and stays until I'm yawning, straining to keep my eyes open. The Lioness' advice was somewhat useful, but I'm tempted to tell her that I got rich by a stroke of luck, avoidance, and the law of scarcity. I leave Melbourne with so much cash that I have to re-evaluate my book-banking system. I wrap the bills into rolls using rubber bands, stuff them into socks, and maintain a white-knuckled grip on my carry-on suitcase as I embark on a queer detour to Middle Earth.

Off-Duty Stripper

I'm crammed in the back seat of a rented camper van on New Zealand's South Island. With me are my two Aussie mates, Mindy and Bo. We have budgeted six days to drive around, gawking at the precious landscape of verdant undulating hills dotted with white sheep.

Mindy is a lesbian who is really passionate about marketing, while Bo is a carpenter by day, drag queen by night. Since Mindy and I both like minge[17], and Bo and I are both into playing dress-up, I fit right in as their novel stripper-friend. We met one night when they came into the club back in Sydney. Mindy refused to tip me, so I berated her by waving my pussy uncomfortably close to her face. We've been prone to adventures ever since.

On the fourth day of our sojourn, we reach Queenstown. Queenstown is a breathtakingly quaint, beautiful community of outdoor enthusiasts, basking in the sun around a gorgeous lake.

---

[17] Minge: Aussie or British slang for vagina.

Within five square miles, one can ski, snowboard, skydive, swim, white-water raft, get wasted, and, of course, visit the strippers.

We roll into town with less than 24 hours to enjoy the town's offerings, so the only activities we can afford to enjoy are the last two. Bummed that skydiving is off the roster, we are resolved to pursue this drinking and ogling with unprecedented zeal.

Mindy parks the van along the lakeshore. Bo slides open the sliding door and crawls out from a beauty rest.

"Let's take a dip!" Mindy exclaims with the enthusiasm of cruise director. If she wasn't so stoked on viral marketing strategies, I'd hand her a pair of khakis and a clipboard, send her to Fort Lauderdale, and watch her take the Caribbean by storm.

Bo and I peel off our filthy road-trip uniforms, leaving our jeans and long-sleeved shirts on the hood of the van while we dart past a half-dozen fully-clothed, dry-haired sun bathers and into the water.

The lake is so fucking cold that after seven seconds of trying to splash, I go into what I can only describe as divine shock. Making like Jesus, I bolt across the surface of the water and back to the warmth of the stony beach.

"I know the internet said it was a 'glacier' lake," Mindy starts, "but how can water be so freezing without turning to ice?"

"Why didn't you tell us it was a GLACIER lake?!" I squeak through chattering teeth.

"I guess we could have looked it up ourselves," Bo offers as we all try desperately to slip on our jeans over our wet, goose-fleshy legs.

"Well, let's warm up then, okay?" Without waiting for any sort of affirmative from Bo or myself—our teeth are chattering too much to speak—Mindy is already halfway up the street. She pushes through a monstrous brown door into a stone building. In the window, a neon sign: "Speight's—Pride of the South."

112

When I first step inside, I feel as if I've been blinded. I can smell stale beer and rotting wood. By the time my eyes actually adjust, I can see a lonely pool table, a dozen mismatched chairs, and not a single soul beyond the bartender, who bears a remarkable resemblance to my childhood Sunday school teacher.

"This pub is lame," Bo says as the bartender pours us our first pint. Silently, we each down seven more. My insides now match my outsides: soggy and limp. It takes several pitchers of Speight's before making a definitive conclusion that the pub is still lame. We leave.

"Excuse me, sir," Mindy shouts with a perkiness to a passerby. Bo and I stumble out the pub behind her. I squint to shield the afternoon sun from my eyes. A severely athletic-looking man in a royal-blue fleece pullover stops. *How is it humanly possible that this spritely woman has just consumed her weight in beer and still manages to skip everywhere?* I've always envied people who could down an entire keg and then walk a tightrope. It might be the ultimate superpower.

The athlete looks past Mindy and straight at Bo and me—we look like we're on a day pass from the looney bin. We are not as skillful as Mindy is at high-functioning alcoholism; neither of us can seem to breathe through our noses.

Mindy smiles, and nods affirmatively at the athlete: "Where can I find the strippers?"

"Uh," goes the athlete, still staring at Bo and I. Shaking his head in disdain, he points up the street. "Around the corner … but I don't know if it's open yet."

Just as we roll up to the club, a bouncer is setting out a red carpet and velvet rope. He checks our IDs, and charges Bo a $20 cover. Mindy and I breeze through some velvet curtains and burst into what we are hoping to be a loud club with horny drunkards like ourselves and a bunch of babes who will pretend to want to fuck us for a small fee.

113

Inside, there are four dancers, and one bull-dyke barmaid.

No matter where you are in the world, strip clubs are always the same. There is comfort in this.

"I'm home!" I shout as the barmaid dims the lights and shoos one of the dancers from her barstool and onto the stage.

A tall, pretty brunette lifts her right hand, and grips the pole. Carelessly, she flings her body forward and tries to spin around. Instead, she slumps in a clockwise kerplunk. She's very tall, lanky and therefore rather awkward. It's not her fault, but I'm thinking this girl would probably be more successful as a model than of a stripper. Teetering on her plastic shoes, shoulders slumped, and gripping the pole for support, she has no poise whatsoever. She also doesn't really seem to give a fuck, which I find kind of awesome. *Still*, I say to myself, *the girl could use a lesson*.

I approach the stage.

"Hey, honey! What's your name?"

I slip her five bucks as she whips her chestnut extensions over her shoulder, looking down on me.

"Thank you," she replies, adjusting the note in her g-string so it butterflies out to attract the attention of the other non-existent customers. "You can call me Jen."

"Listen, I'm a stripper, too," I slur.

Jen looks me up and down, from my sneakers and grease-stained wet jeans to Bo's hoodie, which he was kind enough to have lent me at some earlier point in the evening that I cannot remember.

"I know, I look like a piano teacher. But, trust me when I say I can teach you a thing or two."
Like most strip club patrons, I am being really arrogant right now. But it's just too painful to watch this girl slump around a pole with shoulders that are lunging forward as though she is trying to shield her beautiful breasts from the world; I decide

114

that this is a great opportunity to pay forward some wisdom I've picked up along the way.

I shoo Jen off stage and explain a simple cobra turn—any stripper worth her salt can swing this move.

"Just hook your knee around the pole and lean forward, and you'll be spinning!" I demonstrate in my sexy outfit of jeans and hoodie. No stranger to handling my alcohol in a professional setting, my cobra turn is flawless. "Your turn!"

I decide that this chick is ace at customer service, humouring me, a dirty, drunk know-it-all tourist.

"That's great!" I lie. Jen's cobra turn sucks. I shoo her away from the pole, climbing up it and quickly flipping into an inversion. I can't tell if she's still watching and listening because my hoodie has slipped over my face. I speak louder. "IF YOU JUST CLENCH YOUR THIGHS AND ASS REALLY HARD I PROMISE YOU WON'T FALL."

Jen doesn't seem too interested in learning my tricks, yet she doesn't seem to care that I'm in her light. Mindy, however, is beyond keen to get up there are try her hand at spinning and flipping. I invite Bo up, too, but he replies by gesturing to our beers and mouthing, "I'm just going to keep an eye on our drinks."

Mindy is a compact softball player with strong, sturdy muscles. She climbs up effortlessly, mirroring my moves with the grace of a catcher. On her first attempt, she hauls herself upside-down and screams, with awkwardly flexed feet, "AM I DOING IT?"

I check my pockets to get us a second round of drinks. They're empty. By the late hour of 5:30 in the evening, Bo and Mindy are out of cash, too.

"Time to go," I tell them. Even if I'm drunk as a skunk, I will not be a freeloading gawker.

We stumble back to the van, climb in, and gnaw on some beef jerky before passing out as the sun sets.

An hour or so later, we are woken up by a loud and aggressive banging on the door, which soon slides open.
Two police officers flash beacon-wielding batons on our splotchy and swollen faces.

"You should really lock your doors in this area," one of them begins.

Half-asleep, Mindy mutters, "Hiya, officer." Bo and I try our best to squint into the law-enforcing beams of light. Somewhere along the way, I've learned that averting one's eyes from a cop can only lead to more problems.

"You can't park here," the second cop says, looking at our windshield, lifting a yellow slip of paper from the wiper. "You know you have a ticket." He waves it at us.

Cop #1 shakes his head: "You should be at a campsite. You can't be here."

Mindy sits up, blinking. "We are not in any shape to drive, officer."

The police officer scrunches his nose, deducing from the stench of beer and beef jerky that the roads will be an unsafe place for Kiwis and tourists alike if we deign to jump on them at this hour.

"Well you can't be here," Cop #2 challenges.

Mindy persists: "But, officer, we really ... shouldn't ... drive."

While I watch Mindy and the officer have a stare down, I gnaw at some beef jerky I've found beneath my makeshift pillow of muddy jeans stuffed into a t-shirt.

Cop #2 breaks the silence: "You'd better pay this ticket before you leave the country."

He slides the door shut with the authoritative slam of a man who likes to be in charge. I flop my head back on the pillow and fall asleep.

I wake up with a soggy slice of beef jerky dangling from my drooling lip.

"You don't strike me as the sleep-eating type, Jacq," Bo says, changing from one dirty shirt to another slightly less dirty one.

"I didn't think I was, either," I reply, peeling the jerky from my chapped lip. I furrow my brow. "I must have been pretty wasted."

We grab breakfast pies from a gas station and speed toward Christchurch. We have a van to return that is in serious need of a hose-down before we board a plane the back to Oz. As we speed along the beautiful coastline, I notice that my wrists are itching so much that I can't concentrate on any of the stunning New Zealand landscape. They itch. I scratch. I scratch all afternoon until we see a pharmacy. I urge Bo to pull off.

"Help me!" I beg the pharmacist, showing her my splotchy red-and-white wrists. "Is it scabies?" I ask, fighting back tears. When there is something unfamiliarly wrong with my body I am prone to bursting into tears. Especially when I'm far away from my mother.

The pharmacist peeks through her reading glasses, teetering on the tip of her nose. "Sand flies," she replies, handing me a tube of cortisone cream and box of antihistamines.

"Just don't itch it. Cover it with frozen peas and you should be fine in the next couple of days."

On the flight, I bother the steward several times for ice, Ziploc bags of any sort, and blankets that he informs me "isn't supposed to give out on this flight." Mindy keeps the whisky flowing, which seems to make it all itch less.

By the time we deplane back in Sydney, my ankles, lower abdomen, and hips are swelling with what I'm sure is a new and fatal venereal disease that I must have obviously contracted from sheep jizz that landed on my beef jerky whilst drying.

After a few more days and sleepless nights, the itching gets worse. The bumps are so hideous and plentiful that I call in sick. This body must not be seen naked. I lie in bed, drunk, trying not to touch the itchiness that has by now spread down the sides of my ribcage, too, when I get a call from Mindy.

"I have the scabies, too," she tells me.

"Now?" I screech. "But we've been back for a week!"

"I know. But I don't think it's scabies. I called Bo. He doesn't have any." A pause. For the first time ever, Mindy doesn't sound like she's broadcasting a children's show.

This is it. This is how I'm going to die.

"Babe, I think we caught something from the strippers."

"Don't be ridiculous. I've worked in half a dozen clubs and never have I caught anything." I have no time for Mindy's judgment. I go on. "And when I work, I am buck naked. We were fully clothed and we didn't even get dances, never mind feel up any of those babes!"

"I went to the doctor, Jacq." I still have a hard time recognizing this new, grave tone in Mindy's voice. "They said it wasn't scabies. And I was too embarrassed to tell her where we were, so I looked it up online…"

"Mindy, you know that last week Web MD said I had a melanoma when I really had a zit."

"I didn't use that site. I looked up stripper diseases and there is this place in Ireland…"

IRELAND. Oh, come the fuck on. Middle Earth—as I've come to call New Zealand—couldn't be farther from Ireland. And … stripper diseases? Slightly taken aback, I wonder how popular that Google search is.

"No, in Ireland there was an outbreak of Pole Pox a few years ago."

"POLE POX?"

"It wasn't very specific, but some of the older poles have nickel in them, and they cause the skin to bump up in a nasty rash."

I look down at my wrists, my ankles, my sides … all main points of contact with a pole, and all exposed when I sauntered in there in my wet jeans and borrowed hoodie.

We have pole pox. Stripper scabies. CUNT CONTAGION!

I can't quite say what I've learned from this itchy misfortune. A mother or nun might urge me to leave stripping forever; "It's a SIGN," she'd plead, weaving rosary beads through her fingers to resist the urge to scratch her forearm. But I just. can't. stay. away. I've got plans.

After three painful weeks, my Pole Pox subsides, and my working holiday visa in Australia expires.

New York City:
Purgatory Part One

To those who love me most, I 'still look great.' To those who
might want to hire me to prance around in a g-string, I look
'soft.' Trading two months of platform heels, incessant squatting
and hip undulations in exchange for a road trip through the Bible
Belt (more on this later) will make a gal pack on a few fun
pounds. If Michelangelo were sketching an erotic painting of my
sumptuous curves, I'm sure he would only encourage me to go
for that seventh hush puppy; but mainstream porn enthusiasts
prefer pre-pubescent looking women with flat-ironed hair and
zero body fat. I'm down to my last 200 bucks, and, at this point,
my hamstrings ache when I bend over to pick the pebbles out of
my loafers. I'm rusty, and the pressure is on: Time to mold
myself into a consumable chick. I must cater to my target
demographic.

Lately, it seems I have forgotten how to look sexy to the lowest
common denominator. Looking fuckable to the average penis
possessor is often inversely proportionate to what it usually
means when trying to possess some sort of sex appeal to hipsters
and lesbians, and in most cases, to my detriment, lesbian
hipsters.

In Greenpoint,[18] everything is brown. The brick, the trim, the clothing on the Polish pro-lifers who have set up a stoop sale raising funds for "women with problem." I climb up three flights of creaking stairs to my sublet. It's a boiler room with a loft bed, and it's mine for the next six weeks. I'm going to get rich and have a lot of picnics in Central Park. I hastily unpack all my shit—four cameras, 10 g-strings, some faded summer road-trip garb, and just enough concealer to mask any semblance of the freckle-faced mathlete who maybe went to school with your daughter. My plan is to embark on a recon mission into Manhattan tonight, with the goal to audition in a day or two and start rebuilding that capital that I've carefully strewn across 15 American states.

Gen—my best friend from university—picked me up in Vancouver, and we drove down the west coast, across the south, and back up to New York via Dollywood, the greatest and most fucked up theme park of all time[19]. Along the way we met some delightful weirdos, tore up our gums gnawing on beef jerky, and got wasted. What's so great about the freelance life is that it kisses you with as much time off as your living expenses will allow. Gen and I are really good at cutting corners by pitching tents on little league fields and drinking shitty domestic beer.

Two months later, Gen has gone back up the Interstate to her native Toronto, and I am alone in Brooklyn, staring at a decrepit suitcase brimming with muddy clothes I really ought to haul over to the laundromat. But clean clothes will have to wait: a sandwich in Brooklyn costs 15 fucking dollars, and shitty domestic beer is half that, so it's time to hit the boulevard and get back on the pole. But where have all my slutty clothes gone? Cut offs and sleeveless blouses seem to be all I've worn and all I've brought with me. I think the sleeveless blouses look good.

---

[18] Greenpoint is the second-to-Williamsburg hipster neighbourhood in Brooklyn. The Polish food is divine and the rent is steadily climbing.
[19] Gen and I are serious Dolly Parton fans. Parton erected Dollywood in her hometown of Pigeon Forge, TN, to create jobs. There are now a lot of jobs there, and also a lot of uber-Christians, redneck tourists, and coal lobbyists.

But looking like Geena Davis circa 1990 is going to send every wallet on a cigarette break[20].

Kneeling over my mildewy bag of tricks, I search again. Maybe I missed something tiny and sequined wedged between my Levis.

Not a single cocktail dress or deep V did I pack, never thinking, *hey, maybe I'll have to look nice when I'm DRESSED, too.* Sometimes I wish I could just be naked all the time. Winter is overrated, anyway.

I put on my tightest-of-tight, shortest-of-short denim cutoffs. Just like everything else to my name, they haven't been washed in a while. I step into them. I feel dirty, and not in the enterprising-slut kind of way.

I take out a black linen sleeveless blouse. It almost bears my midriff. If I unbutton it enough, from the right angle one might be able to catch a glimpse of my sun-kissed cleavage. In the south, this would have been deemed too sexy for even the most hedonistic of harlots. In New York, it counts as a full-coverage shirt. In Miami I would certainly be mistaken for a Mormon. I throw on a pair of orange platform heels that I inherited from a disco-era housewife via the Tucson Goodwill. I tousle my windswept, sandy blonde hair and cake on some whore makeup.

I assess my silhouette in a warped mirror on the back of the door to my room. My knees are like balloons and my head is squished, tiny as a turtle's. The only thing I am certain I have working for me is my tan. In this funhouse mirror, the rest is guesswork.

My Real-Girl self tells me I look cute. My hustler self calls me a soccer mom who is trying to look hot for the coach who I know has a wife but who I know through Facebook is away on a girl's weekend to Ellicottville. But natural tans don't show under

---

[20] Guys who always say they want to go on a smoke break before a dance really just want to waste your time without paying for it. They never return from these smoke breaks.

black light so I will, inevitably, look albino upon descending the steps and strutting into the club.

In my questionably eighties-mom get-up, I feel comfortably cookie-cutter walking down Bedford Avenue. Weaving through throngs of bearded, tattooed, and scrappy-looking adult children[21], everyone seems to be trying really hard to mask their pedigree. When your permanent mailing address is still your parent's house back in the suburbs, a lot of effort goes into giving off the impression that the opposite is true. The American dream of rags to riches is still highly coveted in the five boroughs—only in Williamsburg, it's rags to Rag and Bone. And the only reason I feel so confident about this statement is because these are my peers! I, too, still have my bank statements sent to my mother's house. But for whatever reason, I consider myself more virtuous because I am an illegal alien sex worker. And from where I'm sitting, it is more authentically badass than being from Ohio and making your own goat's milk soap.

My 20-minute walk-of-judgment from apartment to train ends with a sweaty descent into the bowels of Brooklyn.

Entering Manhattan, I swap my loafers for platform heels, and exit into Times Square. I shove my way through the crowd of neck-craners and picture-posers, looking for the signs that indicate a titty bar is near. Spotted: a small man in a red vest handing out flyers. Standing several feet beyond this guy is a significantly larger and more serious-looking man and a velvet rope. He is guarding a glass door that he opens to release charcoal-suited men with bowed heads.

This man is wearing the most ornate bellhop costume I've ever seen: epaulettes, a gilded bellman hat, and freshly buffed saddle shoes. He's smiling at nothing in particular, so when his eyes meet mine, I smile back. He also appears to bear a genuine grin on his face: he's obviously seen my type before (starry eyed, nervous, yet hopeful.) Holding open the glass door with a beckoning nod, he allows me to enter, and I descend the stairs into the underbelly.

---

21 Brooklyn hipsters c. 2012

I am inside the club The Lioness told me I should come to: Russian Dolls. Chatting up the grandpa manager, he seems surprised when I say I want to audition. Is it my mom-blouse? My humidified hair?

"We are full at the moment, but go down the street to this address." He hands me a business card bearing the torso of a woman in a white bikini, which is balanced out with too much text:
"Second Chances Sports Bar Bikini Bar Lingerie Waitresses Gentlemen's Club Steakhouse"

FULL?

No one has ever told me that they are FULL. I am the one for whom everyone makes exceptions.

I am extremely confident for many reasons, but it would be a crock of shit if I said it wasn't because everyone accommodates pretty girls and I'm pretty comfortable exploiting this trend for as long as my tits are perky and I don't get hit by a rogue taxi.

But FULL?

Iris, Sharon—whoever you are—you're rusty.

I have eliminated 'rejection' from my vernacular. I don't take no for an answer. That's what stripping has taught me! 'No is just a starting point for negotiation.' But this old and balding grump with questionably long and greasy hair slicked back like a spartan warrior is the last breed of human I would expect to send me packing. The Lioness did warn me that New York would kick my ass.

I climb the stairs and start down the street. My feet are clammy and suddenly my platforms are too tight around my ankles. I'm itching to fling them off into the street and slip back into my loafers, but it's important that I walk down this street with my rejected head held high.

I hear a deep voice call out from behind me.

"AND?"

I turn around and see the colossal doorman. He is looking at me, and still smiling. I'm baffled by what sort of air-conditioned ventilation system he must be hiding under his oppressive uniform of black, gold, and fringe. No one who works the door of a Times Square strip club could ever be that happy. Turning on my platforms, I hobble back over to him.

"They said they were full."

"Don't worry, love, it's a quiet time of year. Come back in September." He sounds genuine. It's the first sincere smile I've been flashed since I got here.

"September?" I ask.

"Yeah, everyone's back to work in September. Come back then." He smiles.

I wade through the crowd that seems to grow even denser as I count the seven blocks I have to walk to Second Chances.

Turning at 45th Street, I am faced with a wall of mostly pre-pubescent teens pressed up against a police fence. Their arms hang lifelessly over the barricade, clutching onto posters of what I gauge to be of Harry Potter. I look over to a stage door and up to the marquis that announces that Daniel Radcliffe is in town for a Broadway show. Not five paces after this cacophony of teenage girls is the strip joint on the flyer greasy gramps gave me.

I will have to pass this crew of youth, innocence, and gawkiness every day I walk to work this summer.

The manager of Second Chances wears glasses with lightly tinted violet lenses. It's his 'thing.' Just like how back in the mid-nineties the youngest Hanson brother wore yellow Dr. Martens and that was his 'thing.' I want to pat him on the head and smile condescendingly; instead I smile with my eyes and give my best maybe-one-day-we'll-do-it-in-the-broom-closet shoulder shrug.

"You want to audition?" he asks while looking past me, toward the television.

"I'd love to," I reply with an enthusiasm I will learn is completely unnecessary.

"Yes, you can. You can right now."

"Oh, I was thinking of coming back Monday," I tell him. In Australia, I had to show up, show my face and work permit, and fill out endless paperwork in order to score an audition. But New York City moves fast. Today is Friday; Monday may as well be a light year from now.

I leave the club with the understanding that whenever I come back, I should be prepared to audition.

Back on the L train to Brooklyn, I try my hardest not to breathe in the stench of piss and my own body odour along with millions of others'. As the subway car rattles along the rails, I scan the changing wardrobe landscape of midtown sex appeal as it morphs into Brooklyn hipsteria. I have a long, hard think about how unsexy cutoffs and a sleeveless blouse are when men in ill-fitted suits are looking for glamour girls. Hipster Daisy Duke is a cute gimmick, but on the flashier side of the East River a girl's gotta leave the tangled hair and frump-sex look behind.

With a disheartened gait and blistering ankles, I return to my shoebox and fall asleep crying to *Steel Magnolias* under the temporary relief of an oscillating fan.

On Monday, I find a curling iron in the shared bathroom of my sublet, and purchase a comb and hairspray with my credit card. Studying a Youtube video on how to turn short, choppy mops of hair into Marilyn Monroe waves, I try my best to duplicate the look.

After combing out my new ringlets, it becomes obvious that I look more like Shirley Temple than the blondest bombshell in the history of humanity. There is one unruly curl that refuses to go anywhere I guide it and instead sits right in the centre of my forehead. I slap on my signature vintage-whore shade of lipstick to push my baby face from *The Good Ship Lollipop* to *Let me suck your Lollipop.* I'm nearly there.

Glancing over at my makeshift closet, I sigh with sloped shoulders as I realize that it looks exactly like it did yesterday. Several carefully thrifted silk blouses, and a few pairs of shorts that have each been modified over the years to look like they're in even worse condition than when I bought them at the Goodwill. I leaf through the hangers, double-checking to see if maybe I missed something that could double as a *come-hither, dear Wall Street* outfit.

And

Ohmyfuckinggod

A dress.

It's ankle-length and fuchsia with a white doily functioning as a decorative neckpiece. I think it's what many people often refer to as a muumuu. Uncharacteristically, I bought it at a church bazaar. I've toted it around three continents and that $3 tag is still on it. It's for in case I ever want to go to the beach, or, you know, babysit 17 babies and cook creamed corn in Costco-sized baking tins.

It seems as though I'm prepared for just about anything except for what I came to New York to do.

In spite of all my fashion insecurities surrounding my silk-and-denim summer uniform, I slip back into my saggy Daisy Dukes, and make for the subway, leaving early to try my hand at New York City bargain shopping before showtime.

By the time I arrive at Forever 21, my makeup has already melted off. Music is blaring louder than any strip-club speaker and mothers are toting around their daughters' selections of shitty clothes to try on. Their matching t-shirts tell me they are from Birmingham for a cheerleading competition. The familiar look of dread is encrypted in the mother's brow: *Please God, don't let these trashy clothes make her grow up to be a stripper.* I see a woman standing still among the swarm of mother-daughter duos. She picks at her cuticles. The only indication that she works here is her headset.

"Excuse me, can you help me?" With the enthusiasm of someone who counts ball bearings for a living, she shifts her focus from her hangnail to my look of distress. My lipstick is bleeding into the creases of my upper lip (isn't that supposed to happen after 40, and like, NOT before 25?). A sweat moustache congeals along the feathered crackling of red.

"Where can I find a tiny, slutty dress?"

The clerk looks at me, raising an eyebrow. She is unphased by my frank inquisition. "Downstairs."

I head toward the escalator, looking down to notice four other 'downstairs' levels, all devoted to selling cheap knock-off garments of shit and shittier quality.

By some grace of the Goddess, I unearth a small, slutty, floral-print dress for under 10 dollars. My personal opinion is that I should have been paid to walk out with this piece-of-shit excuse for a garment. But I decide against getting arrested and charge the $9.80 to my nearly-maxed Visa. I don't have enough cash left at this point to sacrifice a 10-dollar bill. I walk out of the store with the dress on. My slut factor just went from a 3 to an 8 in under 10 dollars! I know this because suddenly all the dads with their pulled-up socks start craning their necks as I weave through the crowd. I am one strut closer to "HIRED!"

I forego the platform heels and keep my loafers on because fuck it.

Arriving at Harry Potter's neighbouring venue, the doorman opens the door and I descend the stairs to meet a similarly balding and bespectacled—albeit different—manager. His name is Andy. He instructs me to follow him.

We pass by a small podium. It measures less than a metre in width. A girl is haplessly making figure eights with her hips while standing on it. I will learn that this is the bikini podium. If you are assigned to dance on it, you have to wear a bikini.

Andy leads me through a maze of mirrors and teal carpeting to a clearing of cigarette smoke and Avon cosmetics. Inside, the house Mama is at it with a one-inch barrel curling iron, giving a Japanese girl eighties feathered curls while remixed Britney blares from an unnecessarily large speaker mounted in the corner. Beneath the speaker, a dancer makes a commendable effort to shovel pad thai into her mouth using chopsticks: judging by her dirty blonde hair and lack of dexterity, she did not grow up using such utensils.

I slip into my dress, and pat the sweat off my upper lip, chin, and forehead using a napkin I found precariously tossed in the corner.

I get on stage and do my thing. Like most clubs, the instructions are that you are clothed for the first song. "Clothed," however, has a different meaning in strip clubs than it would, in say, an airport. What Andy means by "clothed" is that my nipples and vagina are covered by opaque fabric.

For my first two and a half minutes on stage, I am accompanied by two tall, slim, grim-looking girls, and Katy Perry. The two girls whisper to each other in Russian as they lean with their backs against the poles and adjust their panties. If a spectator had a microscope he would be able to observe that these girls are swaying their hips. In strip clubs, hip-swaying counts as dancing.

Aside from Andy's silent observation in a dark corner, my audience is several strippers and four Latino dudes who all appear to be airing out their balls. One of them has a girl grinding on his outstretched thigh, while the three other gents lean back in their chairs, smiling back at me as I flash them my tits.

The second song comes on. It's a rap remix that features a lot of bongos. It's a shitty song for the slow, sultry dance moves these girls are working on stage. For every person who thinks strippers are dumb, I can say with confidence that they have never spoken to a strip club DJ. In my travels thus far, all but one have failed to demonstrate any sort of musical intuition. None has had the sense of how to create a sexy environment to stimulate a generous distribution of wealth. Bless the Backstreet

Boys and Melissa Etheridge, but they are not sexy rainmakers. Yet both are frequently featured in a strip club setting. In the DJ's defence, he is usually the friendliest and least perverted of male co-workers.

Throughout the bongo solo, I maintain a slow sway and try my best at a fan kick. Andy waves me over to his perch in the corner. "That was good ... better than most." The other two girls weren't even dancing; they were gossiping and picking their wedgies. But a compliment's a compliment and a job's a job. I start tomorrow.

Ego high, I exit the club, pass the Harry Potter fans, and make my way up Broadway. Fuelled by my triumph at Second Chances, I am determined to try again at the coveted Russian Dolls.

This time, I meet a different manager who is young, short and unenthusiastic about flashing back a smile in my direction. He agrees to give me an audition.

"You have your heels?"

"Yes."

"Your dress?"

"Yes."

"Okay. Follow me."

I dance. The last time I was here, I didn't bother to check out the other girls; I was too focused on sticking my ass out as I leaned against the bar, smoothing out my unruly hair. Every dancer is really skinny with either tiny boobs or fake boobs. They are either pre-pubescently skinny or of the cocaine-is-my-middle-name level of emaciation. There are more dancers and customers here. It doesn't take long to realize that this is the A-list bar of strippers and the other one, down the street and where I was just hired, is where it sends its detritus.

He would love to hire me, but they're full. "Come back in September," he tells me, motioning to the door.

On my first shift at Second Chances, there don't seem to be any 'fat' girls. But New York fat is like Midwestern skinny, so maybe I'm simply delusional and have yet to adjust my body-image lens to fit into the Manhattan model of kale-and-cocaine diet.

A girl warned me about being downgraded to Second Chances; "It's where they send the fat girls."

Holy shit.

I am the fat girl.

I was a little shocked when the house Madam, Winnie, a former stripper who tucked one last Washington into her g-string in the early nineties, started breezing through the club rules.

At first, I was fine.

RULE #1. You may not refuse a drink, ever.
I had no qualms with Rule #1, since in addition to 11-dollar Bud Lights, your client can also buy you a nine-dollar bottle of Norwegian-import water. When you're doing what equals out to an eight-hour pulsing wall-sit, it's important to stay hydrated.

RULE #2. The g-string stays on at all times.
Admittedly, Rule #2 bummed me out some as I really like flashing my gash. It freaks the younger, less-experienced, and more frugal men out and has a hypnotic effect on the older ones. In a club where clients are allowed a peek of pussy, dancers are showered in Benjamins before you can say SHAVED.

Then Winnie announced Rule #3.
RULE #3. To whatever happens in the Champagne Room, the management turns a blind eye.
My reaction to this, both then and now: THIS RULE IS COMPLETELY INSANE AND UNSAFE. PROCEED WITH CAUTION AND PROTECT THY HONEY POT.

Before stripping in New York, I had never even heard of the Champagne Room, except for that one spoken-word ditty, which seemed to advertise it as a safely sex-free zone[22]. To add to the confusion, the fluorescent sign that reads "Champagne Room" in bubblegum-pink cursive lettering is accented by the silhouette of a martini glass with an olive in it.

Up until Winnie brought it up, I had chosen not to think about it. I decided that it sounded like a nice place to giggle and have a bubble bath.

STRIPPER TIP #19: THIS IS NOT WHAT THE CHAMPAGNE ROOM IS FOR.
What I soon learned through the grapevine of stripper shoes and bitch-stick breaks was that the Champagne Room is a place where you will find some small tables, slightly more comfortable seating, and several couples of entangled bodies. According to the veterans, the Champagne Room often involves saliva and fingers going into no-go zones.

Essentially, in the Champagne Room, sex-worker descriptors collide and each woman is for herself. On a nightly basis, my top-earning colleagues rub out a lot of hand jobs, blowjobs, and beyond.

Being the relatively gay lady that I am, I'm not really into gripping dicks. It doesn't bother me that other girls are doing this, it's just not what I'm personally comfortable with. So after Winnie's run-down and the subsequent light-shedding gossip, I decide to do avoid the place.

"Privet," says one tall, slim, platinum blonde with a half-smile that is contoured with brown lip liner.

"I'm not Russian." I half-smile back.

---

[22] "No Sex (In the Champagne Room)" Chris Rock, 1999.

"Oh," she says, walking away. I do speak a bit of Russian, but I'm too embarrassed to admit that I hardly remember any of it. I can also manage a bit of Spanish, but not at the rate these girls are speaking it. No one in here cites English as their mother tongue. From the tanned brunettes huddled in one corner, to the skinny blondes in the other, it's immediately obvious to me that New York City strip clubs are tribal. The girls mingle with their own kind, while I—also illegal, but not visibly so—am left to gossip with the bartender. Like all strip-club wait staff, she's been here longer than any dancer, and holds herself above us. From her vantage point, we are merely fleeting whores just waiting to get deported. My tribe—Anglo-Saxon, and without a green card—is rare and lonely.

The ceilings in the club are low and there are several wide pillars around the stage that obstruct the view of about one-quarter of the patrons. The stage is small, and at any given moment three girls must sway around two poles. An elevated ledge gives the impression that the dancers are frolicking in a playpen. It's made of marble with skull-crackingly sharp edges: a lawsuit waiting to happen. But since strippers aren't unionized and no one here is even allowed to work in the United States, worrying about lawsuits is a low priority for most clubs. I decide to dance with caution.

The stage lights flow from red to orange to blue to white, seeming to linger on the blue setting. But blue lights show stretch marks and cellulite more than any other coloured lights. It's not that hard to make naked chicks in heels look hot. Any photographer or porn filmmaker will tell you that lighting is paramount to making the sexies look sexiest and strip clubs always mysteriously FAIL at this. It's simple math : red lights + black walls = money pit. It's not that Mobsters aren't good at math; it's that they don't give a shit about making us girls look hot. It doesn't help that the carpet looks like it was ripped out of a Swiss Chalet[23] in 1994 and transplanted into Second Chances after sitting in a mildewy storage unit for a few years.

---

[23] Swiss Chalet: A Canadian family restaurant chain that serves the most delicious rotisserie chicken you will ever taste.

My first night of American stripping has me facing two new
challenges: the first challenge presented to me by New York
City stripping culture is to come to terms with the fact that a
single one-dollar bill is deemed an acceptable tip for a dancing
naked lady. *One fucking dollar*. What can you buy for a dollar in
New York City these days? Nothing. Absolutely fucking
nothing. Second, I must adjust my dance routine for the laps of
moderately to severely obese men. As I mount my first paying
customer, who tells me he's visiting the big city from West
Virginia, I cannot even sit on his lap because there is a rock-
solid keg[24] resting on it. He probably hasn't seen his dick in
several years. So if I can't even gauge where his nob is, how can
I possibly simulate dry humping it? Do I caress his big belly?
Should I just rub his shoulders? How am I supposed to sit
down?[25]

The following night, I watch a very petite Mongolian dancer
saunter over to a big Buddha of a man. She smiles with elation
and starts to rub his belly as if it were for good luck. The
Buddha starts smiling and immediately obliges to several lap
dances. I try the same tactic for a big teddy bear of a man sitting
alone in the corner. I skip up to him and proceed to literally
throw myself onto him, resting atop his belly, hugging my arms
around his stout neck.

"Hi!" I smile, eyes like firecrackers. I wiggle up close to his
very clean, very starched shirt.

---

[24] Keg: Canadian slang for belly. When a thick layer of fat covers a six pack of
abs. "This ain't no six pack, it's one big keg!"

[25] These thoughts are insensitive and judgmental and the result of the fact that I
suffer from a little bit of a fat phobia. Like most women who lived through being
a teenager, I've got residual body-image issues. Consequently, I am scared of
people who have a little or a lot more to love. It's been a number of years since I
would throw up tubs of Ben and Jerry's, followed by a two-day fast where I
would only feed myself with images of supermodels. I was so fucking hungry I
nearly ate the entire September Issue of Vogue.
But in this line of work one must overcome these obstacles. I need to be
comfortable with my own body, and everyone else's too.

135

"Hello," he replies, alarmed, but pleased.

"Can we go for a lap dance?" I ask, bouncing into him flirtatiously.

"Okay."

I guide Teddy over to the bench. Any conventional lap dance moves are thrown out the window- there is no visible crotch to gyrate against, so I am resolved to relive my happiest days of yore as Teddy becomes my own personal bouncing castle. I throw myself against him, my limbs splayed in various formations across his softness. Teddy smiles back at me; he seems to be having as much fun as I am.

Like any customer coming in looking for attention and affection, Teddy just wants to be validated. Pretending I don't see his size is part of the problem. Hell, I love a belly rub just as much as any bitch. After three bouncing and giggly belly-rubbing lap dances, I'm smiling, too.

What follows is an account my first successful thwarting of Champagne Room shenanigans:
It's midnight. Second Chances' house Madam comes up to me and my client, who has offered me a handful of twenties to bounce on his bumpy lap. On this particular night, my client, who bears an uncanny resemblance to Weird Al (if Weird Al had boils on his face) is delightfully intoxicated and shows no signs of wanting to end this off-roading affair.

"Would you like to take the lovely lady to the Champagne Room?" Winnie asks.

"GgggrrrrYeeeaaAHHHhhh whhhaaaa whha-t happensinthechampagneroom?"

"Anything you want."

He's interested. "Anything?"

To which Madam replies,
"It's *full contact*."

At this point, I am still a bit green to the particulars, but as far as I know we aren't going in the Champagne Room to play football—the only 'full contact' sort of American interaction with which I am even vaguely familiar.

I balk.

I strategize.

IT IS OFFICIALLY TIME TO BECOME UNSEXY.

Now picture me again: perched above Weird Al's lumpy lap parts, doing my thing, listening to Madam try to pimp my cheeks out to a guy who seems to deem bathing frivolous. I want to tell her 'That's not in my personal job description—didn't you get my resume?'—but that would reflect poorly on me and seriously fuck with whatever job security I might have in this place.
Madam's already keen on having my head because earlier that night we had an altercation about the politics of my g-string (she said it was too much like underwear, I asked if it was too tasteful.)

Weird Al is getting decisively grabbier with this dangling carrot of champagne football.
I remain silent. I decide against coaxing Weird Al into motorboating my tits (although he clearly doesn't need any coaxing) and continue on with my dance.

Once Madam's on to the next couple I change the tone of my dance from Sharon Stone seductress c. 1992, to something more along the lines of *Pee-wee's Playhouse*, wiggling my hips like a Mouseketeer, with a shit-eating grin to match.

Madam returns for a verdict.

"Naaaaaaggghhh maybelater."

I exhale. My sabotage was successful.

*

Don't get me wrong, I love stripping. I love dancing naked for money. I love the game, and I love the men who come in so willing to play it. And, yes, I understand that the club charges 600 dollars for a visit to the Champagne Room, and yes, that's a lot of money. But if it comes down to allowing dirty fingers to contaminate my cooch, I can do without my $200 cut, thank you very much. Why not legalize full frontal on your dance floor before asking us to deep throat in your back rooms? God knows I'd rather flash some gash than be a sheath to strange cock.

Two hours and a measly $20 later, the DJ calls over the speaker, "IRIS, YOU'RE NEXT ON THE BIKINI STAGE."

It is set in the corner of a narrow corridor that leads to the men's room. The bar runs along the opposite side. Occasionally there are guys sitting at the bar, backs facing the dancer on her soapbox. The only real reason anyone would have any need to pass by this area is to take a piss, shit, or blow a line of cocaine. Naturally, there is a lot of traffic here.

It's always easy figure out what they went into the bathroom for. If they exit the door, head high, shoulders back and sniffing the dank air, they've just had a line or a key bump and they didn't share any of it with me. If they come out fastening their zippers, they've just taken a wee and haven't bothered to wash their hands. (MEN: WHY DO YOU LEAVE THE BATHROOM DOING UP YOUR FLY? ALL YOU ARE DOING IS ADVERTISING TO EVERYONE EVERYWHERE THAT YOU DID NOT WASH YOUR HANDS. YOU ARE STUPID AND FILTHY, PLEASE GO HOME NOW). If they waddle out of the room, walking a little slower than usual, they've just laid a log. Even a blind stripper would be able to pick out the third variety, because the swinging door to the john wafts the nature-fresh, carnivore-shit smell from the toilet straight onto her podium.

Above the podium, an air conditioning vent blasts the air from the Antarctic. I stare at the stage, taking a deep breath before I climb to what will be the lowest depths of my nights at Second Chances. Bikini-clad and goosepimpled, I stand and sway, inhaling methane gas.

I am tortured with this for several increments of 15 minutes a night, four nights a week. That's four hours a week of swaying, frigidly, by the men's room, making a game of how long I can hold my breath. I used to play the same game on the bus in elementary school. When driving by a cemetery, all the kids had to hold their breath. Whoever failed at this task was banished to uncoolness for the entire field trip. At the age of nine, this felt like eternal damnation. But now I feel like in this new game, the stakes are marginally higher. Eternal damnation sounds like a goddamn slice compared to breathing in someone else's Shake Shack[26] farts.

My first night ends with me having grossed just over two hundred American dollars. This is not the American dream I've been chasing after. This is, in fact, BULLSHIT. Is it me? Is it them? Is it the day of the week? Is it this DEPRESSING FUCKING CLUB?

I'm in the most expensive city in the world, and I cannot afford to enjoy any of it; my dreams of making big bucks are flurrying around like bits of trash under the BQE[27]. Just when I thought I was unique, I could not be any more of a cliché. I read Patti Smith's *Just Kids* to prescribe myself a rock and roller's dose of optimism, hand-wash the only g-string I own that the manager hasn't scoffed at, and go back to work.

Three weeks later and I'm even more miserable. I'm not making much money so I'm working extra shifts, and no other clubs will let me walk in the door without a Social Security Number.

I take a seat with an early-30s Joe Schmo. Unlike most of the clients in the club, he's not totally fat. It turns out he's from New Zealand. My nostalgia for the good times down under make warming up to him easy and the bond we share over having the Queen on our coins is enough to elicit a dance from him.

---

[26] Shake Shack: allegedly high-end fast food that is notorious for serving up a delicious cheeseburger and making people shart their brains out. If you can clear your schedule for the next 18 hours, the Portobello burger is really good.
[27] BQE: Brooklyn Queens Expressway. The highway that takes you everywhere and nowhere.

Mr. Kiwi has lived in New York for eight years. He holds strong to his accent. I make a mental note to never call it a 'restroom,' and start swaying. Mr. Kiwi brings his hands to my hips. I chat a bit about having visited New Zealand, finding it beautiful, leaning in closer so he can hear me over the throbbing speaker that we are sitting beneath. His hands slide from my hips, around my ass, his fingers wandering under my g-string and toward my bunghole.

"You can't do that," I tell him. America seems even crazier when you're encountering at least one person a night who thinks he can finger your asshole for $20.

"I can do lots of things."

"NO, you can't."

In Australia, dancers are always paid upfront, and the client is expected to behave. If he chooses to act like a piece of shit, the dancer leaves and he's out 50 bucks. In New York, the dance comes first, and the money is paid after he deems the services satisfactory. In America, I have the freedom to walk away from this entitled fuck, but I will also have to forfeit the 20 bucks. I press on with the shitty dance and take my money, declining an extended show.

The weeks go by and the clients grow shittier; my hunger for money only increases as the men seem to have less and less respect for my boundaries.

I do get to dance once for a cute girl with a short skirt and amazing rack. That was nice. She seems really into me dancing for her, spreading her legs so much that her skirt rides up over her black silk panties. I trace my hands from my knees, up her thighs, and along her sides. Arching her back, thrusting her bust in my face, and grinning, she seems to be giving me consent to touch her breasts. She notices my hesitation, and smiles. Is she challenging me to go there? Gently, I cup her gorgeously plump and ample melons, lifting them to plant my face between them. I've never been privy to motorboating a buxom bosom before— I mean, not unless it was in a shower show back in the halcyon days in Sydney. But you can't perform a textbook motorboat in

140

a shower show; you'd fuck up your makeup. The verdict: big tits are really nice, super soft, and so fun! They also probably hurt this cute girl's back and have spoiled any dreams she may have had of being a track-and-field athlete.

My little 'vacation' into the lap of a luscious lady patron is fun, but, most of the time the clients are shit and I'm losing steam. Of course, they sense this. Looking vulnerable and deflated is easy to pick up on, and, even though I have the best fake smile in my zip code, I'm still just coasting by on a few hundred dollars a night.

Miserable, I lament in the corner, fighting back tears. It doesn't seem funny right now but it will, someday. *I can't win them all,* I remind myself.

*

It just so happens that I'm a lesbian who's hot for black guys.

Nothing has ever come of this. I slept with enough cock in 2007 to not feel any need to return to it for quite a long time. Perhaps forever. But for some inexplicable reason I get nervous and excited when presented with the opportunity to straddle a tall, dark, and handsome smooth talker.[28]

In the workplace, black guys usually look the other way when I do my best strut by. I've got some booty. But it's a white-girl booty. I do some squats every now and again, but my string of DNA will never contort my ass into a shelf. I have come to accept this. Not even Apple Bottom Jeans can save me.

So, on a Monday night, you won't BELIEVE my shock and excitement when a handsome man by the name of Jerome feigns interest in having me give him a lap dance.

---

[28] When the guys come in to the club looking for a certain ethnicity to fulfill their sexual fantasy, I totally have mine picked out before we walk in the door: black guys are hot.

I'm nervous. Just like when girls ask me for lap dances. I get all giggly and stumble around like a fifteen-year-old in her first pair of Payless pumps and it's just. not. sexy.

I lead Jerome over to the bench on the room's periphery and start my dance, with AC/DC accompanying my hair-flipping and rump-swaying.

Thunderstruck comes to an end and he ASKS ME TO KEEP DANCING. Jerome likes my eighties hair-metal moves and wants me to continue doing them. He asks me to hop off for a second so he can empty his pockets.

I hop back on, and under my right thigh I feel his phone vibrating.

"You forgot to take your phone out of your pocket," I offer.

"That's not a phone," Jerome replies, smiling.

Jerome has put a vibrating egg in his pocket for my clitoral pleasure. How thoughtful. Surprised and squealing for his benefit, I tell him he's naughty and cheeky (men love to be scolded like five-year-olds), and that I'm especially looking forward to this dance. I pretend to really enjoy it, and when he extends for yet another song I "NEARLY CLIMAX." Part of me wishes I could genuinely enjoy it, but to be honest, most of it is theatrics. But sometimes lap dances can be hot. And not because there is a vibrating egg on my clit, but because the two people have a connection. Jerome and I totally had a chance at feeling sexy together. He had to ruin it with this tacky-ass sex toy, which is messing with my routine. What ever happened to a good old-fashioned dry hump, anyway? How could that ever go out of style? I'm annoyed and feeling less sexy with every bass thump. Playing sexy all the time rarely feels sexy, but I WAS HOPING that this time would be different. But I'm just working. Even when one's job is to pretend—or not—to want to fuck people for money, thinking about sex at one's workplace can only lead to decreased productivity. There was one time I did cum on the job, but we'll save that for another day[29].

Finally, Jerome runs out of money. I dismount the Vibrating Express, exhausted from the quad workout and not, unfortunately, from the alleged climax. He won't know the difference. (Men seldom do.)

He hands me my payment, and hiding between the twenties is a business card for a sex-toy shop. Go figure.

***

Russian strippers are infamous. They are extremely efficient businesswomen. Mostly of supermodel calibre, they will stop at nothing for a greenback. I call them "matryoshka dolls." I love watching them work. Occasionally, I've had to pick up my own jaw from the primary-coloured eighties splashwork carpeting of a club.

I meet Joseph, another arrogant, lonely man sporting a polyester golf shirt and a fresh haircut. I take a seat with him and ask him about his weekend. STRIPPER TIP #20: Never ask a client about his day if the day is a Monday, a Friday, or any day in between. They don't want to talk about their shitty jobs that drive them to drink and sit between our thighs.

He starts a monologue about how he wants to buy a condo in South Beach; that he needs a break; that he wants some company. I've obviously asked him the right questions as he places two twenties on the table next to my clutch. As he continues on his rant, several of the matryoshka dolls come up to him, kissing him on the cheek, and playing with his hair. It turns out that Joseph is quite celebrated at the club. Stripper etiquette 101 is that if a girl is sitting with a client, he's off-

---

[29] Ok , fine, I'll tell you now: It was back in Sydney during a shower show. This really drunk and scruffy man just wanted to simulate licking my asshole through the glass. And man, was I ever *into* it. At some point during the performance I directed the shower head towards my clit, and came. It was great.

143

limits to everyone else—unless of course he invites you over himself.

As I listen to Joseph's woes about being lonely and uncompromising, he slips me another two twenties and his business card, for "If you ever want to go for a nice dinner."

Meanwhile, at a table opposite us, one of the matryoshka dolls is sitting and glaring at Joseph.

"I think Sasha is giving me dirty looks," he remarks. "May I invite her over?"

"Of course." I could say no, but that would be rude and so I'll just blame that on my north-of-the-borderness.

He waves Sasha over. Sasha, otherwise known as Anna Kournikova's doppelganger with a cheaper dye job, saunters over and sits in Joseph's lap.
"Do you two know each other?" Joseph asks us. We don't. I don't know anyone at the club. There are no other women in my Anglo-Saxon tribe, so I've been a lone wolf since I walked into Second Chances.

"Hi, Sasha. I'm Iris."

We shake hands as Sasha grinds into Joseph's lap. Joseph tries his best to go on about how accomplished he is and how he likes the beach and the colour turquoise while Sasha offers up a free lap dance. She starts to bite on his cheek.

"Let's go play," she whispers between my ear and his. "Do you like girls?" Sasha asks me, giving me the "SAY YES, BITCH" eyebrows of death.

For the first time ever, I'm tempted to say no. I'm really in no mood to fake finger-fuck a doll who smells like Patron, but I manage an unconvincing nod in complicity.

Sasha takes Joseph's head in her bejewelled hands and smushes her face into his. Joseph, embarrassed, presses on about Floridian real estate. He is unsuccessful as Sasha is determined to change the subject to Champagne Room follies.

I start to get embarrassed. I'm sitting there prudishly, asking about Joseph's aspirations to incorporate more white linen into his wardrobe, and here's this chick on top of him trying to get me to scissor her for 200 bucks.

"Should I leave you two alone?" I ask.

"No, I'd like you to stay," Joseph manages to say through the mop of brassy extensions that shroud his reddening face.

I, too, wanted to stay and get a couple more twenties passed in my direction for sitting pretty and listening. But Sasha has other plans and well, I've already explained how determined the Russians are.

I get up and leave, assuring him that I'll join him later when he's not so preoccupied. Within seconds, three more matryoshka dolls are clamouring for a piece of Joseph. A few minutes later, I look over to see the progress of their hustle and he's disappeared. So have the dolls.

***

Second Chances is a total dump. I knew this from the get-go. But, New York usually sends its most recent immigrants into a panic, and I am no different. Johnny, a client of mine, recognizes that I am pretty unhappy, no matter how many times I reassure him "I'm FINE! I LOVE my job! You can't ALWAYS win. Some days are better than others …"

"Listen, let me take you around to a club or two so you can see what else there is. You don't fit in here."

I agree to go with him, and it just so happens that every other club in Manhattan is infinitely less depressing than the one in which I've been fighting back tears for the past month. Vaulted ceilings. Vast stages. Couches that aren't damp.

At a club in Gramercy, I try to convince Johnny to get a lap dance from a pretty and perfect-titted French girl, Aurelie. He declines, instead offering me the dance.

Then I realize that I've NEVER. HAD. A. LAP DANCE.

Never.

I've given maybe a thousand. Never once have I sat and had a strange girl press her tits into my face for money. It's just always been the other way around, and I've never given much thought to why I haven't sampled the services I offer (for market research purposes, of course).

Aurelie sways and dances in front of me to the latest Lady Gaga single. I don't know which one … bless Gaga, but they all sorta sound the same. Then she grinds between my legs. This doesn't really do much for anyone without a schlong. Nonetheless, I appreciate the choreography.

Unlike nearly every male client I've ever had, I must mention how I have no desire to touch her. Here is this woman offering her gorgeous body for my entertainment and viewing pleasure, and I don't see any need to reach out and hold on. Surprised by my lifeless hands, she takes them and places them on her breasts. They are nice breasts; I love boobs. But grabbing on to this nice pair belonging to a woman I hardly know doesn't exactly make me cream.

It was a nice dance. 'Nice' like when your waitress makes an extra special effort to make sure there are no crumbs left on the tablecloth. Not 'nice' like when you get home to your girlfriend decked out in leather and lace.

Chicks: We're just wired differently.

I go back the following day to audition at the sexy Gramercy club, but they've been shut down by the IRS and are filing for bankruptcy.

Dragging my ass back to Second Chances, I say 'yes' to an adventure to the Champagne Room with a young, arrogant banker sporting a patchy goatee. It's time to face my fear and plunge into the unknown.

Goatee, Pimp Winnie, and I push through the gossamer curtain and walk the length of a long and narrow room, partitioned every six or seven feet with a couch, a table, a single tea light, and a partition screen. Only an idiot would call this 'private.' Once your eyes adjust to the pitch-black darkness, everyone can see everyone. I pass three sets of entangled bodies when it becomes clear that 'The Champagne Room' should actually be called 'The Peer Pressure Room.'

Goatee pays Winnie $600, then Winnie pays me $200. Joy! I'm getting paid my yet-to-be-hard-earned 33 percent up-front! The incentive, now, is to work harder (read: put out) for a tip. Goatee and I have an hour to enjoy each other's company.

I stand tall as Goatee sinks into the couch. I start to sway to no beat in particular when Goatee lunges at me like an excited baby.

"Not yet," I say, trying to buy time.

I can see next to me that another dancer is clearly giving a guy a handjob. I've never been the most enthusiastic hand-jobber. Even if I was, this little bitch before me would have to pay me hell of a lot more that $200 for one.

"I'm not going to do that," I say, motioning over to the entanglement next to us.

Goatee doesn't say anything; he just looks at me, excited and expectant. He paws at me, and I continue to dance, keeping my distance.

When I do finally sit on his lap, he clutches to my hips like a child clinging to a toy.

"Gentle," I tell him. STRIPPER TIP #21: A drooling man is a baby. Sometimes you have to talk to him like one.

For an hour, Goatee wordlessly pleads with me to put out, and I dance evasively around him. It's embarrassing. A single lap dance like this is bad enough, but when they are allowed to touch you, it gets awkward. I guess that's why everyone reverts to just giving handjobs and blowjobs and. It's what the clients want, and significantly easier than extracting a conversation out of them.

147

The hour ends. Goatee stands, thumbs down his boner in disappointment, and hands me a $50 tip.

I leave the room and decide that this experience has been pretty uncomfortable and terrible. I was a pretty late bloomer, sexually; now, I'm reminded of those make-out parties, where everyone would just hook up and dry hump each other, that I was so not into. I felt uncomfortable and pressured into locking my braces with Branden Teeple when really I just wanted to hang out, eat cheetos, and bop to the beat of some angsty Blink-182 anthem.

I decide that the Champagne Room is not for me, and pray for September to come sooner.

September

It's a Sunday night and The Russian Doll House is packed. Girls mill about almost silently, dragging men to the lap dance area, rubbing up against them briefly, only to pick up a new customer not a minute after finishing with the last one. This is the Holy Grail of fast cash in New York City, and I just left a pint of sweat and repressed tears on the stage for my audition. Kurt watches from the corner. We've met before. He would sometimes work shifts at Second Chances. We had a conversation once about his kids and little league and I decided that he wasn't half bad. He doesn't recognize me; I've lost about 10 pounds on the knee-pounding torture device Lisa Rinna calls a treadmill, and I'm now a platinum blonde, thanks to sitting under the sting of a heat lamp with bleach in my hair for the better half of yesterday afternoon. My scalp is pink, raw, and painful. I've turned myself into the closest thing to resembling Jenna Jameson without subjecting myself to UV radiation[30] and prosthetics.

"Okay," Kurt says, loud and flat. He's looking left as I stand to his right. Kurt's gaze is now scanning the wall on the opposite side of the room. He rolls his eyes: "Now, I'm going to go ahead and *hire* you." As I look at him not looking at me, it is clear that

---

[30] Canadians aren't into tanning. If we were, it would just be one big disappointment. True, I could spray one on. But I could also spray myself in a mixture of Pam and vanilla extract and probably wouldn't know the difference. Also: Marilyn never tanned.

Kurt's tone is insinuating that he is doing me a massive favour. I remember Kurt quite fondly but the man yelling at me—but in an opposite direction—is proving himself to be a douchebag. The industry does this to people. You can be generally awesome, and then one day you're just NOT anymore. You're spoilt. It's dangerous. *Poor prick,* I think to myself. *He's got kids and everything.*

"When can you start?"

"Tomorrow?"

"Okay. You're going to come in tomorrow at 7:30 and you're going to meet Jerry Jr. He's the Monday night manager. He's going to sort you out and give you the orientation."

I scurry back to the dressing closet, slipping on my Real-Girl clothes and flats. I do my very best to strut nonchalantly out of the club, giving my best mega-babe swagger, all the while trying hard to contain my excitement.

I'M NOT TOO FAT! MY HAIR IS ABOUT TO SNAP OFF IT'S SO FUCKING WHITE. I'M FUCKING HIRED! I'M 24 HOURS AWAY FROM BEING RICH.

On the subway, I tap my feet and smile so hard that a middle-aged woman next to me scoffs and moves down to the other end of the car. I want to call everyone I know* (I know about four people in NYC, and I came out to them as a stripper. I was really nervous, until my friend Sophie said, "Oh, don't worry, honey, Everyone in New York is a whore." If anything now I just have some pretty impressive street cred.) about my latest ascent in the stripper ranks. *I'M IN. I GOT IN. NO MORE NIGHTS OF WEEPING ALONE IN THE DARK CORNERS OF SECOND CHANCES!* But I don't really have any friends in New York yet, so I just go home and watch *Flashdance* for the 50th time.

The next morning, I wake up dancing. I can barely contain my excitement as I wait for night to fall. I prance over to yoga to calm my nerves and centre myself, but it's useless. Throughout the first sun salutation, I set a target for how much I plan on making on my first night as a Russian Doll. *It's Monday night,* I reason. *But I'm keen, I'm fresh, I'm THRILLED.* I set my target at $500. Most of the Russian Dolls are rumoured to earn thrice that sum, but I don't want to be too hard on myself on my first day.

Pressing into downward dog, I plan what kind of extravagant cheese and meat spread I'm going to buy for my victory feast tomorrow afternoon.

"Stepping or jumping your feet toward your palms, hang your arms into doll pose."

Grabbing my elbows, I hang my head and stare between my shins at the other yogis.

There is no fucking way any of these bitches are thinking about harnessing the energy of the universe with their chakras for love and compassion. This is New York Fucking City...Williamsburg...Whatever. That girl in the $90 Lululemon pants is thinking Prada, too.

It's pretty fucked up how high I get off the idea of earning money. Money is what makes the world go 'round, and it seems to spin faster when you've got more of it.

I'm supposed to be meditating and honouring my flow. I decide to try to reconcile myself with the wisdom put forth from the instructor: "Wisdom is knowing we are all One. Love is what it feels like and Compassion is what it acts like."

I take a deep breath and bring my arms above my head, palms pressed together, fingers to the exposed pipes lining the ceiling: *Thank you, Universe, for my relatively symmetrical features, especially my plump, pert breasts and their generous earning potential. May they never sag.*

Stretching into a side-bend, I ponder what sort of designer bag I'm going to reward myself with at the end of the week. I've always wanted to have the courage to walk into the Prada store in Soho, but I've never been able to. I swear the clerks are hired based on their intimidation tactics alone. The only courage that will push me through the heavy, fingerprint-less glass doors would be the manifestation of hard hustling: a rolled-up wad of hundreds, hot in my pocket.

Wearing heels all the time gives a person incredible balance. But when the yoga instructor brings us to Standing Tree Pose, I can't for the life of every squat I've ever done in stilettos balance on one leg.

Okay, mind, I acknowledge that you're really excited, but please leave me alone so I can at least finish my practice with an ounce of sincerity.

But I just. can't. wait. to. get. back. to. work. My thoughts of money (and restored confidence) will just not go away.

I'm one of those assholes who SMILES during her shavasana. The beauty in the universe is mine and it's about to manifest itself as large amounts of money that are ready to be claimed by my greedy, freshly manicured hands.

Fuck Second Chances, that smoke-filled dressing room, and the corner of shame. Every Russian Doll makes a fortune and I'm about to join their ranks.

Most of my friends hate their jobs. A lot of them are professional Tweeters and Facebookers. As much as I love an unhealthy dose of newsfeeds, I deem myself one lucky bonermonger.

*

Passing through the doors and into the dressing closet as if it's my own personal boudoir, I am as eager as a beaver to step into my cunt floss and mount every suit I just passed sauntering through Midtown.

"Hi!" I announce to the house Mama. "It's my first night. I'm Zoe."

Characteristically, she doesn't give a shit, and demonstrates this with a frowning nod.

I slip into my dress and shoes and saunter through the club, over to the man Kurt told me would be in charge tonight: Jerry Jr.

154

"I KNOW THIS GIRL," he says, pointing at me with his clipboard.

"I know her," he says again, telling the other managers who are crowded together, going over the roster.

Jerry Jr. thrusts the edge of the brown clipboard under my nose. I feel like I'm being picked out of a lineup for kidnapping. Since when knowing me a problem? The clipboard in my face is suggesting that it most definitely is a problem.

Eyes wide and blinking, I look at him like he's speaking Greek. Do I say I have a stripper sister? With darker hair?

"…I auditioned here ages ago. You told me to come back in September!" I smile. My smile usually makes people change their minds. Thank you, Mom, for insisting that I get braces.

"Listen, I know Kurt hired you last night. But really, we don't have any room for you here right now. I have too many girls."

I've heard this speech before. Verbatim. Fuck.

"Look, all I'm doing right now is hiring girls for the other clubs. I can send you to our other two clubs but right now I've got 90 girls here—"

"Jerry. Jerry." I try to get him to look in my general direction, which is especially hard given the mobster trend of looking out a window or at a stage of naked chicks when addressing anyone personally.

"JERRY," I plead. "Be real with me for a second."

Jerry squints, and tries to look at me. He fails, settling his gaze on my forehead.

"Is it my look? Do I need to lose weight? My hair, is it too short? Just TELL ME, please, because I am not going to those clubs. I hate those clubs. You know how dumpy they are."

"No, no, it's not that. You're fine," he reassures me, albeit unconvincingly. This is the most personal moment Jerry Jr. and I will ever have. It passes quickly.

"How long do I have to wait?" I ask. I'm desperate. Me, a fucking babe of a stripper who knows her hustle and is highly skilled in the art of making everyone love her, is desperate. Fuck you, New York, for making me feel this way. I have no idea what's wrong with me but I know that something must be if I'm being rejected for a second time after being told to come back.

Jerry Jr. starts to walk away. "Can … I work the day shift?"

Jerry Jr. turns around. Dropping his chin down in shock, he asks, "You wanna work the day shift?"

"How long will I have to work the day shift until I can work nights?"

"I dunno, uh … a couple weeks—a month."

"Fine. I'll do it. I'm just not going to those other clubs. I'll wait."

I don't know what the fuck I've walked myself into. New York City is not a place to WAIT for your turn to get what you want. Capitalism is about stomping on post-Soviet drone heads to get to where you need to be. I thought I'd already reached my lowest point in the Big Apple, but apparently not.

"I'm on the schedule for tonight, and I'm dressed and ready to go." I hold my arms out, sinewy and pleading. "Can I at least work tonight?"

"I don't want to get into bad habits," is Jerry Jr's response.

The wind is out of my sails. My shoulders are not the sloping type, but somehow they manage to roll forward. "So do I come in tomorrow?"

"Yeah, come in at 11:30."

156

Purgatory Part Two

There are two distinct differences between the clientele of the Day Girl and the Night Time Dream Team: First, a Day Girl's clients are die-hard fans of naked ladies. They've been there before, they know the drill, and they're not shy to dish out the dollars. You don't have to explain to them what a lap dance is, how much it costs, and that nipple-sucking is not ever included in the $20 special.

Second, her clients are hardly ever drunk (read: impressionable). This means she has to actually talk to them in complete sentences and expect a coherent answer in return. This process must be repeated several times before a successful coax into a lap dance is possible. On my first day, I am lucky enough to have this conversational exchange with a man in coveralls perched at the bar:

"Hi…" I begin, trying to forget that it's a quarter past twelve on a Tuesday. I lean in to pass a whisper to his ear, "How are you today?" He smells like hard labor and Old Spice.

"I'm great." Chin up, he scans the room, his hands planted firmly on his knees. "So many beautiful tits around I'll be whacking off like a madman later."

"You're right. There are a lot of nice tits around here. Wanna go for a lap dance?"

"Yeah," inspecting my rack, "sure."

I take him over to the bench and lean in close to his neck, hovering over his head. This is how my lap dance routines always begin. STRIPPER TIP #22: Let them smell you. I don't know what it is, but without trying too hard, strippers are like fresh baked-cookies: hot and edible.

"No, NO, not so close. Move back so I can see," he demands.

I stand up and sway, ensuring he has optimal tit-viewing from his vantage point. It's less of a lap dance than it is me standing in front of him with my tits out.

"Do you ever let guys blow their load on your tits?"

"Never."

"NEVER? Oh man ..." Over his coveralls, he starts to flick at his dick. Guys rub and readjust all the time while I'm dancing, but never have I seen a guy flick his penis at the sight of something pleasing. "Oh man, I would blow such nasty loads on your tits."

The third characteristic of Day Girls is that it is assumed that we all have babies screaming for us at home. For every two clients I approach on Day One of Purgatory Part Two, one will ask if I have any children. They don't believe me when I say no.

By 7:30 p.m., the customers start piling in. Suddenly, the club is buzzing with excitement and average-looking men in expensive suits and I sigh at the relief that at least in my final half hour I'll be able to sprint through all these fresh and eager faces. A guy in a navy blazer and a pocket square pays $13 for a Stella Artois and sides up next to me. "Long day?" he asks.

"No, it's been great!" I lie.

We flirt for a moment or two; I make him laugh. STRIPPER TIP #23: Laughter is a great way to segue into, "So can we go for a little dance?" After someone laughs, they are way more likely to follow up with a yes.

I graze his forearm with my index finger, ready to slide into action.

"Oh, no thank you. I'm waiting for the Night Girls."

Finally, what it means to be a Day Girl is to be surely bummed when the whistle blows on your hustle at 8 p.m., and the Night Time Dream Team shows up to make the real money. Every single end of my shift, I am exhausted and jealous that I can't stay for the gratuitous generosity of drunk business men. I have go to to sleep while the grown-ups stay and play. Every single work day ends with a total bummer moment where I must accept that I'm on the B-team and I earn, like, an eighth of what these other babes are about to rake in.

I give myself a pep talk: *It's just this month. The weather's still warm. Things will perk up in October.*

The Day Time B-Team is supervised by Day Girls of days gone by. The managerial squad consists of three women who never smile.

The first manager is Amy. Amy is pretty and petite with a mane of shiny black hair she haphazardly does up in a pony-loop. Although she was born in Korea, the nasal cadence in her bossings-around has me certain that she has spent every spare moment of her 35 years on Long Island, rearing 12 sons alongside a deaf husband with poorly functioning hearing-aids. Just like her fake tits, she's firm and unmalleable. Amy doesn't like when I chat with the waitresses, my only colleagues who are sort of cordial with me. Rather than communicate this to me with a simple "no fraternizing, sweethaht," she instead grabs me by my upper arm, dragging me several paces out of earshot of my only acquaintance.

It's nothing personal, Amy, but I've concluded that you're a bitch. You are more than welcome to redeem yourself at any time. But I know you don't give a fuck about redemption. And, this, Amy, is the part of me that wants to like you.

The second manager is my favourite person in the club on whom I get to exercise my gaydar. Her name is Liz, and she wears brown orthopaedic pumps beneath khaki flares. Liz has feathered blonde hair that probably looked really sexy when she first styled it that way, back when Farrah Fawcett was on the

161

bedroom walls of teenage boys across America. There is just something about the way that Liz tucks her fitted blouse into her belted khakis that hat makes me think she bats for my team. The tautness of her blouse stretches just enough over her biceps that lead me to believe she can definitely throw a softball. I could not throw a softball if my life depended on it, and this is one of many reasons why I am a bad lesbian. I refuse to play any organized sports and I don't compost. But I can still sniff out a rug muncher, and that's all that matters in the end, right? There's something in Liz's staunch gait and detached professionalism with my fellow strippers that screams REPRESSED LATE-40s ASPIRING FINGERBANGER, and naturally I want to reach out to her. But she's too busy crossing her arms and rolling her eyes at dressing room dramas to let me serenade her with a little a cappella Melissa Etheridge jam.

The matriarch of daytime management is Louise. By default, Louise is the friendliest of them all. This is because she isn't usually mean on purpose, and when she is she delegates the reprimand to be dished out by Liz or Kim. If she wasn't Jerry's sister, Louise could be a really intimidating linebacker for the NFL. Like the house Mama, she accentuates her bahama-mama-ness with crushed velvet patterns inspired by Emilio Pucci's resort collection from 1982. Louise sits on a perch at the side of the room with US Weekly, The National Enquirer, and a desk lamp. She has been known to attempt a crossword.

Louise draws up the schedule for the Day Girls. When I tell her I can't work next Tuesday, she asks, with husk and aggression, "WHY?"

"To go to a concert," I reply.

"Who are you seeing?" *Wait. What. Is Louise feigning interest in my personal life?*

"Hanson," I inform her.

Louise's mouth curls into a sneer. But a sneer in strip-club lifer[31] parlance is considered a smile.

*

Depending on who is managing, power-tripping, or just plain hating on my ass, each day at Russian Dolls is different, but equally shitty. Every morning, an authority figure tells me that something about my appearance sucks, and that I have to change it.

One Thursday morning, my hoochie dress that has hitherto qualified as 'long' suddenly becomes 'too short.' White and sequinned, the halter dress hugs my hips and thighs, with the hemline dropping two inches below my knee. Whenever I wear it, people call out to me "Marilyn!" (Any platinum blonde stripper with hair above her shoulders is 'Marilyn.' Any long-haired, curvy brunette with a tan is 'Kim!': Horny men are seldom cultured or creative.)

Louise calls me over: "YA CAN'T WAY-AH THAT DRESS, HONNAY."

"I've been wearing this dress all week," I tell her.

I hate this dress. I was forced to buy it a few months back at Second Chances when my other one wasn't 'white enough' for the white party no one told me about. I am quite happy to NOT wear this dress ever again. But I was ordered to buy it on an occasion not unlike the one that I'm describing now. It is so cheaply made; the seamstress didn't bother putting a lining in it before adding the $100 price tag. The sequins scratch through the fabric, making me feel like I've subjected myself to one of those masochistic religions where you have to wear a shirt made of hair. I wear it because I've been putting off going to the sex shops to find yet another hundred-dollar dress that comes in a box just big enough to contain a pair of socks.

---

[31] Lifer: A stripper who will never stop working in strip clubs. She dances for 20 years, becomes a manager for the next 30, and then either takes over the world or dies of lung cancer.

163

Louise stares at my hemline, arms crossed, head rotating left to right.

I look at the other girls. Most of them are wearing 'gowns' (read: two panels of fabric stitched together at the waist). On top of her spray tan, one of the lifers is wearing a lilac dress. Her dress is the same length as mine, but no one is calling her over for inspection.

Louise brings my attention back to her haranguing,

"YA NEED A GOWN. IT'S GOTTA GO TO THE FLOW-AH."

I look back to my lilac-dressed colleague, whose dress certainly does not go 'to the floor.' I look back to Louise, expressionless.

"Go to the back and ask Mama if she has a luong dress fo ya."

Of course, Mama has several dresses that fit the dress code. I rifle through a box of fluorescent Lycra, unearthing one black sequinned piece. I slip it on over my head to see what it looks like. The gown dangles down to the floor, as it should, with a slit up the left leg and ass cheek. The top piece is an upside-down triangularly shaped piece of fabric that, at the base, is connected to the skirt. The other two corners have string attached to them, forming a halter. The one thing working in this frock's favour is that it is lined, so my nipples won't be raw by the third time I take it off this afternoon. The dress has a sticker on it that tells me it's going to cost me $140. I'm thinking it definitely cost no more than $6 to make, and it is hideous. But if I want to stay and work, I have to scribble an I.O.U. on a cocktail napkin and pay her out as soon as I make the cash.

I keep the dress on and shove the rejected white one into my backpack. I stand up, taking a look at myself in the full-length mirror. It's 11:48 on a Thursday morning and I look like a caricature from a prom-themed porno. I take a deep breath and console myself with the words of Dolly Parton: "It costs a lot of money to look this cheap!" Instead of evoking surprise, the cost of this 'gown' has me working really hard to fight back a flood of tears. But this is not waterproof mascara, and this is not a safe space for feeling vulnerable and down on my luck; this is the waiting room for going on to do bigger and better things and crying will only send me back to Second Chances or onto my mom's couch in suburban Ontario.

This is not why I strip. I didn't come here to be bullied. I came here to work my own hours on my own steam to make the money I need to live—as Oprah would put it—my best life. Instead I feel humiliated in this stupid 'gown' under these stupid rules and now I have to convince myself that I am the sexiest sister to ever grace these sticky floors. So I walk out into the club and wait for the horny lunch-breakers to file in.

One of the cute Brazilian girls who I only ever see chain-smoking in the emergency exit stairwell is sitting with the first and only man in the club. Scrawny and precise, her client has two trial-sized toiletry bottles on a table, along with a die. Miss Brazil looks away from him, arms crossed, with her leg jutting out and resting on his thigh. Carefully, he removes her shoe, squeezes some oil onto his hands, and proceeds to fondle and rub the arch of her calloused foot. Miss Brazil's arms are still tightly pressed against her chest, her gaze fixed on the wall. Smack, smack, smack goes her bubble gum.

Eventually, Miss Brazil is summoned on stage. I decide that my feet could use a rub, too, so I waltz over to take her place. I plop into the chair, the seat still warm.

"Why do you have a die?" I'm too fed up to bother with pleasantries.

The Gambler folds his hands together on the table, and smiles as if he's 40 years older than his fortysomething age. He looks to my hands.

"Would you like a hand massage?"

I give him my right hand.

"You should probably take off your rings."

I oblige.

165

"Will you excuse me for a moment?" he asks, his voice barely audible. "I like to wash my hands between each massage."

When The Gambler comes back, he squeezes a few drops of what he tells me is almond oil, and rubs it into his hands. He takes my right hand with both of his, and proceeds to caress my palm.
"You see, I don't really have much money for lap dances, but I just love women's hands and feet." He is pressing so lightly on my hand that it almost tickles. It's the most pansy massage I've ever received. "So I bring in the die. If you roll the number you guess, I'll get a dance. If not, well, you just get the pleasure of a massage."

The Gambler reaches for my other hand, repeating the same lifeless routine of fondling my fingers. This is the day shift: perpetually nonplussed, but with nothing else to do.

"Well, thank you for the massage, honey. That was nice," I lie.

"Would you like to roll the dice, then?"

This guy is offering me a one-in-six chance at earning $20 from him. More humiliation. But there's nothing else to do, nothing else to be earned.

I call a four, and roll a two.

The Gambler nods with a slow blink and I'm off to another corner of the club to hope that someone else comes in soon. Someone who will pay me.

*

A man moonwalks into the club. Clearly drunk, he lifts his arms as though he's airing out his pits, and attempts a spin but ends up walking into a pillar. Catching a glimpse of my sequinned radiance from the corner, he points at me: "You." He waves me over. "Wuh-wuh-will you dance for me?"

Without a verbal response, I grab his arm and drag him over to the side of the room and, in a frigid haste, remove my new gown and plop it on the floor. I start my dance while the inebriated

166

moonwalker rolls his head back and forth beneath me; he's seemingly unable to support it—much like a newborn baby.

I dance for three songs before he mutters a slurry whisper. "Spit on me."

"Pardon me?" I heard him, but I just want to be certain that this is the moment I've been waiting for for the past year: the moment when I get to hork up a globule of Sugar-Free Redbull residue and fling it at a client's face.

His head is still lolling from side to side; his eyes give up on trying to stay open: "SPIT. ON. ME."

With pleasure!

But then ... I balk. ME. The naked, dancing megababe is getting stage fright.

Reaching within the depths of my esophagus, I cannot find enough mucus to generate a sizable bulb of goo. I spatter what I already have in my mouth at his face; whatever moisture was left over from some previously barren conversation about stock trading mists onto his balding head.

"AGGGHHHhhhhhhh...RRrrrr." The Moonwalker's legs collapse under me. His mouth is agape. Nearly falling from my post, I ask: "Did you just cum in your pants? You know that costs extra." STRIPPER TIP #24: If a man cums—whether you put in a little extra elbow grease or not—demand a tip. Our job is to tease, so any enjoyment extending beyond that merits a tip. The Moonwalker is unresponsive. He's in the fifth dimension of drunkenness and masochistic ecstasy. His wallet has flopped open and rests in the open palm of his lifeless hand. I take what he owes me and move on in search of my next $20.

Another physically nondescript john is sitting at the bar, gazing up and over at me from reading glasses that are teetering on the tip of his deeply porous nose. I smile at him. He smiles back. A smile is a green light for a stripper: I saunter over and throw my arms around his neck and shoulders.

"How are you today?"

167

"I'm great. I love my day off."

Charlie is a firefighter from New Jersey. He gets one free day for every nine and this is how he spends it: "I get on the Path and get into the city, go to mass at St. Patricks, have lunch at Hooters, and then come over here."

"And what do you do next?"

"I'll probably go home. That's all I wanna do," Charlie replies. I find his matter-of-fact sincerity endearing.

The days roll on and the day shift remains the fucking day shift. It's slow, it's tedious and I just can't understand why I am still unwelcome on the night shift. I lost weight, destroyed my hair … I've gone from Skipper to Barbie for this place, and I'm still only allowed to order from the lunch menu.

***

Running from the train, down Broadway and into the club, I gasp for breath as Liz greets me with, "Nice bag." Combing back her feathered bangs, she eyes the stitchwork of my Coach tote. I got from a client who designs them. He wanted to go for a beer and I casually asked him if he would bring me one of his designs. He obliged, and then accused me of using him. Lying, I denied it, and never called him back. It's a pretty nice bag. It was worth the beer in Murray Hill. I resolved next time to manifest a designer for Prada.

"You're late," Liz says.

"It's 11:45!" I reason between gasps for breath.

Liz lifts her Motorola Razr, tapping the screen with her unmanicured finger. It flashes 11:46.

"You can pay the $25 fine when you make it. I'll just take the $75 house fee now."

As I'm peeling my eyes open with a mascara wand, I see a tall and leggy blonde saunter into the dressing closet. She is chatting

168

away on her phone in an English that has clearly spent some time in Cleveland. She's wearing a tattered and billowy t-shirt, black skinny jeans—bereft of factory-made holes or rhinestone embellishment—and a canvas tote spewing glossy magazines. Staring at her through my drying eyelashes, I conclude that she, too, must live in Williamsburg.

How curious! There is someone here who I might be able to talk to! I return my gaze to my own sleepy eyes, finishing the application of my raccoon makeup routine by kissing it off with a slash of my signaturely ironic Russian Red lipstick. It really wasn't meant to be ironic. I was an honest Russophile for a while. My degree says that I am fluent in Russian, which, like the degree itself, is total bullshit. My Russian sucks balls. I'm partially relieved that I don't have to lie about my linguistic competencies anymore. Whenever anyone says, "Say something in Russian," it makes both of us look like assholes. Now I'm just a "dumb stripper." When people assume I'm dumb as a dump truck, it's hard to disappoint them. This is incredibly liberating. No one wants to hear about the thesis I don't remember writing because I was too jacked up on Adderall! They just want confirmation that my tits are real and my pussy is wet.

I clamber over a few spray-tanned bodies, past Mama, who is really having a hard time with her emphysema this morning, and out of the dressing closet. It's 11:54 and I'm ordering a tequila sunrise to ease into an afternoon of listening to suits talk about stock trading. (I am continually surprised by how guiltless they are about taking people's money, and subsequently charging them for having it depreciate several hundred percent. These guys are swindlers and yet I'm the one who gets the flak for lack of morals … all for dancing around in fucking underpants. Ruining children's college funds is totally acceptable, but giving a guy a boner is grounds for eternal damnation!)

I take a seat next to a starched-collared chap who is expressing interest in my hobbies. This is not uncommon in strip club patrons, and I've devised several responses to keep it entertaining: Occasionally I say I like 'movies' and list *Thelma and Louise*, *The Graduate* and *I Shot Andy Warhol,* which usually fucks it up or pigeonholes me as a freaky man-hater. Other times, I cite *27 Dresses,* or anything else featuring Katherine Heigl, and in those moments my fate is sealed as an enterprising and blonde basic bitch for the rest of the afternoon.

But today I am caught off-guard and accidentally utter what I *actually do* when I'm not whispering sweet nothings into the ears of self-loathing financiers.

"A WRITER!" the client bellows with grandfatherly enthusiasm. "Well, WHADDYA KNOW. A Writer. Ha! Isn't that something? What do you write about?"

Before I can even open my mouth to spin another sort of half-truth, the leggy blonde walks up to our conclave, leaning in to ask Sir Bellows, "Would you like a neck and shoulder massage?"

"OH BOY, I SURE WOULD. What's your name, sweetheart?"

"Carla."

"CARLA. Nice to meet you. I'm really stiff today. Beat the darn tootin' crap outta my shoulders, will ya?"

Sir Bellows gestures over to me while Carla dabs some essential oils onto Sir Bellows' temples.
"THIS ONE RIGHT HERE, SHE'S A WRITER. ISN'T THAT SOMETHING, CARLA? A WRITER." Most clients at Russian Dolls expect to meet a Lithuanian supermodel with a sick cousin at home, so I've grown used to this kind of surprised-you-speak-English reaction. Oftentimes, they look disappointed. "I was hoping for someone … more exotic," one freshmen told me one day after I sat on his lap for no drink and 20 minutes.

"A writer," Carla inquires. "I *thought* I overheard you speaking English!"

Carla brings Sir Bellows to a state of sandalwood-infused semi-consciousness while we prattle on about being the only native English-speakers at Russian Dolls.

"Yeah, management kinda hates American girls here. I auditioned a while back to switch from massaging to dancing and they told me I had to go to their bastard clubs downtown."

My jaw drops: Carla—tall, blonde, leggy, and with what I assume to be fantastic real breasts under her bustier—was denied a job at this club where some of the girls on stage have vintage tit jobs sagging like silicone melons in tube socks. (Fact: Boob jobs don't look good forever. Every decade or so, you have to get them redone. It's basic biology and physics: skin stretches under weight. If those siliconed fun-bags are bouncing around a stage for a 40-hour workweek, they won't have that levitating look forever.)

"They denied you a job?" I repeat, dumbfounded.

"Yeah. It seems like they only want European or Brazilian girls. I see American girls come in to audition every day. They never make it past Jerry."

Suddenly everything makes sense. Even though I am Canadian and not American, I see how an untrained ear and keenness for Eastern European frigidity and Latina heat may not have picked up on this. Young women without green cards or proficiency in the English language tend to obey orders, and they don't complain about horrendous working conditions. I was just *shocked* by the fact that Jerry wasn't squirming with joy at the prospect of having a maple-syrup-toting smartypants on his Night Time Dream Team. I decide that from here on out, if I want to get on to the night shift, I will have to be French.

I leave Carla with Sir Bellows and make for the dressing closet.

I'm just going to be French from now on, I tell myself. *It can't be that hard. I've been speaking French since the age of 5 and have watched enough New Wave films to think myself Parisian at heart. This has got to win me a spot with the Night Time Dream Team.*

"Allo!" I greet my next suit with a coy fake frenchiness that I've borrowed from *Last Tango in Paris.* "Ow arrrre you tu-day?"

"Well, hello there. Where are you from?"

"I am from France. Ave you been zere?"

"No, I haven't," my newest Francophile replies.

171

"Would you … uh …" I hesitate, trying to find the English word that has suddenly escaped me. "… like to go forrrr a dance wiz me?"

"Well, yes, I would."

I start my dance, explaining in broken English with many pauses and mispronunciations how much I love America and New York and how different it is from my home country.

"I just looove ze expressions you use herrre. Zey are so interesting!"

"Do you know the expression, 'Eat pussy?' Because I would like to do that to you."

"Oh, I sink I know what zat means … You arrre naughty boy!"

STRIPPER TIP #25: 'Naughty' is a word I use to call a man a pervert. It's a way to scold him for being a pig without explicitly calling him a piggy piece of shit. It's complimentary, and keeps them wanting more. If a dancer wants to get paid at the end of her dance, she's got to keep her audience sated, yet still begging for more, till the end of each two-and-a-half minute set.
I press on with my French charade, as I seem to be getting dances without having to bother with tedious chatter. The only time I decide against employing my fake accent is when I see a man with either a well-fitted suit, a pocket square, or both. These are two clear indicators that a man is European, and therefore possibly French.

American men seem to be fascinated with the *je ne sais quoi* of European women; or perhaps they just like the idea that we'll compensate for our poor English comprehension skills with submissiveness. If my French self can't find the word, I make up for it with a pantomime in which I grab his dick and bite on his ear. In this way, I can skip whatever point I was trying to make and go straight to a lap dance before he can say MY HOTEL.

My fake French is not flawless. At one point, upon announcing that I hailed form a small town in the Alps by the Swiss border, a client responds with, "You don't sound French at all."

I save myself by explaining in broken sentences that I was an army brat, and had lived "all over ze world." I don't know anything about growing up in the military, so I grip his thigh, clawing his poly-cotton blend trousers, and whisper some sexy and grammatically incorrect nothings into his ear. We go for several dances and my alleged backstory is never again disputed.

The day drags on and I start to believe my own bullshit. I feel as though I am actually French. When I'm in the bathroom stall, muttering to myself, checking my phone, and counting my twenties, the mutterings are of the same lilt that I've been using all afternoon. I'm in character, and I don't want to fuck it up. (Plus I've always sort of wished that I grew up on a diet of cheese and Nutella with wine in my sippy cup.)

I approach a young Japanese man sipping chardonnay at the bar. "Allo, Ow are you tu-day?" The schpiel begins. I tell him I am from France, to which he replies, in French, "I'm French too! Although I was born in Japan, I'm actually a French citizen. It's so nice to meet a French girl here. Where are you from?"

Fuck. My strategic method of assuming French/non-French clients has totally excluded the fact that FRANCE IS PRETTY FUCKING MULTICULTURAL. *Je suis une dumbasse.* I balk at my ignorance, smile coyly, and grip his thigh. Although I am a fluent French speaker, I am not in any way French. I speak French Canadian with an English accent and often swap masculine nouns with feminine articles, and it may be endearing, but one thing it is not is perfect French. If the club wasn't so dark, my reddening face would give me away. It doesn't matter, though; he's already figured me out.

The Japanese-Frenchman is sweet enough to decide against calling me on my bluff and obliges to a few dances. At the end he tells me—in English—"Thank you. Have a nice day." I stuff the bills into my purse and scurry into the dressing closet. Lies are really hard to maintain.

By the day's end, I am exhausted—not from doing an eight-hour pulsing wall-sit in four-inch platforms, or from fake smiling and girlishly giggling, but from the acting. Pretending to be a fantasy girl is work enough, but being Chloe the French hustler is an added pressure that has me nearly weeping in despair as the clock nears 8. I still have a 40-minute commute home in my whore makeup, warding off evil predators with my white earbuds. By the time I get home, it's 9 p.m. and I crash onto my unmade mattress, tuckered the fuck out.

For the rest of the week I am resolved to continue with *mes charades européennes.* I figure that in order to get onto the night shift, I'll have to convince myself and all of the American managers that I am, like the majority of the other girls, European and lacking in English language comprehension. If I keep this up, after a few weeks they won't even remember my initial Canadian twang! And, when I finally get onto the night shift, the act won't be nearly as exhausting, because it's too busy to have a real conversation with anyone. Evenings at the club are a whirlwind of girls and crotches and dance after dance where very little is said between client and entertainer. But in order to have the opportunity to be a French lady of the night, I have to keep jumping through these absurd hoops of daytime shenanigans, coaxing and flirting with oldies and fatties for intimate moments in dark corners where they can breathe in the scent of young flesh without fighting for their attention over the rowdy bachelor parties.

I fucking hate working the day shift. *This is temporary*, I tell myself. I just don't know *how* temporary—this is the stressful part. I'm not sure if it's within my power to change it or if I really do have to sit and wait patiently. Who am I kidding? New York never requires waiting and patience if you want to get anywhere. It's about the hustle. Hustlers don't wait in purgatory. I haven't seen Jerry or Jr. in a few days, so I approach Louise to see when I can speak with one of them.

"Allo, Louise, I was joost wondering… when does Djarry come in tu ze club? He told me tu ask him about ze night shift."

Louise raises an eyebrow, but says nothing about my ridiculous accent. Maybe she doesn't notice. But there is something all-knowing about her that makes my blood boil because clearly she can't be fucked to shed any light on this situation for me.

"Tonight. He'll be in tonight." She returns to US Weekly. (Someone is maybe pregnant, and there are three different potential fathers.)

This could be my last day as a Day Girl. The gates of wealth will open to me tonight.

*

Later that evening, Jerry waltzes into the lair, fat as a cat, hands on his belly, a cigar wedged between his canines. Mobsters really are parodies of themselves.

"Allo, Djarry!" I exclaim with a French (read: subdued) flirtation. "Yu said tu me a monts ago zat I could dance in za evening dis monts … Can I—"

"I got too many girls on at night," he interjects with a frown. "Maybe next month."

I want to tell him that I just saw three new babes getting hired as I was leaving last night. But I'm just in denial. When managers tell you, "Maybe later," it's the same as when a customer replies with, "Maybe later," after you ask them if they'd like a dance. "Maybe later" doesn't exist in New York. It's just a tactic for avoidance. "Maybe later" really just means, "No, nope, never, and I won't even dignify you with a proper rejection."
I'll never be on the night shift. And the only person who didn't know this the whole time was me.

A GUY JUST CALLED ME "THE GIRL NEXT DOOR." WHAT DOES THAT EVEN MEAN?
IT MEANS YOU'RE WHITE, ENGLISH-SPEAKING, AND THAT YOU DON'T HAVE ANY PLASTIC SURGERY.
SO I'M NOT "EXOTIC"?
NO.

Paris

Sliding a meaty, calloused palm up my skirt. I press my hips into the thickness of his fingers. Breathless, I beg: "Fuck me, Gerard."

"Excuse me, mademoiselle, would you care for some water?"

I lift the scratchy, complimentary sleep mask onto my forehead. Flashing her best fake smile, an immaculate flight attendant hands me a plastic cup filled halfway with Evian.

I'm having a sex dream about a client I'm on my way to see. My chest is heaving. Parched, I sip the water, lifting the window screen. Blinded by the morning sunlight, I squeeze my eyes shut, seeing only red. I try to shake the memory of Gerard's hands I was so hungrily forcing between my thighs, but I only see red.

"Good morning, passengers, we are beginning our descent into Charles de Gaulle. It is 7:30 in the morning in Paris, slightly cloudy and 7 degrees Celsius. Thank you for flying with us."

One month ago:

I press my bare shoulder into the broad, silvery chest of a well-dressed man. His custom-tailored navy suit jacket is flung

177

perfectly across the back of his barstool. Gold monogrammed initials ('*PFG'*) stitched into an inside pocket are just as telling as the Limited Edition Omega Speedmaster[32] heavy on his wrist.

"Hello," I say, drawing my index finger from his collar, down toward his belt. I've had a drink or two this afternoon. The only way I make money during this day shift is by drinking through it. Alcohol makes me sluttier, more open-minded, and less likely to look down at my watch.[33]

A cocktail, a smile, a lap dance, and discussion of oysters prompts Gerard to ask me, "So, if I take you to ze Champagne Room, will you … give me … a hand job?"

My eyes lock with his icy-blue expectant eyes. Lips pouty and pursed around my straw, I sip leisurely on my fourth vodka soda. Swallowing with a smirk, I mouth the word: "No."

I should probably say, "maybe," since "no" stops the world from spinning in places like this. But today, booze has me feeling boldly honest.

Gerard squints, and pulls me closer. "I respect dat." Pause. "I like you, Chloe. You are special."

I'm not special. At this point, I'm a bad businesswoman. I should have said "maybe," taken the money, and run. But dare I say I am enjoying sitting on this Frenchman's lap? A few more drinks, a few more lap dances, and I am drunk and Gerard asks me, "When do you get out of here?"

"Eight."

"Will you join me for dinner? And oysters?"

---

[32] Limited Edition Omega Speedmaster: a very expensive watch that doesn't look particularly expensive, but any hustler worth her salt knows it is.
[33] My watch: A gold-plated Tissot that my mother bought me for my graduation from University. I love this watch. It's also worth one tenth of a Limited Edition Omega Speedmaster.

The one bonus of working the day shift is that I've been making a career of joining men for dinner after my shift ends. In a few months, I've ploughed through the most decadent wine lists, oyster selections, and porterhouse steaks—so much that I'm on a first name basis with the maitre d' at Per Se[34]. The second bonus is that I've started to have a social life. I made a few friends in New York. I even met a cute girl. But then when my new friends ask me what I 'do,' and I tell them I'm a day-shift stripper, and then it all feels shitty again. I haven't quite figured out all the reasons why I like stripping, yet. I'm just doing it, and for the most part, it's rad. But the reason why I like it so much so far is the money. The day shift never really makes me much of that.

Gerard and I paint the Upper East Side red with vintage wines, Malpeque oysters, lobster tails, and chocolate ganache before enjoying a nightcap in the bar at the Peninsula Hotel. Howling, drunk, and begging a buttoned-up, weary-eyed bartender to pour us a fourth round of B52 shots, I decide that I really like this man. He is a retired hot French man who wears his lady-killer days like a badge beneath his monogrammed inside pocket: *Discreetly*. I peg him as Marlon-Brando-circa-*Last-Tango-in-Paris*-hot. After he clues me in to the fact that he sold his medical-appliance company for 40 million euros last year, he looks even hotter.

We slam the empty glass thimbles onto the mahogany table. Wiping a hand along his square, assertive jaw, a band of gold catches the light of the sinking candle set between us.

"Chloe, come to Paris wiz me."

"Ha!"

"I could show you all of Paris."

Wiping my mouth with a stray napkin, I bob my head and look around the room. We are the last ones standing at the Peninsula.

---

[34] Per Se: a staggeringly expensive and remarkably delicious French restaurant in Midtown.

"Maybe," I say. *Maybe* is a stripper's favourite word. It's bursting with empty promises and rarely leads anyone to believing that the answer is actually "no." The answer is almost always "no." But sometimes even the most professional extortionists exercise bad judgment.

"I haven't had fun like zis in a long time, Chloe."

Like the drunk blonde that I am, I look up to my left, then right, tapping ragtime onto the bar with my nails.

"Would I have my own hotel room?"

"Of course!" A grave frown, a single nod: "Separate rooms!"

"As friends?"

"As friends."

"Will you take me to the Moulin Rouge?"

"Whatever is your desire, my Chloe."

"*Maybe.*"

Friends. Separate hotel rooms. Maybe he just thinks I'm a lot of fun. A fun, platonic friendship party in Paris!

On the red eye from JFK to Charles de Gaulle, I dream of wanting to fuck Gerard. But when I wake up, I feel shocked, disgusted, and scared. I don't think I actually want to have sex with this man. *Is my subconscious feeling guilty? No fucking way. I am SO not that kind of woman.*

The last night I spent in Paris was at the Hotel Nation, a by-the-hour hooker hotel in Montmartre. My friend Gen and I were on the final legs of a hitchhiking Tour de France, and down to our last few euros. Through iron bars, the concierge assured us that it was, indeed, "the cheapest hotel in Paris." The mattress was plywood and the walls were lapped with a coat of filthy lavender paint. A mid-40s woman in a red feather boa stopped me on my way to the shared toilet to ask if I, too, was "a dame from

180

Beverly Hills looking for her big break." That was three years ago.

Today, I check into the Hotel St. James on Rue de Rivoli. The marble lobby, the quintessentially bitchy bellhop, and perfect view of Jardin des Tuileries indicate that this hotel is definitely not for the penny-pinching traveller.

Gerard has meetings all day, so I have today to wander around the city as I please. I traipse through Jardin des Tuileries only to turn around and wander the dining room, fitness centre, and gift shop of the hotel. I slip a few dresses onto wooden hangers and dial '0' for steak frites and *un café, s'il vous plait*. Paris will always be here; the time I have to luxuriate in this world of privilege is finite. On the door to my quarters, a card hangs, listing all of the items that are available for in-room dining. Ticking a few boxes as I skim the items, I opt for a *mi-cuit* boiled egg, a 6-euro grapefruit juice, fruit salad, a pot of coffee, and the International Herald Tribune.

A hesitant woodpecker taps at my door. "*Service aux chambres.*"

I open the door and welcome a small man in a smaller suit into my chamber. With a bow, he salutes me—"*Bonjour, madame*"—and places the tray of provisions on my unmade bed.

I should really be a travel companion more often.

I draw a bubble bath to soak away my jetlag. Wrapping myself in a cloud of spongy white terrycloth, I tie off the sash and collapse into a pit of pristine, pillowy decadence. I fall asleep to *True Grit*—a yawn of a movie—that I rented for 20 euros and charged to the room.

The next morning, a phone rings on my nightstand.

"Are you ready, my Chloe?"

My cheek smiles into the receiver. "*Oui, Gerard.*"

"Meet me outside and to ze right of the hotel by ze red door."

Here we go.

A massive red door cracks open no more than an inch. A single, searching pale blue eye peeks out from beneath an arched and bushy silver eyebrow.

"Okay," Gerard whispers. "Walk down ze street and I meet you at ze corner."

The red door squeezes shut with a heavy click.

Along the sidewalk, in the taxi, all the way to Montparnasse, Gerard huddles behind a hat, a turned up collar, or the flat of his hand. He looks down at my firetruck-red, ankle-length coat I like to call my 'theatre coat,' and groans. *This is my most sophisticated and least worn-in coat*, I thought to myself as I packed it into my suitcase back in New York. As the cab bumps through a handful of arrondissements, a moment of self-awareness kicks in: blonde hair, red coat, and 30 years his junior, I could not look more like a mistress if I tried. What's worse is that I look like a crass, American mistress. Not even the Parisians working the corners wear red.

As he hides behind the wine list, all I can see of Gerard are squat white knuckles.

"What wine do you like?" Ice-blue eyes peek above the burgundy leather binder. "Red-white-white is best wiz oysters what did you do wiz your hair I liked it better before have you always had short hair?" A heavy exhale through pursed lips. "Oh boy, Chloe."

Why are you so nervous? I want to ask. *We're just here as friends!*

My fork pokes at the oysters, the fish, and the foie gras mousse while Gerard's eyes dart around the lunch crowd. Several sips of wine seem to smooth out the furrow in his brow. It's raining, so we opt for a second bottle to wait out the drizzle. Gerard starts mansplaining[35] wine, photography, and air travel while I peruse the desserts.

As we wander the slick streets of Paris, my Pentax K1000[36] swings around my neck like a brick.

"Those old cameras are a waste of time," he says, picking up a state-of-the-art Nikon and handing it to the clerk alongside his credit card. I stuff my precious relic into my bag, and start snapping pictures. Gerard dodges every shot.

Opening another taxi door, Gerard announces that he must meet briefly with his former colleague and good friend, Jean-Marcel.

"I must warn you, though, that he is quite, uh … crude."

Pushing through an iron gate and clopping up a marble staircase, Gerard and I enter into a blinding-white studio overlooking Place Hugo. Three slender young women in high-quality, low-impact pencil skirts assess the stitchwork on an expensive dress that closely resembles a freshly pressed t-shirt.

"Gerard!" A voice bellows from a hallway. "Welcome back. I just have to deal with this stupid bullshit and I'll be with you in a second. Have a look around."

I finger through a rolling rack of gunmetal-grey, draped silk dresses while Jean-Marcel consults with his design team: "This is shit, I don't like it." The girls bow their heads. "Why am I even here? You're so boring, I don't even want to fuck you! But I'll fuck your friends!" The flick of his lighter and first drag of his cigarette is the only moment he pauses from badgering his employees.

---

[35] Mansplaining: a portmanteau of the words "man" and "explaining" that describes the act of a man speaking to a woman with the assumption that she knows less than he does about the topic being discussed on the basis of her gender. It's condescending, and far too common.
[36] Pentax K1000: A dope-ass SLR camera that is really popular among photography students. The model I have was made in 1971.

Jackass-Marcel spits insults and criticisms in every direction. It's in French, so I don't catch everything. If I did, I might not trust myself not to strangle him. But I'm not here as myself, a woman who speaks her mind and stands up for others, a woman who calls out bullying and assholery; I am merely The Company. Sit, stand, peruse grey garments, and look pretty. Although we barely make eye contact, I identify with these women. They are designing clothes and I'm selling a fantasy, but our working conditions are nearly identical: we appeal and pander to the Jean-Marcels of the world to finance our ambition.

After customizing his insults to each of the women in the showroom, Jean-Marcel finally acknowledges my existence: "*Alors c'est vrai que Chloe a une belle poitrine.*" Which roughly translates to, "We can all see that Chloe has a nice rack."

Everything sounds better in French.

***

Passing a luminous oil painting in a gallery window, I fall back to breathe in the brush strokes.

"Zat one is not very important," Gerard says, inspecting the plaque at the gallery door. "Zis gallery does not really carry anything very good ... but it's not ze worst." He peers through the darkness to a sculpture in the recesses of the sleeping museum. "Zat figure is worth something. It's quite an important artist. I bought one of his some time ago and sold it for much, much more." He goes on: "I have a good eye." I look at him in the reflection. His eyes are fixed to the plaques, descriptions, and the red dot that announces if the art is a hot ticket or not.

"Yes, but which ones do you *like*?" I ask.

"I like the ones that make me money," he says with a swift rise of the eyebrows.

I don't feel like the friends I thought we were that drunken night at the Peninsula. Do I even remember it? I feel tedious. Gerard is nervous and fidgety.

At Flute l'Etoile, Gerard raves about his youth in Hong Kong as a young bachelor.

"Maybe in January I take you zere," he muses as he slides an oyster into his mouth for the second time today.

Over steak tartare topped with onions, cognac, and a quail egg, Gerard tells me that every now and again, he sleeps with prostitutes. "I haven't slept wiz my wife in two years. But she is a good mother." He sighs. "If it weren't for my children, it would have been over a long time ago."

I choose not to opine that an unhappy marriage is not a good place to raise children[37].

We stagger our entrances through the red door and climb to Gerard's suite. It's a colleague's condo he uses for his mistresses. Although it is allegedly serviced by the Hotel St. James next door, the suite hasn't seen a vacuum or duster in ages. It's loaded with new gadgets, a greying black leather L couch, and a fridge that has only expired condiments and champagne. It smells like every house my dad has ever rented.

A bottle of bubbles pops in the kitchenette as I settle into the cold of the couch. Slipping off my heels, I tuck my feet under my legs. Champagne flutes in hand, Gerard approaches the electronics wall. Eric Clapton joins our twosome, soothing my nerves and lubricating Gerard's expectations.

After a few tentative sips, Gerard takes the flute from my hand, places it on the glass coffee table, and lifts me to my feet. Sturdy and confident, he waltzes me around the L of the couch. We dance to the coo of *Layla*. There is really nothing better than a good lead. I cackle and Gerard hums along with the chorus. I feel as if I'm dancing with my best friend's dad at a wedding.

---

[37] POLARIZING PARENTING STATEMENT ALERT: When my parents could not stand the sight of each other any longer, they pulled the plug. I was 9. I lived with my mom for most of the time while my dad took on the role of the responsibility-shirking, absent father. They still hate each other so much they cannot even agree to a proper, legal divorce, but at least they weren't putting on a sham show. Kids aren't stupid, and fake-nice is a game strictly for grown-ups.

But we are not at a wedding and he is not my best friend's dad. Why aren't we out painting the town red like we did in New York? Because, on the inside, Gerard is still an 18-year-old man with a conquesting dick in his pants, and I am the prize.

After a few spins and do-si-dos, I rest my head against his chest. "This is so *fun* Gerard, but I think I ate too much. I'm so *tired*." A theatrical yawn brings our first night to a close. Obligingly, Gerard shoos me back to my room. With a sweetness, he whispers after me, "Sweet dreams, Chloe."

I exhale a sigh of relief as I close and deadbolt the door to my own, separate hotel room.

The next day we wake up so early I don't even have time to have my morning coffee, grapefruit juice, and gander at the Tribune. We are invited back to Jean-Marcel's Versaillesque bachelor pad. Today ,the design team is replaced by five screaming children and two sweating nannies. Jackass-Marcel has five children from four different wives. It's his day to spend with them, so he's invited Gerard and me over.

They chat hurriedly over coffee about how shitty US Airways' first-class seats are, and which airline has the ugliest flight attendants. Jackass-Marcel boasts about how many cities they have flown through that week. Just yesterday, he returned from Morocco, where he spent the afternoon. They drop their cups in the sink for the help, and off we shuffle down the street and around the corner to spend a small fortune at a fromagerie.

At the cheese shop, Gerard buys me a few wheels of Brie, a brick of Roquefort, and something else deliciously stinky that the fromager vacuum packs for me upon learning that I will be taking my dairy treasures on the plane with me back to New York. Vacuum-packed cheese will not be detected by TSA beagles (which would result in swift confiscation).

As we exit the fromagerie, Gerard is still visibly stressed and nervous to be seen with me. I'm beginning to believe he thinks this is a real affair.

"A lot of people from Miami know me in this part of Paris," says Gerard, looking over his shoulder. The bulk of men who engage in affairs are usually so wrapped up in the sex that they fail to pursue it with any stealth or strategy. In my experience, a man likes to show off his women; whether she's his wife or mistress is irrelevant. Boasting to his peers is more important than the sanctity of his marriage. I guess it's tricky to showboat if he doesn't know his way around town. I almost feel bad that he feels so guilty over doing something wrong when I am determined that there will be no wrong-doing for as long as I am conscious and exercising my free will. As the airtight heap of dairy slips with a thud to bottom of my shopping bag, I realize now is not a good time to calm his nerves. *"Coo coo, don't worry, boo, I'm not going to let anything happen that will compromise the sanctity of your marriage. I'm just here for the cheese!"*

At the Michelin-starred restaurant in the Eiffel Tower, Gerard orders a vintage Bordeaux with fidgeting hands. The food is bland and I don't know how much it costs because female patrons are handed menus without prices. He asks the garçon if he can keep the menu. Gerard lifts it to his face when he catches sight of someone he thinks he recognizes.

"False alarm," he says, reaching for the wine.

Gerard pokes at his plate, focusing mainly on emptying the bottle of Bordeaux. "You see, Chloe, women marry men hoping they'll change. And men marry women, hoping they never change." His hands fidget less. A smile stretches across his face. Gerard is most at home when haranguing about his philosophies derived from *Men are From Mars, Women are from Venus*. I don't agree with most of his statements, but he professes in this way that doesn't let me get a word in edgewise. The chemistry of the quippy banter we had back in New York is gone.

More wine.

Gerard sets down his knife and smirks. "You know, in a hypothetical, mythical world, we could have a contract of six months where we travel anywhere and everywhere, and at the end, it's over and we go back to our lives." He looks down at his

187

plate. "We would have to be lovers, though," he adds, disguising his visceral desires as an afterthought.

He's a bit arrogant, but he's sharp and likes to please. I'm having fun. But now he wants to fuck, and I'm thinking *fuck, this is so much worse than being a whore.* He wants to fuck me because we actually like each other. And since he hasn't explicitly paid me for a fuck, only implicitly paid for my travel expenses, I'm being coaxed with a tinge of guilt to suck this man's dick. *What the fuck have I got myself into?*

"… and then you can write about it," he whispers to me. "You can call your novel *The Contract*."

We pass by La Perla and Gerard buys me a bra and panty set that costs half my rent back in New York. I change into the set, and slip my favourite green and black velvet brocade dress over it. I dab on a red lip, and off we go to the most ridiculous, campy spectacle that I have ever seen: *Le Moulin Rouge.* The dancers look like sad whores slapping a sore smile on their face as they flash their tits and tote livestock across a dusty stage. As Gerard's hand slides up my thigh, I feel a deep connection to their struggle.

In the taxi back to the hotel, Gerard says to me: "Do you feel guilty for not having given me a lap dance yet?"

"No," I reply, trying to sound casual and aloof like every good whore should.

But the silence in the taxi makes me feel like maybe I should. We need to end this night on a high note, and *Le Moulin Rouge* was not it. I may as well give him a lap dance in this expensive-as-fuck lingerie.

Back at the on-loan bachelor pad, Gerard pops another bottle of champagne. Swapping Clapton for Dire Straits, he beckons me to his lap. I start to sway.

He looks into my eyes, and says, "I just want to cuddle."

If you're with someone you care about, these words are music. If you are feeling the slightest bit uncomfortable, 'cuddling' is the last fucking thing you will ever want to do. *DO YOU KNOW HOW MANY TIMES I HEAR THIS, AND OUT OF ALL THE TIMES I HEAR IT HOW OFTEN I BELIEVE IT?* I believed it the first time. I've heard it several hundred times, and mostly I find it offensive because we both know it's not true. I don't know whether to be flattered because he thinks I'm dumb enough to believe it, or to be mildly amused by the fact that this man seated before me who is old enough to be my father is *still* using this same tactic to get under my skirt. I know I'm in trouble. That my insistence of 'separate rooms,' and the fact that I don't DO extras in the Champagne Room in New York is irrelevant now. I'm in fucking Paris on this rich and powerful man's dime. The second I leave the club, the clearly established boundaries I have in my head are not recognized.

Gerard leans in with his big face and rough lips. I meet him halfway because what other choice do I really have at this point, sitting on his lap and sobering up by the millisecond? I don't want to kiss him, but I do it anyway. I don't know why. Guilt and expectation, I guess.

My lips meet his. No tongue, no inward undulation of the hips, just lips touching. Ten thousand years later, I pull away. With great effort, I smile. It hurts.

"You see," he starts, "I don't want to do anything you don't want to do."

I don't know what would be easier: making the arrangements up-front about the SEX and the CASH, or navigating this sort of courtship. I'm no sage, but I know what every man means by this is: *BUT I WANT YOU TO WANT TO HAVE SEX AND WILL KEEP TRYING TO CONVINCE YOU OF THIS UNTIL YOU AGREE OR COMPLY.* It's the bougie man's version of *'hey, baby, just have another drink.'*

"And what I want from you is what you do not want to give me. A real kiss."

You are a dumbass, Jacq.

I try to rationalize what I've done to get here but all I can hear is *YOU ARE SUPPOSED TO FUCK HIM BECAUSE THAT IS*

189

WHAT A MAN EXPECTS WHEN HE BUYS YOU THINGS. It's hard to hear my own voice when that same record's been playing on repeat for a long time. All I know is that what Gerard just said is right: I do not want to give him a real kiss.

So I get up, kick off my shoes, and dance around the room in my new lingerie.

I slip my dress off one shoulder, then the other, and finally down to the bra, panty, and stockings we bought earlier that day. I'm usually so comfortable doing this—moving around, performing, dancing. This is what I do. And if I'm really quick, no one can catch me. I jump onto the couch and bounce with a silly sway of my hips.

But there aren't any lights. There's no stage, no rules enforced by imposing black men standing in the corner. No matter how many sips of champagne I take between prancing around this couch, I feel awkward, like a 14-year-old girl trying to look sexy. My discomfort overshadows my professionalism. And this is a whole new level of 'professional.' This is some blue-ribbon cock-teasing shit.

"I like this show much better than the one we saw earlier tonight," Gerard whispers. "Those women are beautiful. But not as beautiful as you ..." He slips a stocky finger beneath my bra strap. The tried-and-true, never-fail one-line opener: *You are the prettiest girl I've ever seen.* (If it ain't broke, don't fix it.)

Gerard sits behind me and starts rubbing my shoulders. He moves down my back, and slips my bra strap odd with his calloused index finger. *That's the biggest hand that's touched me in my entire life. I don't remember the 20- and 30-year-olds having such ... meat hooks. It must be an old-man thing: fat, strong hands.*

I'd really rather be sitting alone in my hotel room, watching *Last Tango in Paris*. But this **is** *Last Tango in Paris*. I'm here and I'm supposed to fuck this guy, even though we both agreed when booking the tickets that it wasn't part of the plan. It is *always* part of the plan.

"Let me give you a massage," Gerard offers, gesturing to the length of the couch.

Prostrate on the cold and squeaky leather, I am stiff as a board.

Dear god, let there not be a frozen stick of butter in this 21st-century adaptation.

Gerard proceeds with a full-body grope that he tells me will be "ze best full-body massage of your life."

He reaches for the waistband of my panties. With a whimper, I tell him, "No," brushing his hand away with mine … I just feel large, imposing hands on me. It's a thousand times worse than any Champagne Room, and this guy is allegedly trying to give me a massage.

"Why not?"

"Well, if I get naked, you won't be touching me anymore." I maintain that my Paris Rules are not unlike my Strip Club Rules. The more naked I get, the more rules and restrictions are enforced.

"Why not?" he asks.

"I don't want to."

You only want to do what I want to do, right? That's what you said.

Gerard looks down and to the side, exhaling. He accepts the boundaries I've set up, but not without a serious sulk.

"Well, I guess I knew from the beginning that I would never really have you."

My heart pounds as I weigh the strength of my convictions against the brute hardiness of this six-foot man as we sit alone in this room.

"Okay," he says, patting my thigh. He gets up and moseys toward the door.

The cold, damp night air outside the hotel tastes like freedom and relief. *Only one more day in Paris. Thank fuck.*

Safe in my room, I crack open my journal,

This has been quite the experience. I have enjoyed the spoils of Paris and decadence and room service and my new camera and spectacular views but I hate bumming out poor Gerard[38]

I had an old sugar daddy back in Montreal; he was about Gerard's age. His name was Sam, and he just wanted to watch me eat and take me shopping. He never even tried to kiss me. I guess that sort of set the bar for what I thought older men wanted from younger women. Like, did Anna Nicole actually have sex with that guy? Or did she just giggle on his lap? I don't know much about the sex lives of baby boomers. I dance for them, chat them up, but never have I asked, "How often do you have sex? Do you get as hard as often as you did 20 years ago?" These questions might be a bit abrupt, but they probably would have helped me plan this trip. Or at least say no to it altogether.

Gerard wants a mistress. He was just so old that I didn't think he was actually gagging to fuck when I thought I made it clear that I wouldn't be. I was obviously not very clear. If I had been, I wouldn't have been invited. I guess I wanted to think that I was so lovely and fun that time with me without putting his dick in me was worth the time and money. I was wrong.

I stop feeling guilty about all of these feelings of miscommunication and disappointment when Gerard tells me over dinner—at a deliberately bland restaurant—that I am a sadist, and that he could have raped me.

---

[38] *WTF DID I ACTUALLY WRITE THAT? BECAUSE I LIKE HIM AND I FEEL A LITTLE BIT GUILTY FOR BEING HIS PERSONAL COCK TEASE, BUT I REVEL IN THE FACT THAT I'VE MADE IT THROUGH A FREE TRIP TO PARIS AND HAVEN'T DONE WHAT EVERY MAN WANTS AND EXPECTS ME TO DO. AS A BALL-BUSTING, VINDICTIVE WOMAN WITH A FEMINIST AGENDA THAT THAT REFUSES TO GIVE MEN SEX BECAUSE THEY ALLEGEDLY DESERVE IT, I WIN. AS A PERSON IN AN UNCOMFORTABLE SITUATION, I LOSE.*

I chew the food, but I taste nothing. Such a shame. It's foie gras pate, my favourite.

"You are LUCKY, Chloe; you are playing a dangerous game. One day the stakes will be higher."

Spilling the Cotes du Rhone from the carafe into his glass, I read through the lines: *If I press on with this, I will be raped.*

I was raped once. I called it non-consensual sex for a while, but, as much as I didn't want to admit it, I knew it was rape. My rapist was someone I considered a friend. We had slept together a few times before. I didn't want to anymore—not this time. He decided that he did.

I don't talk about it very often, but when I do, everyone asks for CLARIFICATION. The women ask, mortified, for fear of acknowledging that time she said no and he said yes; for fear of admitting to themselves that they've also been raped. Men ask for clarification. When. How. What did you say. What did he say. They never want to believe it. Maybe because they've raped someone, too, but they think of it as something … other: 'Rough;' that she was hinting at it; being flirtatious.

"I see in your eyes that you are very cold," Gerard says, searching for cracks in my character through my unblinking eyes.

I remain silent. What's the protocol for when someone threatens to rape you, or tells you that you're lucky that he didn't? I opt for staying still with my back straight. Sometimes all you have left is your grace. I don't feel bad anymore. I just feel angry.

"I don't know what happened to you, but there is something that makes you revel in torture … It's not the sex. It's sex with purpose." *Whatever the hell that means.*

Maybe it's that I don't like to have sex with any other purpose than love or lust. I don't have to. I haven't had to. It is a game, and the game is tricky, and the game is certainly not fair or just.

I'm doing all I can to disassociate from this tedious and terrifying conversation. I just want to have sex with a woman

193

right now. That Kryptonite from the bar. The one with the soft skin, tiny, flirty hands, and cheeky smile. The kind of smile that doesn't revel in being stronger than me. The night I met her, back in New York, I told her about coming here: "Yep, I'm going to Paris to see a client. And I don't even have to fuck him!" Other girls at clubs have talked about travelling with clients and never mentioned fucking them. Did they have the same humourless time as I am having now? Or did they just fuck them and *FAIL TO MENTION THAT?*

I love the power of denying men their desires. This—I know—is fucked up; these are my Daddy Issues. My dad would always tell my sister and me 'no.' He was constantly deflecting his fatherly responsibilities, and didn't want to do anything for us that was not also convenient for him. It sucked and it manifests itself in my adult life in lots of weird little ways. Here I am in Paris telling this guy 'no.' I had told him no to a hand job once before, and he seemed cool with it. But my desire for a trip to Paris overshadowed my knowing better: powerful men don't like to be told 'no,' especially when you're costing them time and money.

"I'm sorry it didn't turn out the way either of us wanted." I won't apologize for not wanting to have sex. I still have to remind myself this from time to time. Like right now. I don't want to apologize, but I feel I should because it's written in some scripture somewhere that a woman who denies a man sex after he buys her nice things and pays for her to travel across an ocean to see him needs to apologize. "I had a really nice time. I'm glad I came. I don't regret anything."

"Well, I didn't have such a nice time, but I don't regret anything either." He looks at his plate of untouched food. At his half-empty glass of wine.

Coming all this way for such a game was a really bad idea. This entire job is about being elusive about my boundaries to keep men spending. I stop being in control the moment I leave the safety of a club with big, burly male bouncers. I'm finding it really fucked up to think that I'm only safe when I'm under the protection of another man, so I'm trying to change it. Why does this make people think that I'm stupid and naive?

I've always liked taking men up on their ridiculous offers and disappointing them. Such as:

"I'll buy you a house."

"Oh yeah?"

"Yeah."

"Okay. I want a Manhattan penthouse. You busy tomorrow? We can go to the real estate agent."

"Uhhhhh …"

I guess the difference in this instance is that I let this guy fly me to Paris, right? So he spent a bunch of time and money on me. But men spend money on women all the time without any sort of guaranteed return on their investment.

For days, I agonize over this trip with little resolution. In my head, there is anger. Outwardly, I am embarassed. Embarrassed to tell the story, because whomever I tell—even the girl I'm seeing—pegs me as a dumb whore. I feel like an idiot for thinking I was bigger, smarter, faster, and stronger than this system. Maybe I knew this all along, and I'm just a vindictive woman who went there to teach him a lesson, and I failed to teach him this lesson in a way that serves me. Did I see him as a father? Successful, generous, and intellectual … that's what I've always wanted in a father.

The hardest part is my friends thinking I'm stupid and naive for going. It's like everyone is on Gerard's side when I explain how we met, and the terms of our agreement. Friend-zoning when you're a sex worker is impossible. Friendship as companionship … is that so unfathomable? My attempts to experiment with these boundaries and expectations are pushing me to new depths of sadness, futility, and anger. This situation has me questioning my ability to do this work. I need a moment of respite where the rent is cheap and I'm indebted to no one.

IF I CAN'T
TAKE MY
PANTS OFF,
HOW AM I
SUPPOSED
TO FUCK YOU?

-Billy, 66, Georgia

Santa Fe

New Mexico is magical, vast, and eerie. I breathe in crisp, high-altitude desert air and exhale relief that I'm not seeking the praises of Jerry or dodging the sexual advances of elderly Frenchmen. I'm here to write this book. I've come to Santa Fe to buy some sage, type out whatever I can piece together from scratchy notes written in the drunken haze that has been the last year of my life, and to cleanse my liver. I plan to take baths, write, swim, hike, and pore over books I've been carrying around but have always been too hungover to ever read. My rationale is that *this is how writers are supposed to live.*

Or maybe that's only the fiction-writing ones?

By the third day of my writer's retreat I get as far as watching and rewatching *Flashdance*, and buying apple cider vinegar from Trader Joe's.

I commend myself on my baby steps, pour myself a glass of chardonnay, and check my email.

Sophie: *Did you make me a sugar daddy account? I just got a confirmation email. Or did I make myself one while drunk?*

I confess to trying to get every woman I know on the enterprising babe bandwagon. Sophie and I went to university together, and have since shared many a sublet in various Brooklyn neighbourhoods. She is young, smart, and beautiful and therefore in a prime position to Anna Nicole[39] the next 10 years of her life. Although I have no recollection of signing her up for a dating site, it doesn't mean it didn't happen.

Rich man/pretty girl dating sites are really just the most honest and efficient social-media communities facilitating the eternally symbiotic relationship of the overpaid male and underpaid female dwellers of New York City.

***

Upon my arrival, my favourite Santa Fe discovery is that there are two public pools within walking distance of my urban casita. I pay $29 for a month of unlimited lap-swimming in a pool that I will end up sharing with no more than two swimmers at once. No shared lanes, no getting kicked in the face by deliberately slow swimmers, and no shit-evacuations (this is what an average workout is like when you're a swimmer in New York City).

Every afternoon I walk across town and am greeted by a smiling man with a thick and shiny black ponytail, which he weaves through a battered red baseball cap. Noticing my New Yorker frown, he smiles even wider and says, "Welcome to your place!"

In these moments, I feel like an asshole. Being a bitch at work is par for the course, kind of fun, and great exercise. But in Real Girl mode I still fancy myself a smiling girl with kind eyes and a secret stash of pepper spray. My accommodating Canadianness has totally vanished since Russian Dolls. I've become the frigid bitch against which I once defined myself.

I used to hate the repetitive nature of swimming laps, so now, naturally, I'm addicted to it. It's cathartic and anti-social, and

---

[39] Anna-Nicole: verb. Using youth, beauty, and charm to get what I need and want from those in power (read: usually old, rich, white men). Origins: Anna Nicole Smith, the patron saint of strippers. May she rest in peace.

198

since iPhones aren't yet waterproof, I can actually disconnect from everything. Stripping makes you kind of hate loud music, anyway.

With every lap I resolve to be better, healthier, and more organized. Through saliva-slathered[40], aqua-tinted goggles, I visualize how the next six months of my life are going to look. Every now and again I attempt a flip turn (I suck at flip turns). Swimming is the only honest thing I do. So I limit myself to 30 minutes a day.

I throw a hat over my wet hair and walk back to my casita. I make a conscious decision to procrastinate with gossip and bullshit. Gchat is great for this.

Jacq: *How are the dating 'arrangements' coming along?*
Sophie: *I haven't replied to anyone yet. I'm in the office calling EVERY SINGLE FUCKING VENDOR to change the credit-card information on file. There are at least 30.*
Jacq: *Oh, so you're being water-boarded.*
Sophie: *Yup. Kill me. How is Santa Fe?*
Jacq*: Fucking beautiful and brilliant and empty.*
Sophie: *And what of the writing?*
Jacq: *Well, I'm pretty sure I slept through the first five days, but now I'm getting back on track and writing is actually happening, I think. Like, I'm not just talking and thinking about writing, I am actually sitting my ass down to write, which is great because I have yet to properly regain feeling in my legs (Russian Dolls ruined me.) All I can see is that there is a lot of hair growing on them—so novel! I like it. If a fly lands on my leg, I can feel it crawling around so I can swat it away before it bites me. And bushes are so divinely feminine and pretty. I forgot I could grow one. I don't know how I'll ever return to New York. But Kryptonite is there and it's hard not to visualize wanting to eat crackers in bed with that one.*
Sophie: *There is always something eerily masochistic that brings us all back here. Maybe this sugar daddy dating will*

---

[40] Saliva: If you want to avoid fogging up your goggles, you can spritz them with an anti-fog solution ($7) or spit in them (free).

make it at least less expensive. I'm getting a lot of foot fetish inquiries, which is annoying.

Jacq: *What's wrong with foot fetishists? They are so easy! It's usually just getting a foot massage, going shoe shopping, or possibly having them jerk off between the arches of your feet. If I had to choose any part of my body for a guy to jerk off on, I'd probably pick the extremities farthest from my mouth, hair, and face. Plus the entire concept of a man worshipping your feet means that he's probably quite submissive, which can be tedious, but quiets my fears of 'am I going to get raped doing this?' A guy paid me 200 bucks to suck on my toes, which led me to discovering that sucking on toes is HOT. Rarely do we learn new things whilst earning money.*

Sophie: *But my toes are broken; I have calluses and no pedicure.*

Jacq: *Maybe they'll be into that? Men are obsessed with ballerinas.*

Sophie: *Perhaps. The most intriguing one thus far—not, to my knowledge, a foot fetishist—is 51, from Switzerland, and he is in New York NOW and wants to pay me to hang out.*

Jacq: *That usually means sex*

Sophie: *Yeah, that's what I think, too.*

Jacq: *I wish men had more tact. Or maybe we're safer because they don't? I mean, if men had the tact to accompany their generally stronger physiques, we might all be dead.*

Sophie: *I'll keep browsing. What I'm still stumped on is wardrobe ...*

Jacq: *Wear a dress. Always a dress.* STRIPPER TIP #26: A woman is 8000 times more likely to get what she wants when she's wearing a dress. *Not stilettos—just enough of a heel to fit the 'I'm a bitch in heels' trope. Just make sure you can still stride confidently in them, and also potentially make a swift and stealthy exit should things turn to shit.*

Sophie: *The shiny leopard muumuu thing, is that doable if I belt it, with heels?*

Jacq: *NO, Sophie. NOT THE MUUMUU. Sorry. I love you. And I love the muumuu, darling. But sugar daddies don't get it. Unless they're in real estate, they don't even know where Williamsburg is, never mind the fact that muumuus are currently being marketed as these fiercely fecund panty-less fashion staples.*

Sophie: *This one guy's profile description says: "EAGER TO HELP THE PROVERBIAL ARTS FUND"*

Jacq: *MARRY HIM.*

I close my laptop, throw on an eggplant-coloured poncho and go for a walk around town. Santa Fe feels as if it's perpetually Sunday. Every woman I pass is also wearing a poncho and walking alone, head held high. Apparently I'm not the only one who came here to write her memoir.

Sophie: *Please advise on Ian the Professor:*
- married
- fun flirty emails that aren't entirely stupid.
- First time using the internet to meet a sugar baby
I'm thinking of suggesting sushi … on Sunday?
I CAN'T WAIT FOR MY FIRST ONE. I will simply WILL my shoes and clothes to actually be sufficient, and don some Jacq-inspired confidence, and smile the shit out of those fuckers.
Jacq: *Dating a married guy is EASY. And I'm pretty sure it's some sort of tragically adventurous rite of passage. You won't have to dote on him, and he can't exactly dote on you, either. You can have fun when you decide to make time for it, but otherwise it's completely non-committal. Of course, if you actually like each other in serious, long-term ways, things can get pretty bleak. He sounds fun and relatively intelligent. And if there are sparks then you can fuck in every penthouse suite in New York City and order room service (other bonus of married men: they have to rent a hotel room. The rich ones always get nice places). Sunday night may be a tricky suggestion if he's a family man, but ask anyway, and if he tries to push it to a Tuesday, don't take it personally. You do realise you're going to be very good at this, right? Older men love being around free spirits who don't have obligations like mortgages and bosses. You're like a unicorn. Let them bask in your light. Santa Fe is lonely. Mostly I really like it. But then I go days without talking to anyone but the internet and it feels shitty. Our correspondence is my lifeblood.*
Sophie: *I am getting a torrent of emails. Why did whoever wrote the bible decide on only seven days in a week?*
Jacq: *You can date lots of guys at once. Whenever you feel like a free meal, just ring one up. I know a ripper who has 50 different birthdays. She writes her alleged D.O.B. in her phonebook under the client's name. Basically, she has crafted a steady stream of presents and gentleman callers. She geniusly guilts all of these men into coming in, chasing down a litany of*

*'birthday shots,' and subsequently spending thousands of
dollars. The tricky part is knowing all the astrology. Who am I
kidding? Men hate astrology.*

Sophie: *I just had the weirdest experience: I was at a bar when
this really tall, really hot guy with an accent and tasteful beard
hit on me. He didn't ask me for drugs or sex; he just kept asking
me why I didn't have a boyfriend. Such a gentleman! I thought
his breed was extinct. He is definitely going to fuck with my
sugar daddy game.*

Jacq: *Date him, too! Date all of them. Do not agonize over
feeling like you need to pick one right away. What a waste of
precious energy. We won't look like this forever.*

Sophie: *I have six possible dates this week. At this point I'm just
trying to figure out which ones to blow off. I'm going to try to
balance this like a puzzle ... Is it a bad idea to schedule two in
one night?*

Jacq: *I would advise against double-booking your evening with
two separate dudes. You never know how the first date might go;
maybe you'll want to have it last a little longer, or, if it's shit,
you won't be in any mood to entertain the likes of another
potential asshole. Or, if the second dude is nice, you'll be in a
shitty mood anyway and likely bomb the date. One at a time,
girl.*

*It's nice having an epic list to choose from, isn't it? That's what
stripping's like. The OBJECTIVE is to flirt with as many people
in the room as time will allow, and the pay-off is CASH. Being a
slutty opportunist is worthy of praise while the shy, 'virtuous'
ones get less respect. IT'S REVOLUTIONARY. Maybe one day
I'll craft just the right sales pitch to get you to come to the club
with me. What does The Professor look like?*

Sophie: *As far as I can tell he looks sort of like a hermit.*

Sophie links me to a photo: a low-angle self-portrait taken of a
man in a light blue shirt, longish grey hair that older professors
always think they are entitled to have, and a morose look on his
face, which has rather okay bone structure. A bookshelf and
yellow wall fill the background. This is a selfie that should have
been deleted, and reattempted.

Jacq: *This Professor just needs a woman to spruce up his look
and life. I mean, THAT is the picture he sent YOU, a total babe,
whom he is trying to COURT. Man needs Hitch or some shit.*

He's not ugly or gross; just pathetic-looking. At least he has his Ikea-shelved library of textbooks in the background to reassure you that he's literate. This guy has no game. He's going to be easy to swoon, but harder to get scrill out of. Not impossible, but you'll have to do some coaxing. You'll probably have to discuss the 'arrangement' you are seeking as if it were a syllabus. Plan ahead.

Sophie: *You realize you've been signed up as my sex-work guru right? I am going to ask you for stupid advice on EVERYTHING? Like when to ask for chocolates vs. a laptop vs. La Perla panties?*

Jacq: *I'm happy to be your guru. I miss making money! It's been three whole weeks and I feel like I've lost a part of myself. I think I'm going to audition at the only club in town on Thursday. I am suffering from stripper withdrawal. My thighs are getting fleshy and I think I've forgotten how to fake-smile. OH MY GOD, WHAT IF I'VE FORGOTTEN HOW TO CLAP MY ASS CHEEKS? Get on that dating bandwagon. Dates beget more dates. Shoes beget more shoes.*

Looking around my cabin, books, notes, and Real Girl clothes scatter across my bed and spill onto the floor. I figure I won't be having any guests, ever, so why bother tidying? I'm enjoying the solitude and sobriety, but I'm a little bit bored. A piece of me is missing. I don't know where my Real Girl self ends and my stripper self begins, but it's hard to enjoy my cotton briefs without the lace g-strings to balance them out.

Sophie: *Happy Valentine's Day, Doll! What are your plans? I'm going to a burlesque show in ... Midtown.*

Jacq: *Happy Valentine's Day to you, too! I'm busy stuffing my face with two boxes of salted caramels and truffles that arrived on my doorstep from a certain tattooed princess whom I may or may not have referred to as Kryptonite ... Of course, I'm less bitter now. And I knew I liked this girl, but now I'm starting to think she must like me too? My plan for today is to masturbate, if I have the energy. I probably won't. Going out and gathering all these stories was far more exhilarating than sitting down to write them. Burlesque! Midtown! Do you know your Rolexes and Cartiers? Obnoxiously diamond studded ones mean they like to spend in a showy way (on you, very possibly); Cartier means they're classy, but have some serious scrilla. Keep your eyes peeled for the rich, lonely looking ones (read: ALL OF*

203

THEM, if they don't already have a lady velcroed to their side—
it's fucking Valentine's day, for fuck's sake. Every single man in
New York City is getting drunk tonight).

Sophie: *I need to take a watch class.*

Jacq: *If it's big and shiny —but not too shiny, those ones are
fake—and looks like it has several time zones twirling around its
face, STAY. If it's a Casio or Timex, RUNNNN. And that's
Watches 101.*

Sophie: *First sushi date tomorrow with The Professor. My
confidence is fading.*

Jacq: *CONFIDENCE MUST NOT FADE! Sushi is easy to eat
with class! Those rolls and those floppy pieces of sashimi will
only make of him think of you putting his floppy or moderately
hard dick in your mouth. You'll be great. Wear your hair down.
At Russian Dolls we ARE NOT ALLOWED to wear our hair up.
Men like the swishy movement, the thought of running their
hands through it, pulling it, imagining how it will whip across
your back if they will ever be so so lucky to stick it in you. Order
a drink when you sit down to calm your nerves. Tell him you're
nervous! That you've never been on a date like this before! He
will find it endearing. I lied to clients for my entire first MONTH
of stripping, saying it was my first day, every day, and they were
all super friendly and generous about it. They don't want you to
be discouraged ... they want to make sure they don't give all
moderately ugly rich guys a bad rap ... Also, I would go with a
stain or a tint rather than a really bold lip. I'm reading this
AMAZING book by this badass French feminist—it's called
King Kong Theory[41]. She talks about about how being bold is
intimidating and men want to be reassured by intelligent women
that they're still mostly interested in pleasing the cock; that they
are 'not that smart;' that being sexy and submissive is more
important than being autonomous. So all of this is totally
FUCKED UP, but, that being said, look sexy and sultry without
being too intimidating. So like, a red tint, but do without the lip
liner, and blot it a bit ... y'get what I'm sayin'?*

Sophie: *Not one but THREE of the random loser hipsters I have
met lately called or texted me last night, at like 1-2 am, asking
what I was up to and, for example, "can i bike 2 where u r," or
"what r u doing" ... walking home shivering from Valentine's*

---

[41] *King Kong Theory* by Virginie Despentes. Read this fucking book.

disaster in the rain and my wet sequins, these sorts of calls make me want to die. Your words are little grains of courage I will arm myself with as I march to my dates. With lipstain and flowing hair, of course.

Jacq: *Fuck the hipster boys. Let the daddies shower you with chocolates and electronics.*

How is he rich again? I always thought academics were poor ... I'm going to audition at PINKS tonight, Santa Fe's one and only strip club. The only review I can find about the joint states the following: "Albuquerque is only 45 minutes away, Vegas is eight hours and Los Angeles 16 hours. Any are worth the drive."

***

From my little rented Adobe casita, I walk to the bus stop where I'll be hopping on the number 2 down Cerillos Road.

I take the bus down the main artery of the city, alongside a half-dozen other passengers, each carrying several weathered bags that I can only guess contain all of their worldly possessions. Meanwhile, I'm all whored up, mentally preparing to wow the judges by listening to Britney Spears' breathiest tracks.

A man looks over to me, saying something, but I can't hear him. I un-bud my ears to learn that he would like to know what time it is.

"It's 7:30," I tell him.

"Thanks," he says, reaching into his backpack, pulling out a faded and peeling sleeve of *Love Me Tender* on VHS. "Do you know who this is?" he asks, between clearing a throat that's corralled decades of cigarette smoke and pointing at the tape.

"*YOU AIN'T NONTHIN' BUT A HOUND DOG*," he starts, with impressive pitch.

"It's Elvis," I answer, smiling in earnest.

"You like him?"

205

"Yeah. My grandma loved him. He's very handsome," I say, pointing to his pouty lip on the battered sleeve.

"You like him?"

"Yeah, I do."

"You see, a lot of people didn't like him." He looks out the window, going on with a scratchy rendition of *Love Me Tender*.

"Did you know he had a brother?" I offer.

"Yeah. He died. I lost my brother Billy in Nam. I want him back, but I can't have him back."

It's never easy listening to strangers talk about loss. I know that all you're really supposed to do is listen, but I don't have the self-possession to just listen, so instead I change the subject: "Are you going home to watch that?"

"I'm homeless," he replies, with a matter-of-fact shrug.

"Oh, sorry," I say, embarrassed.

I get off at the Sonic Burger, which I'm told is the landmark for the strip club, whose sign is harder to decipher in the twilight. Looking harder past the blue and yellow beacon of drive-in burgers, I see the fluorescent flashing of purple and pink that my deductive logic tells me is this small town's only ripper joint: PINKS.

Beneath the sign is a giant concrete block in the middle of the parking lot. The block doesn't seem to have any windows … or doors. Just a big yellow spray-painted arrow telling me to walk to the right. I walk around one corner, only to see another yellow spray-painted arrow. It tells me to continue walking in the same direction. I walk a bit farther, and am confronted with another stupid fucking arrow. At this point I'm around the back of the building, out of view from the street. This is where rape scenes happen in the movies.

I take a deep breath, and follow the arrow around the last corner.

I gasp in horror as I bump into two very large men. They nod politely, and then return to their cigarettes. I exhale when I look through them and notice not another yellow arrow, but a hot pink door. I push through it.

There is something so reassuringly familiar about the stench of beer-soaked carpet.

"Hi, I'd like to audition," I say with a smile to the first face I see: a big guy in a white shirt that glows purple under the black light. He is like an orb.

"We don't really audition," he tells me. His voice is soft and sweet. "We just need you to fill out some paperwork and we'll go from there."

I'm wearing a massive winter coat, scarf, gloves and snow boots. Without taking any of the aforementioned items off, I am hired.

Here's the kicker: "You have to wear latex," I am told by Softy.

I hate having to go shopping for new shit. It used to be novel, but now it's just a fucking chore and a business expense that would be tax deductible, if I were legit enough to file taxes.

"State law of New Mexico states that if your nipples aren't covered, you are, by default, soliciting."

So if I flash a pink nip I'm a whore. We're all whores! I'm fine with this! I say whore like I say cunt! With love, affection, and admiration! I don't think New Mexico and I share the same feelings on this, though. American rules are funny, and they get even funnier and more complicated as you break them down state by state. Back in New York, only 40 percent of a strip club's business can provide 'adult entertainment,' while the other 60 percent has to be devoted to good old wholesome boozing, dining, or—the most customary loophole—bikini baring. In Tennessee, the buttocks are all too tempting so dancers have to wear booty shorts—revealing a butt crack or butt cleavage is grounds for arrest.

"Most of the dancers go to Walmart" Softy suggests. "They get fabric glue and paste that over their nipple; it's less irritating than nail polish."

I don't know which lawmakers think that slapping nail lacquer on one's nipples is less dangerous than letting them dance in the breeze of a good beer belch, but whatever. The more lap dances I give, the more I learn that there is very little that makes sense in the world.

I start next week.

Sophie: *The Professor and I had drinks and didn't even get around to sushi. Why do men never want to eat on first dates? Is it because we're fat, they're nervous, or is it just a depressing combination of both? Anyway, he was ... fine. Definitely not classy, and sort of drooling a lot. I mean, he's leagues above a lot of the twentysomethings just by showing up on time and sober. As soon as we sit down, he hands me a book, and reminds me not to open it in public due to the 'present' inside ($200!). And then, after drink number two, says, "I hope I at least get to kiss you before I set you up with my friends." Firstly, I wonder if I can pull off a thing with someone who so obviously wants to fuck as soon as possible; second, I wonder if there is any more sugar involved or if that 'present' was just to show he deserves to be on the site. Which, by the way, he is not anymore; he disabled his account. If it comes down to even $1000 a month, having to fuck someone a couple times, I think I am not adverse to that. Wow, honey—you may have cracked open a box of Whore in this girl.*

Jacq: *Presents! Persist with The Professor. Lots of them delete their accounts—it doesn't mean that he doesn't want to see you. Or maybe I'm just biased because he put the money in a book and that makes my heart sing. PINKS is a dank titty bar and I'm pretty sure I'm going to like it. We have to wear pasties, yet somehow under New Mexico state law, pasties have morphed from sequinned titty twirlers to dried fabric glue. I also ordered a Jessica Simpson wig in the mail. I figure the American Man hates my pixie cut, which is proving impossible to grow out. Maybe it's all the bleach I keep applying to my roots? My manager back at Russian Dolls told me one morning, "You look like Peter Pan," as if it was to bolster my fucking confidence. Don't get me wrong, I LOVE PETER PAN. He is my childhood*

208

hero, second only to Pippi Longstocking. But when was the last time you saw a porno with characters who look like either of my aforementioned idols that wasn't targeted toward the gays? That Louise is a SADIST, I TELL YOU. Anyway, I've decided to embrace the fact that it's my job to look like a porn star, and this headband-wig (a 'fall,' I've learned to call it) seems like a fun experiment. All of these relationships require upkeep, so if you have to make notes on each guy, DO, because sometimes you can mix them up. They mustn't know that you're dating them all for sport. So if you're not available, make like Kate Moss and NEVER EXPLAIN. You're busy, that's all.

Sophie: *Somehow this note keeping actually seems like the most useful use of my college-derived skills. But the **kissing**, Jacq, how does a sugar baby avoid that?*

Jacq: *Ah, kissing. I'm not as good at this particular negotiation as strippers have a pretty staunch Pretty Woman policy. You can play hard-to-get, just always be polite. Don't forget that you're a princess who needs spoiling. Just **typing** that sounds so cheesy and disgusting, but so are most sad truths. Maybe throw him a kiss of reciprocity when he buys you something. The phrase 'no money, no honey,' is cliche for a reason.*

Sophie: *You clearly have a way with making men want to buy you things! I have yet to master this.*

Jacq: *I'm good at making men want to buy me things NOW, but I wasn't always so skillful. I couldn't convince my dad to buy me ANYTHING, ever. (Yay! Daddy Issues Make You A Successful Ball-Buster!) And the first time I asked a sugar daddy (pre-stripping) for a huge chunk of change back in Montreal, he never called me again. You just have to realize that they do WANT to spoil the shit out of you, but it has to please them, too. So, like, you're going to have to buy lingerie and stupid heels you'll never wear, and, occasionally pick up something you actually NEED.*

Sophie: *Here's a toast to the financial and material gains of having Shit Fathers.*

Jacq: *I would be so broke if I didn't hate men as much as I do.*

Taking the bus back down the freeway, I mentally prepare myself for my first night at PINKS by listening to Fleetwood Mac. To avoid another embarrassing exchange where I ignorantly ask a homeless person if he's on his way home, I press the volume button on my headphones to full capacity and keep my head down.

209

I walk into the dressing room, where a tiny Native American woman with lustrous jet-black hair looks at her reflection. She runs a boar-bristle brush through her mane, which falls below her waist. She's wearing black patent-leather thigh-high boots, and nothing else.

"Hi, sweetheart. Is it your first night? She flips her hair, sets down the brush, and picks up a Ziploc bag. Pulling out a white g-string, she slips it on. "I'm Shana." Her voice is raspy and sage.

"I'm Annika," I say into the mirror, dropping my backpack on the counter. "And yes, first night here."

"I haven't danced in years," she tells me, pasting fabric glue to cover her areolae. Almost instantly, it dries clear and sparkly. Even if it dries transparent and one can still clearly see the anatomy it's designed to conceal, a pasty is a pasty.

I've bought some glue from a nearby craft store, and I start smearing it on my nipples. The goo is cold, which makes my nipples hard, causing the glue to clump. I try to smooth it out, but now it just looks like I have diseased grey chunks growing out of my breasts.

"Here, Annika, use mine." Shana hands me her white bottle of goo. "You need to warm it up in your hands first. Also, that brand is terrible. Just throw it out."

Following her instruction, I apply the thin layer of pearlescent 'pasty' and watch it dry instantly. It looks as if I've plastic-wrapped my nipples. You know, to keep them fresh.

"I've danced all over the country. I don't wanna be here," Shana goes on in a defeated flip of her gorgeous locks that bounce off her strikingly high cheekbones. I slip on my hairpiece. It pinches at my ears.

Shana looks at my new hair and nods approvingly. "I'm old … I got grandkids." She looks back to her reflection. "I'm taking them on a hike this weekend … Need some money to get them something nice."

We assess our bodies: standing tall and straight, we each do our embarrassing sultry mirror face followed by a simultaneous twirl to check out our posteriors. The transformation is complete; we are ready to leave the dressing room cocoon and get to work.

The cleaning lights are still on. Shana and I sidle up to the bar. Death metal bleeds from the bartender's headphones as she saws a dull knife across a lime. Shana waves to get her attention, holding up two fingers. Death Metal looks up with a scowl. Shana gestures to me, then to herself.
Death Metal pours two shots of Crown Royal as Shana passes her a twenty.

"First days are always tough. Welcome," Shana tells me as we clink the plastic shot glasses back down on the bar. Death Metal flips the rubber caps off the booze and flicks on a switch, which ignites a buzzing sound followed by a flickering of black lights. Shana smiles, her veneers bright and blinding, just like my hairpiece. Looking in the mirror behind the bottles, I see two radioactive cyborgs: part human, part plastic. Everything that's fake in a strip club gets accentuated when the black lights come on. Just like in CSI, black lights bring out all the things we try our best to hide. Only in the club, nobody gives a fuck. Entertainment isn't about authenticity. It's about being present, having a good time, and appreciating what's in front of you without agonizing over how it got there.

Across the room, a DJ has appeared. He turns on John Denver to kick off the night. Death Metal groans, then returns to her bucket of limes.

With a relaxed slowness, the DJ walks over to our perch to introduce himself. His name is Carlos, and he is also the manager. Carlos asks me what kind of music I like to dance to, and what I would like for dinner.

"Dinner?" I ask.

"Yeah, I own a restaurant that's not too far away. It's traditional New Mexican fare. Are you hungry?"

"How much is it?"

"It's free."

MY STRIP CLUB BOSS IS OFFERING ME SOMETHING FOR
FREE. HE DOES NOT SEEM TO BE IMPLYING THAT HE
WOULD LATER LIKE A BLOW JOB. I decide that NEW
MEXICO FUCKING ROCKS.

Two more girls trot out of the dressing room and crowd around
me and Shana. They wear matching hot pink wristbands and
introduce themselves as Jessie and Kelly.

Jessie is heavily spray-tanned with a messy mop of brassy hair
and a painfully cute smile. Kelly looks like Kristen Stewart's
doppelganger: dark hair, porcelain skin, and piercing hazel eyes.
She's extremely thin, only she has this juicy booty ornamented
with a tribal tramp stamp. She's fucking hot; I want to hate her
but I also really wouldn't mind fucking her. Dark-haired girls
always get me with their sly coolness. But then Kelly opens her
mouth: "You look like a model!" she exclaims, blinking twice
and smiling like a pageant queen. Her disposition is like an
explosion of giggling Playmates. She is blondest brunette I have
ever met. Vampire on the outside, Reese Witherspoon on this
inside. It's weird. New Mexico is weird.

"Last night my boyfriend beat me up," she starts, sipping on a
Shirley Temple. She says it casually, like she went to see
Twilight and the popcorn was stale. I'm about to ask her if she's
ok, but Jessie breaks the two-second silence with a change of
subject: "There are a lot of girls tonight, huh?"

Instead of processing the reality that domestic abuse is a fact of
life for some of these girls, I sheepishly fall in line with small
talk: "Were you at a music festival?" I ask, pointing to their
fluorescent wristbands.

"No, it means that we're under 21."

A fifth girl sidles up to the bar. Her name is Talia. She confesses
to me that she just started dancing for the first time last week.
Talia is a single mother of five, with sharpied-on eyebrows and
a warm, toothy grin.

212

"I'm still really nervous," Talia says to Kelly, Shana, Jessie and me.

"Just remember to breathe," Shana offers as the DJ announces Talia's first song.

Stepping onto the stage, Talia's shoulders hunch forward as she places her hands on her knees, bobbing to a beat none of us are hearing.

In between smacking her gum, Kelly confirms the obvious: "She can't dance. I tried giving her some tips yesterday. She's too stiff."

She is indeed too stiff. She is dancing like a shy child. If I didn't know that she has had five children, I would be certain she was a virgin: dancing with her knees, and not her hips. I feel like a creepy pervert just watching her.

Jessie takes a break from sipping on her pint of Diet Coke: "Give her a Xanax."

Kelly shrugs: "I already did."

In my first night, I meet a man who digs for gold, a burly nurse, and a Mexican cowboy to whom I manage to sell a dance *in Spanish*. (Thanks to my Grade 10 Spanish teacher—Mrs. O'Donnell—who taught me the language of love through the lyrics to every Shakira song).

"It's not always this slow," Carlos tells me as he hands me a hot and weighty Styrofoam take-out container of refried beans and pupusas. "It's the first day of Lent."

I really need to mark all religious holidays in my calendar. Not so I can remind myself to repent, but to avoid showing up to work. For whatever reason, God-fearing people are always better customers than heathens.

At PINKS, a customer favourite is called an 'air dance.' It's topless, lasts for one song, and costs five fucking dollars. A dancer is not allowed to touch the customer, except for his

213

shoulders. No matter how much I beg to differ, shoulders are deemed by the New Mexico state government to be a sexless part of the body.

The only VIP room I sell is to an average Joe with the Manliest Deodorant Smell Of All Time. 'VIP' in New Mexico is a $25 dance in a room with a few couches in it. The dancer may then sit on Joe, touch Joe, or even maybe, possibly dance for Joe, but Joe must keep his hands to himself.

The headband that keeps Jessica on my head is digging into the back of my ears. When I try to adjust it to relieve the pain, she slips off. I abandon my dreams of fiercely whipping my hair while spinning around a pole and decide to look into Rogaine. In the meantime, I dance slowly and cautiously.

Joe decides to continue with a second VIP dance. He reaches for my ankle, and rests his hand on my heel.

"Hey man," Carlos says, leaning a shoulder though a crack in the door. "Would you mind taking your hand off her ankle?"

Joe nods obligingly. "Oh yeah, of course. Sorry, man." I smile at Joe assuringly. I barely noticed.

As I sway my tits at eye level, Joe looks up with an embarrassed frown: "Sorry 'bout that."

I almost scoff at the sincerity of this place but instead decide that I really like it. I barely make enough money for lunch, but I like PINKS. Time seems to stand still here. I like the girls, the haphazard decor (a pastiche of neon beer signs), and the cross-section of New Mexican locals who are shy, polite, and generally odd. I miss human interaction. PINKS is great because it seems less about putting on blinders and extracting every last penny from every man who passes through the hot pink door, and more about hanging out with friends. I'm charmed.

Plus nobody actually staves off chocolate, booze or tits for the entirety of Lent. Everyone knows that.

214

Sophie: *So after my first few successful-ish dates, I am now having the unlucky ones. Tonight's gent was two sided—first off, he is very sweet, and has inherited money so has all the time in the world to collect Pre-war Films (i.e. I got to impress him with my knowledge of said topic); second, he lied about almost everything. He is a total introvert, and while he is rolling in dough, has never had to work so has no concept of what it means to need money. We didn't eat, and he was so sweet and clueless I couldn't get it up to ask for cab fare. How was your debut with Jessica at PINKS?*

Jacq: *People who inherit wealth are usually really shitty people to be around; brats with no interest in anyone but themselves.* PINKS *was quaint, oddly hilarious, and hardly profitable. If I needed the money right now, I'd be crying. Thank fuck I saved all the necessary funds for this writer's retreat with my miserable New York day-shift dollars. Since the scrill I make is just for fun-spending, it doesn't really matter, which in turn makes the hustle more relaxing, and therefore *theoretically* and *hopefully* more successful. Alas, we only make money when we act like we don't need it. Jessica is kind of uncomfortable. I can't whip my hair too hard, otherwise it just falls off. Not that there was anyone to dance for, but still, the whole fucking point of having long hair is so you can whip it. Disappointing.*

I go back to PINKS the following night because I don't like this solitary writer's retreat unless I can contrast it with horny weirdos and free empanadas.

I wear a powder-blue babydoll dress that, when paired with Jessica, means I bear an uncanny likeness to Alice in Wonderland. It's the second day of Lent, the sinners are out to play, and my fresh-meat status has me getting *all the dances*.

"What do you do for fun?" I ask, peeling off my babydoll to commence my air dance.

"I do custom cars," says a thirtysomething man with elaborate ink on his forearm spelling out 'Estrella.'

"Cool! What's your dream car?" I flip Jessica over a bare shoulder.

215

"Any car and every car. I'll fix it up so you won't even *recognize* it."

"Oh yeah? So what do you think I should drive?" I ask, cupping my tits.

"1973 red corvette. You got that whole white chick thing going on. You'd look good in a red car."

I use my New York hustle to sweep every man who walks through the fuchsia doors, leading him straight into the VIP room. I'm an air-dancing MACHINE. As I rush back into the dressing room to re-pin Jessica to my scalp and reapply some concealer on my ass, Softy calls me over to this office.

"Hey, Annika," he starts. He looks embarrassed. "Some of the girls are concerned that you're, uh, giving away a bit too much for the air dances. Just remember that you can only touch their shoulders, and, well, it's just an air dance."

I'm taken aback by the most sheepish of reprimands I have ever received in my life, never mind at a titty bar.

Now I'm embarrassed. Maybe I was giving too much for a five fucking dollar dance. I've just been told that I'm the cheap floozy. The one who lowers the standards and fucks with everyone's business. I am the Russian concubine who makes out with clients for a measly $20 dollar dance back in New York. I am that girl. The extras girl. The one who ruins it for everyone. I was feeling like a queen, only now I'm realizing that being queen can mean being an asshole. That's not how it works here.

No one is going to tell me how to do my job. "Don't work so hard" is not really a common turn of phrase in America. And being Top Bitch means having haters. But this isn't New York. My rent is $300 a month, and I don't have five babies at home. I've compromised Santa Fe's small business owners. I feel like Walmart.

Sophie: *Last night I let James (the ad exec from Montreal who has a semi-hard dick and who I never want to fuck but always end up doing so) take me for dinner, and wine, and a movie, AND a cocktail—and due to my newfound confidence as a flirty*

216

conversation maker I not only hopped directly on the G train home after without so much as a cheek kiss, but I felt no guilt! If nothing else, all this pseudo hustling has given me self worth. Odd.

Jacq: *I'm SO GLAD to hear that you didn't feel obligated to kiss, suck or fuck your ad exec friend. Fucking should never be an obligation. I'm glad these daddies (both shitty and pleasant) have compelled you to either a) only fuck a guy if you want to, or b) make sure you're getting something out of it that isn't just dinner. WINNING!*

Sophie: *A man from Craigslist wants me to model leggings for an hour for $100. I'm doing it.*

*

"Hi, Annika!" Kelly squeals, plopping in a chair next to me. I'm back at PINKS, and I've resolved to just take it easy tonight.

Kelly opens up her purse, digging around with her bitten-to-the-quick fingertips. Looking back up to me, with a hush, she asks, "Do you take pills … smoke weed … anything like that?"

"Uh … sometimes."

Kelly's posture snaps up with excitement. "Do you want a Xanax?"

"Are they strong?" I ask.
"No! They're FUN! I just took threeeeeeeee," Kelly says, reaching down to her leg, stroking it as though she's luxuriating in the sensuous pleasure of pulling up a silk stocking. She throws her head back in a cackle. "Really, just take one. They're fun!"

"Which one is Xanax again?"

"It just makes you feel nice!"

Kelly doesn't really answer my question, but I know better than to turn down free prescription meds. "Okay, well, I'll just take half —"

"They're really small. Just take the whole thing." Eyes alight, Kelly daintily drops a tiny, white, oval-shaped pill into my hand. I don't want to take the whole thing, not right away. One of my drug-experiment rules is to always take half of the recommended dosage. But Kelly seems pretty insistent on me downing the whole thing in one shot. She did, after all, just take three. All 90 pounds of her.
"Okay, well, I'm just going to take it in the dressing room. I have a bottle of water in there."

Kelly nods enthusiastically, giggling.

Clip clopping across the sticky carpeting, passing the pool table, poker machine, and Death Metal, I slip into the dressing room and pull a bottle of water out from my knapsack. Staring at myself in the mirror, I place the pill between my two front teeth, and bite down. The second half of the pill goes flying toward the mirror, ricochets off my reflection, and disappears onto the floor.

Fuck.

I only wanted to take half, but what if I wanted more than half later? I hate being wasteful.

I get down on all fours. I scour the carpet, whose swirly-eighties-*Sesame-Street*-on-an-acid-trip pattern doesn't make my hunt any easier. As if reading the secrets of strippers past in Braille on the floor, I run the flat of my palm over bits of peeled off pasties, earring backs, and used Q-tips.
I don't know why, but I need to find this Xanax.

I pull my cell phone from my bag, illuminating the screen and pointing it on the ground. I shine the light under the vanity and into the dark recesses of the Stripper Detritus Vortex. The bright white of a tampon applicator shines back at me.

Getting back on all fours, I feel a prick under my right knee.

Small, white and jagged, I seem to be the junkie victor as I examine the shard between my thumb and index finger: The Beloved Other Half to my Xanax Gift. All of this hard work has me realizing that it would be foolish to risk losing this half-treat

218

again, so to insure myself against any future losses, I blow the dust off, and pop the remaining Xanax into my mouth.

I take note of the time: It's 7 o'clock on the dot, Friday night.

I sit at the bar and gab with Shana, Kelly, and Trixie. Trixie is Kelly's best friend. They both have three-year-olds at home, and sometimes they work together to share the cost of a babysitter.

Kelly starts with her usual shocking statement: "Last night I got arrested for getting in a fight with a girl."

"You WHAT?" All of this is still shocking to me. I've been in town two whole weeks now, and the parole speak is starting to become commonplace, but Kelly just isn't the 'arrest me' type. She's just so fucking *cheery* all the time. Tonight I learn to credit the Xanax for this.

Trixie drops her chin, throwing a serious stare at Kelly. "You have to go and see your parole officer next week, Kel. You can't be doing that!"

"SHE THREW A ROCK AT MY NEW FUCKIN' CAR!"

"Yeah but you gotta be careful, babe." Trixie picks some dirt from beneath her bubblegum pink nails. "I gotta go too. But I'm worried …" Trixie trails off.

"Just eat cotton balls diluted in bleach!" Kelly squeaks. "I do it all the time." Slathering on a layer of petroleum glitter across a calculated pout, Kelly jumps off the barstool and adjusts her pink-and-black bikini top. "Alright, I need to make money. My car payment is due tomorrow. It's stick, so I can't really drive it, but it's sexy," she winks, and saunters away.

Shana, ever stoic at the bar, sips on her Crown Royal as the rest of the girls trot off.

"Why would they need to eat cotton balls diluted in bleach?" I ask.

"It makes you pass the piss test." Shana flips her hair, exhaling long and slow. "I used to party. Those girls gotta be careful.

219

Especially Kelly. That girl has seen too much." She stares at her glass, tracing the rim with her finger. "You know, she met some guys here once, and they convinced her to go back to their motel room to party. They tied her up, naked, to the bed, and left her there for five days, coming in and out, partying … you know, gang raping her and stuff. And then finally, one day, when most of the guys were out of the room, she convinced the one watching her to let her go. She went running out of the hotel buck naked. And the guys were coming back in, they tried to stop her, but she kicked them, and got help, and … well, she's still here, and she's sweet as pie. But I worry every day for that girl."

Being the born-and-bred WASP that I am, I can't believe what I'm hearing. I'm used to seeing it on TV. But this is New Mexico, "Heroin Alley," where half the population has never left the state, and opportunity doesn't knock as loud at your door as the pushers do. As it starts to sink in that there is a lot of darkness in these places that I romanticise as 'isolated' and 'spiritual,' I still can't believe that of all the people in this place, it's the perkiest girl in the room who's got the darkest story.

"But she's just so … bubbly … like, all the time." I feel naive for thinking she was genuinely happy like that.

"When you go through as much as she does, eventually you just let it roll off you. And those pills certainly help." Shana gets up to approach an older fellow in crisp jeans and a ten-gallon hat, which he tips as she cracks a shy smile. I lean forward to get up, but suddenly I'm … *heavy*.

As far as I know, Xanax is prescribed to treat anxiety. Basically, it chills you the fuck out. I'm about to learn that Xanax is not the drug to be taking on a Friday night at a strip club.

Slowly, I use the bar to press up onto my feet. I feel a smile spread, warm and detached, across my face. I stare at everything, at nothing. For a long time.

At some point, I lose my post at the bar, so I decide to walk over to the first guy in my line of sight. He's sitting alone, smiling. I lean in, pressing a heavy hand onto his shoulder.

"Hi," I hear my voice but it sounds far away. "Do you want a lap dance?" I don't need to remind myself to smile because it's still plastered across my face.

The guy looks up to me, smiles back pleasantly, and says, "Sit down, join me! I'd love to get to know you a bit first." He pulls out a chair, setting it next to his.

"You're too much *work*," I tell him, pushing his shoulder. It sends him reeling back in the rolling chair while I stumble backward into a poker machine.

On this particularly booming Friday night, I manage to make $45 dollars in the span of eight hours.

*

Sophie: *So aside from the moderately gross private dance studio (in a large Midtown building, which on its other 15 floors houses sweatshop factories), nothing really sketchy happened with Leggings. First five minutes: We sit on folding metal chairs and he tells me again what he is expecting. This is almost verbatim what he'd said in the Starbucks, except he elaborates a little more about where the 'interest' comes from—when he was 5, he had an eighties-fabulous babysitter who wore pink spandex, and while they were playing Connect Four he became obsessed with the feel and look of how they hugged her leg. Hereafter, she was referred to as 'Connect Four Girl.' Minutes 5-12: As we are short on time, Leggings decides I will not go try on other pairs of stretch pants. I stay in the new black pair and he stands behind me (I've figured out he likes intense, attentive eye contact for about one minute, separated by anonymity for about six), and he doesn't stand close but rubs the sides of my thighs. When it's clear I'm not going to scream, and will continue to indulge him in chatting about the pros and cons of commuting from his house in Long Island, he cups my ass. I am fine with this. He asks me to reach to the chair, as if I were "picking something up" (um, like, BEND OVER? Cool). More cupping ... about as aggressively as a kid playing with his napkin at dinner while avoiding eating his peas. Minutes 13-14: "Well, actually I have three—well, I hate the word 'fetish,' but anyhow, leggings is just one. I guess I will just let go and tell*

221

you the other two. They're sort of normal." Fetish #2: Leggings
loves stand-up comedy. He loves Nickelodeon. Fetish #2
involves the IDEA of slapstick pranks, like green goo falling on
someone, only instead of a class-clown type the prank is on a
girl who is a little proper and embarrassed by it. Fetish #3:
Girls 'passing gas.' This one is like, pretty normal, except it
turns out I don't think he really likes girls to fart (like about 50
percent of all the men I've dated have)—really, this is Fetish #2
in a different pair of leggings. He likes the IDEA of a prim
proper girl farting by accident or being forced to or ...
WHATEVER. At this point, I get it. He is a guy who watches too
much It's Always Sunny, who is probably afraid of vaginas and
women who aren't some lovely combo of Girl and Warden.
Minute 15: Leggings says we can sit on the chairs again. Me:
"Oh wow, are we out of time? It feels like it's only been five
minutes!" Leggings: "No, we have 20 minutes left. I just feel
more comfortable this time than the other girl. She just had air
between her ears. So, how are you at telling stories?" My throat
drops. I don't know what kind of story to even begin to tell.
Minutes 16-35: Leggings tells me a story that he would like me
to repeat back, but in the first person, with 'ad libs' and
embellishments. It's basically the Nickelodeon-goo fantasy
mixed with the fart fantasy mixed with his stand-up comedy
obsession, but tailored to me ("you have to have a fundraiser
for photo equipment so there are all these people and a stage
and ..." etc.). I am to lie facing the wall, on the floor, away
from the mirror. He sits sort of behind me with his hand on my
thigh, and the stroking all but stops once I start to tell the story.
He wants me to really get into it. Holy fucking awkward. I
manage it, making sure to describe how embarrassed I am to
fart in front of these people for slapstick fundraising, but how I
really have to do it so my new boss will keep me on the team,
etc. All the way to the goo part, which had to be "coconut
flavoured" (????), to which I add that it was 'so unexpected'
and that I was uncomfortable with how my hair got all gooey
and it plastered my production t-shirt down and it stuck to my
leggings. So, um, I don't think he was aware of this being a
juvenile cum fantasy, but holy crap. He may or may not have
been very slightly jerking off. He definitely did not want me to
know, if he was. He is like a slightly twisted lamb.
Jacq: *WELCOME TO THE WORLD OF SEX WORK! This is*
the greatest first client you could ever have. It's mostly mental
gymnastics at a second-grade level while not having to touch the

222

guy. The way you describe it sounds like he really likes you. Fetish girls have to be smart. It's like improv actors—they're fucking brilliant because they have to be able to take anything and run with it, making it what the audience wants to see and hear. I knew you'd ace the kinksters. It's pretty underwhelming, isn't it? The job itself. The secrets and the scandals and how unorthodox it is, and of course, the cold hard CA$H is what makes it magical.

Sophie: *Tonight marks the opening of a rabbit hole, methinks. The possibility of rejection, normally paralyzing to me, is simply part of the invigorating sense that there are SO MANY twisted and confused men it doesn't even matter if a particular one likes you. In the words of Bree Daniels, "I am in control."[42] You're so right about the waterboarding effect. I've only been in the office half the day and it feels like a ridiculous, tedious waste of time. SOMEONE CUP MY ASS AND HAND ME SOME TWENTIES.*

---

[42] *Klute,* 1969. The story of Bree Daniels, played by Jane Fucking Fonda (!!!) as a whip-smart New York City call girl who gets swept up in a murder mystery. Watch this movie for the fashion, buy 10 copies for the ritual worshipping of polyester couture and woman power.

Man Camp

Back in Sydney, Jessie-Lee mentioned making a mint in the oil
fields of Alberta, Canada: "They fly you out there for two
weeks, set you up in a hotel and you get paid a DAY RATE on
top of what you can hustle! But they *throw coins at ya.*"

Apart from the coin-tossing, all of this still sounds too good to
be true. Plus, I figure it's about time I earn some legal money
that I can deposit into an actual bank account. So I book a flight
from Santa Fe to Alberta, the province that, coincidentally, is
where every person for whom I have ever danced believes me to
be from.

I thought it a savvy business strategy to be from a place no one
has ever heard of. I tell everyone "I'm a mountain girl," and
follow up with "I taste like maple syrup!" The reality is I have
only been there on two separate and brief occasions—the first
time was for shitty summer job developing photos and the
second time I was on a family ski trip. The only shred of truth in
my tale of origin is that I do taste like maple syrup. Obviously.

After three connecting flights and several complementary micro-packets of salted peanuts, I am frozen in a parking lot in the middle of the Northern Alberta tundra. My ride was supposed to be here half an hour ago.

"Just wait there and I'll be at the pick-up at gate number seven soon," twangy and accommodating, the distinctly Canadian voice tells me over a payphone. "I'm in a white SUV."

Standing frozen in the bone-chilling wind, I wait with my bags at my feet. Several couples pass me, half of them charioted by white SUVs. Picking up, dropping off, the ladies struggle to keep their blowouts in place with their splotched red-and-white porn-star-manicured fingers. A monster truck rumbles by with a teacup-sized monster dog scratching at the window. Through a cloud of smoke, the thick-knuckled driver cranes his neck to check his 14 blind spots. It's too cold to crack a window to clear the cabin of the second-hand smoke.

Sixteen lap-dance songs-worth of time past our scheduled connection, a white SUV, as promised, pulls up to the curb. A timidly smiling woman presses a button on her dashboard and the passenger window lowers. Her hot-dog-shaped canine pops his head up and greets me with moderate indifference, before focusing his attention on the lock knob, which is covered with a chrome skull.

"Hi, Annika!" she shouts from across the vast expanse of space that separates her side of the car from her puppy. SUVs upset me. I get all earthy and shit. My Burning Man longings to roll around on a bed of granola bubble to the surface and I mistake a pang of hippie emotion in my otherwise unfeeling lower half for a hernia. Silently, I acknowledge that it's nice to feel something at all, and hop in the vehicle.

The hot dog nuzzles into my neck as we drive westward, on the same stretch of two-lane highway, for 150 kilometres.

Dannika, my chauffeur, is the owner of the club, and she personally picks up each of the Slick Chicks who fly in for their two-week contract. Eyes on the road, she routinely checks her mirrors for the non-existent cars that might creep up on us and

226

pass as she hovers one or two kilometres above the speed limit. Her French-manicured hands rest exactly at 10 and 2.

"So how did you get to owning a strip club?" I make small talk.

"I always wanted to own a business. I've always been an entrepreneur. So when I learned that the club was for sale, I bought it."

"You had no dreams as a child of becoming a Madam?"

"Oh, no. I just wanted to run a business. Any business. I bought Slick Chicks seven years ago."

"Were you ever a dancer?"

"No," she says, with a definitive drop of the chin. She doesn't sound defensive, but instead insistent about making this distinction clear. This is common in the business of enterprising naked women. Generally, clothed women who work in strip clubs are happy to be there, but ultimately distinguish themselves as separate from the cash cows who do the trotting around with their tits out. Until Dannika gets up on stage and shakes her tits for an audience of growling brutes, she will never truly understand or respect it. She won't see how terrible it can be or how fucking brilliant and hilarious it is. She won't see that walking down the street as a 'civilian' is not that different from working as a consumable woman—except that for us, every holler rings with an opportunity to turn a profit.

The narrow strip of road is dark and straight. All there is to acknowledge is a dashed yellow line, separating us from the hypothetical oncoming traffic.

Eventually, a white dot appears on the southern horizon. The dot multiplies to become a vertical line of white and turquoise dots. As we near the lights, they seem to reach even higher into the sky.

"Is that a space station?" I ask honestly.

"Is what a space station?"

"Right there. Right ahead of us, on your side. Is it a silo?"

"What are you talking about?"

"Look. We are passing it right now." It's the only thing I could possibly be pointing at, given there is absolutely nothing else we can see.

"That's a rig. An oil rig."

"Oh." I am in oil country! "I've never seen one before."

"I see them all the time. So I don't really see them anymore. Sorry, I didn't know what you were talking about. You'll see more and more of them as we get closer to The Patch."

I know we arrive in The Patch because the next lit-up structure to feast my tourist eyes on is an artistic interpretation of three oil rigs. Three red 'rigs,' standing pretty in a row, reach 10 feet into the frozen night air. Each rig has a white neon-lit animation of spewing oil. Beneath the sculpture in large block letters the intersection reads: Welcome to The Oil Patch.

Dannika pulls into a hotel parking lot that looks and feels like Walmart. The sign boasts free WiFi, complimentary breakfast, Wednesday night karaoke and—

"Oh my god, there's a POOL!" I squirm in my seat, crossing my fingers that it's still open so I can take an evening dip.

"The pool's closed." Before rolling off into the darkness, Dannika tells me that the front desk is expecting me, and that the club manager will meet me at the club at 5 p.m. tomorrow night.

On the desk of my basement hotel room, I am greeted by a sign that reads "DUE TO THE HOTEL ROOMS CONTINUALLY SMELLING OF POT, THE RCMP[43] HAVE BEEN INFORMED AND WILL BE PERFORMING ROUTINE

---

[43] RCMP: Royal Canadian Mounted Police. Cops, on horseback, dressed in red with black hats. Sexy as hell.

CHECKS WITH THEIR DOGS THROUGHOUT THE
YEAR." I find the sign rather ironic, since the overwhelming
stench I am trying not to inhale is that of stale cigarette smoke.
There's a clean ashtray next to the sign, and above the sign, on
the wall facing the desk, is a no-smoking sign.

Day One of my stint as a Slick Chick has me schlepping through
a whiteout in late March. I'm told it's a 15-minute walk from the
hotel to the club. I bundle up in a long black coat, my favourite
two-metre[44] scarf that can wrap around my neck several times,
and a tuque fit for a seven-year-old. Lifting my legs high,
pressing into the fresh and fluffy snow, I embark on the
kilometre-long walk to the club. I'm worried that no one is
going to show up, given the inclement weather. In New York,
even a light drizzle has everyone calling their delivery guy for
cigarettes, toilet paper, and Chexican delicacies.

I pass a dollar store, a grocery store, several liquor stores, and
endless rows of structures serving unclear purposes. Later, I will
learn that these buildings are squats, motels, or something that
lies eerily between the two. There's a lot of work here, but not a
lot of housing. The contractors can't keep up with the demand
for labourers. People seem to be making do with trailers, motel
rooms, and the kind of pop-up shacks you buy on the internet
and assemble with an Allen key.

The second I reach Main Street, a mud-caked half-tonne pick-up
truck slows to the pace of my snowstorm stride. In spite of the
shrieking wind and swirling snow, the driver rolls down his
window to serenade me with a scratchy sing-song: *"You're sexy
and you know it."*

The Oil Patch: population 7,000, 6500 of whom are men—
burly, belching men wearing overalls and steel-toed boots, men
with big trucks and deep pockets. Men from all over Canada
flock here to drill, weld, or drive their way to riches. All a
dancer's gotta do is show up. Eighteen-year-old Manitoban farm
boys who didn't finish high school are pulling $500 a day, every

---

[44] The measurements in this chapter are going to be metric. Deal with it. The rest
of the world already does.

day. Financial planning extends as far as deciding which stripper to spend their entire paycheque on this Friday. This is boomtown. This is what the Canadian Dream looks like in 2012.

Continuing down Main Street, I pass a pub, a grocery store, a steak house, a Chinese food restaurant, and a tanning salon that doubles as a laundromat. After the local elementary school and church is a burger joint, skirted with picnic tables covered in a foot of snow. Next, four windowless cinderblock walls, no wider than the length of two Chevy half-tonne pick-ups. This is Slick Chicks.

As bleak as it looks, I'm told this place is a money pit. I consider myself an open-minded woman, so I pull open the hollow steel door.

It's unclear whether this place was once a restaurant or an automotive garage. There is a single stage to the far left of the room, a bar on the right, and a smattering of tables and chairs on the grey stone-tiled floor in between.

A woman with jet-black hair pops up from behind the bar.

"Hey bebe. I'm KoKo. I'm da manager." Her voice is raspy and tinged with sounds of home. 'Ome, that is. KoKo is Quebecoise and therefore has a remarkable knack for swearing, and for throwing h's in front of words that start with vowels, but doing away with them completely when they do *hexist*.

Beneath her black, second-skin tank top is a rock-hard pair of plastically engineered party blimps, and at her rear is the ass-that-won't-quit of a former gymnast and woman who has never heard of sneakers. Pointing out from the hem of her bedazzled flares are a pair of black leather stilettos, with which she stands at five foot nothing.

KoKo danced for 24 years, and only retired a few months ago to take on the role of running The Blue Oasis.

"Oke, bebe, I need you to put your makeup on, an den you're gonna go for your photoshoot wit Hallex. Den you're gonna go to da print shop an' make posters an' magnets and be back here for six terdy, kay?"

I am guided to a repurposed broom closet, which functions as the dressing room. The walls are painted diarrhea brown. On the underside of a shelf I read, "Believe in god and he shall forgive you," scribbled in black Sharpie in what I can only assume was the depths of a drunken despair. Beneath this alleged truism, and in significantly larger font, a steadier hand has penned "GOD IS REAL."

I set down my bag of tricks and transform from Real Girl to Whore in three minutes. It's a routine that is no longer fun and exciting, but essential in the transformation from the girl trudging down the side of the highway to the flawless entertainer from a faraway land. It takes a lot of bronzer to look like an innate Goddess.

I start by slapping on the lightest liquid foundation over the bags under my eyes, down the bridge of my nose, and along my jawline. I smear it in with a brush, evening everything out so my face seems uniform in its applied tint: Soft Ivory. I consider it an upgrade from the shade it was this morning: Red Splotch. Plucking a finer brush from my bag, I trace my eyes 10 or 12 times with black powder. Drawing wings out toward my temples, I blink a few times to rid the excess black gunk from my eyeball and assess my work: Bedroom Eyes, check. Strip clubs are always dank and dark, but there's no telling what sort of high definition contraption this photographer will be using, so I'm careful to make sure the line is straight and mirrors the angled swoosh of the one on my opposite eye. I've never been very good at the whole eyeliner thing. I always apply one, then the other, and when I pull back to see myself in the mirror it looks as though I have birthed a lazy eye. I can never get the angles right. I shrug it off by reassuring myself that I don't care enough, that I can just tilt my head to give the illusion that they are even, or, more aptly, that my customers won't even notice.

Mascara, blush, pressed powder, blush, blush, bronzer, bronzer, and blush. If I'm feeling particularly ridiculous and self-aware: glitter.

As I overzealously dust on the final touch—a layer of shimmer for that healthy sun-kissed glow after a long day in a basement hotel room—KoKo punches open the door to the dressing room with the heel of her hand. The door must be made of drywall and toothpicks, because it flies open, only to be stopped as the doorknob gets stuck in a hole that has clearly been made by a routine action like the one KoKo performed. The surprise makes me turn one of my 'just-kissed' cheeks into a brown smear of too-much-fun-in-the-drag-queen's-sandbox.

"Oke, Annika, Hallex is here for you. You ready? You look ready!" She raises her eyes and smiles.

I gather my things back into my bag. As I slip my coat, sweater, scarf, and mitts back on, KoKo pokes her head back in,

"Han' we godda change your name. Hit's too similar to Danika's name. I'm gonna fuck id up on da mic so you godda pick a new one."

***

Alex picks me up in a navy minivan. He's a big guy, a little weird, and mostly nervous. Sitting in the passenger seat, he hands me 'his work.' One look at his portfolio of fridge magnets and it's immediately apparent that Alex is one of those perverts who calls himself a photographer, and has the gear and the business cards to prove it, but then you click into his website and it's full of the worst pictures someone's weird uncle has ever taken. Either you start masturbating because you're into bad-quality soft-core, or your eyes bleed. But this is part of the contract I signed: Albertan showgirl culture involves the buying and selling of sexy promo.

Alex's studio is set up in the living room of his one-bedroom house, which he elects not to heat.

I throw together three different outfits: A black negligee (The Old Hollywood Glamour Girl), a baby-blue babydoll (The Jail Bait), and a pair of Daisy Dukes and a push-up bra (The All-American Girl Next Door).

I stand, freezing, on a backdrop that I am certain he stole from an elementary-school picture day: light blue and grey dancing together like the waves on the shore near a BP oil spill.

With shaking hands, Alex glances at me, then back to his lights, and then back at me, mouth agape. "Now I'm just going to adjust the lights to receive optimal lighting on the most relevant features for the shoot ..." I'm hardly charmed by his overcompensating professionalism.

As he fumbles nervously with his tripod, my mind trails off, and I recall from that the contract I did a once-over on that this is costing me $150.

I strike a few provocative poses, bending over, suggestively tugging at my bra strap, smirking, scowling, looking impressionable, then horny, then angry.

"You know, the top sellers tend to be the nudes," offers Alex, stuffing a fist into his pocket.

Scanning through the images on his IBM Thinkpad from 1999, I see that I've held up my end of the bargain rather well. I look cute, sassy, and vulnerable, yet totally capable of giving good head: the perfect hybrid of those babes in the philistine magazines that my mom refused to buy in the grocery store— the ones that dedicated 70 percent of their content to baseball scores, the rest to babes and racist headlines. And I haven't forgotten to include a dash of Seventeen magazine jail bait. When you're a stripper, you take the lowest age you could possibly pass for, and then subtract five. That's your stripper age. So, as a 25-year-old stripper, who could be 22, I look like a perfect 17-year-old. I get this industry now. It feels amazing. And also totally fucked up.

Alex assures me that the photos we selected for magnets and posters will be fit to print the following day. "You know, you can always do calendars and lighters and—"

"I'm only here for two weeks. As much as I like the idea of a guy lighting up one of his Lucky Strikes with my tits, I'm going to stick with the bare minimum."

Since my promo prints won't be ready until tomorrow, tonight I'll have to improvise with loonies and random objects in the dressing room.

Alex drops me back off at the club, where the night has already started. A handful of weary men sip on Molson[45] to the slow, comfortable twang of Garth Brooks. Two girls are perched at the bar, wearing down bomber jackets, legs wrapped in car blankets. As soon as they catch sight of me—a woman, and therefore certainly 'new talent'—they smile with a bob of their unlit cigarettes, which are stuck to their lips, and beeline out the door, which has yet to close behind me.

"You godda name yet, bebe?"

I was really into being Annika. It was sweet and innocent-sounding, all the while near proof that I am in fact, a Swedish goddess and not just a post-grad nightmare from suburban Canada. I was actually starting to believe that I was that goddess. I shrug.

"Whaddabout 'Madeleine?'" she offers.

"That's the one with the story of the girl who was a menace, right?"

"Yeah."

"And she had no parents?"

"Uh, yeah."

"It's perfect."

"So Madel—"

"But I don't like it. It makes me feel too much like an actual virgin and not enough like a faux porn-star virgin, you know?"

Inspiration fails to strike. "Let's just go with 'Anna.'" I can't waste any energy on creative mind exercises; I have a long night ahead of me.

---

[45] Molson Canadian: the most widely consumed beer in Canada.

"Oke, Hanna."

***

Sitting on the stools are a variety of men in their most authentic Canadian tuxedos[46]. Their denim is more flawlessly worn-in than the 'pre-stressed' ones you can buy for $400 on the Lower East Side—you know, the ones you buy with a black Amex and pair with Louboutins to traipse around all coked up in an after-after-afterhours club that no one has allegedly ever heard of. But slouching before me is a crew of men using denim for its original purpose: work. Before I can thoroughly revel in the authenticity of this place, my waist is shepherded by a callused palm.

"Hey there, darlin'—haven't seen you here before." This man smells of beer and hard labour. His leathery face shows a grey and toothy grin. "Let's go for a dance."

I take him to the counter where he pays KoKo. He pulls out a black Velcro wallet that looks as if it may have once been royal blue. Tearing back the closure with a loud rip, the wallet springs open and shows at least two dozen crisp twenties and a few fifties. I know this because, even in the dim lighting, and because I am not colour blind, the bills are green like my grandmother's wallpaper[47] and red like my rag-stained briefs[48]. I forgot how easy it was to distinguish between Canadian denominations.

"We would like to go for a dance," I announce, smiling like jail bait.

KoKo leans over the counter, resting her tits on her forearms. "'Ow long you wanna go for?"

"I think we'll go for two dances," he says.

---

[46] Canadian Tuxedo: Denim jeans and a denim jacket, worn together in perfect harmony. Also commonly referred to as 'Double Denim.'
[47] Green: Canadian $20 bills.
[48] Red: Canadian $50 bills

235

"JUST TWO?" KoKo asks. "She can 'ardly get naked in two dances! Take 'er for three."

He smiles and drops his head to his shoulder, happily suffering the wrath of a woman scolding him and telling him what to do. "Alright. Three it is."

I didn't have to sell ANYTHING. I didn't have to approach him, and didn't bother with trying to upsell him with premium mayonnaise like I did the last time I ever worked at an establishment that sold food.

He hands KoKo five $20 bills. As she relieves him of the burden of so much cash, she asks,
"Hand da rest his a tip for my girl?"

"Yes, ma'am."

I take him by the hand and walk him toward the back room, which is in fact the front room. The two designated spaces for private dances are like cubbyholes, and they are right there as you walk in the door to the club. I set the timer on the wall for 12 minutes, or 'three dances.' As I start to get naked, I cannot help but be reminded of a space just like this where I used to hang my coat and lunchbox in kindergarten. With every door that opens, freezing cold tundra air blows right onto my snatch. Fortunately, my client mistakes my shivers for arousal. So far, in Alberta, even when you feel like you're losing, you're winning. Is this what it felt like in the eighties in New York?

I sit on a small bench, upholstered with velvet brocade and two throw pillows. I let the shivers pass through my body and watch my client's knees sway back and forth in his chair.

"It really is a shame I can't touch you," he offers with a tone of accepted defeat.

"Where are you from?" I ask, changing the subject. STRIPPER TIP #27: Never dignify such tedious statements with any sort of response that even remotely suggests I DO NOT WANT YOU TO TOUCH ME, MOTHERFUCKER. Instead, my quivering desire to be prodded by strange and filthy fingers is conveniently obstructed by Alberta provincial law. Back in New

York, when a guy asks if he can touch me for 20 bucks, I'm prone to whimpering the following: "But the law here is that we can't do that … and how could I possibly trust that you're not a cop?"

But this guy doesn't bother persisting with trying to get his meaty hands on me. Instead, he obediently obliges me with an answer:

"Red Deer."

"And how long have you been out here?"

"Six months. I haven't seen a naked woman—'cept here—in six months."

"You haven't been home in six months?"

"No, ma'am."

"Isn't Red Deer, like, two hours away?"

"They got me workin' 20 days on, one day off, and even then I like to pick up a shift on that day if they let ya."

"Do you like it?"

"I like the money."

I will have this conversation at least 20 times tonight. Sometimes they're from Manitoba, Newfoundland, or right here in The Oil Patch, but beyond that they all go on just the same.

"So what do you do for fun?"

He scoffs. "Drink, I guess. No time for fun here."

"Well, what about when you go back home?"

"I got a quad. That's fun, I guess."

"What's a quad?"

237

"Are you serious?"

"I'm not from here."

"A quad's a four-wheeler. You ride around in the mud."

I lean back on the bench and lift my legs, spreading them in a V, resting my ankles on the walls of the cubby. This is the move I call 'the silencer.' It stops them mid-sentence. I trace a finger from the back of my thigh, down my ass crack, ending with a hint at touching my twat. I refrain from actually interacting with my vagina, because I know where my hands have been so far tonight, and they have touched things that other hard labourers have touched, who I have seen exiting the washroom[49] while still doing up their pants. Unless I've twice-rinsed my hands in bleach followed by a soothing milk bath, I've decided to refrain from ever touching my undercarriage at work.

While I'm calculating how much money I am making per panty-removal, I realize: I HAVEN'T flashed my gash for cash in quite some time. She's been tucked away and off-limits to the American audience. I'm happy she's back

My moment of feeling vagically liberated is stunted when I start to worry if I did a good shave job. Then I consider the dim lighting and the fact that this gent hasn't seen a cunt in half a year and my worries are swept away with the snowdrift.

When the timer beeps, I bring my thighs together, and drop my ankles back down to the floor. I sit up, placing my hands on my knees like my kindergarten teacher would and tell him, "Time's up."

He exhales.

"Shall we keep going?"

"I'd better not. I need a smoke. Maybe later?"

---

[49] Washroom: Canadian bathroom.

To my surprise, "later" in Alberta actually means "later," unlike in New York where "later" means, "No thanks, I'm a cheap bastard" or "you're not my type," or a confusing combination of the two.

Before "later" happens with my first client, I am swept back to the cubbyhole so many times that I lose count.

The night is a whirlwind of walking around and smiling for an eighth of a second before I am asked to privately entertain my next client. All I have to do is exist, and money is flung in my direction.

Hours pass and the bar becomes increasingly packed with more of the same feral clods. It's a tiring and monotonous routine that is suddenly halted mid-stride as the current Nickelback song is muted by a screaming KoKo:

"HALRIGHT GET YOUR FUCKING LOONIES OUT, YOU PERVERTS, CUZ I GOT A LADY COMING HON DA STAGE IN TWO MINUTES."

A girl I hadn't noticed yet parades around the room in a bikini and Ugg boots: carrying a beer pitcher in one hand, and a massive Louis Vuitton tote in the other, she smiles, coaxing the pigs toward the trough. As she climbs onto the stage, the tipping rail is chock-full of grinning men with rolls of coins stacked high beside their Molsons.

I sidle up to the bar to watch the show. KoKo nudges me, and covers a microphone with her hand.

"Dese rig pigs[50] love to spend all deir money, bebe. Just watch Marissa han you'll see."

Marissa starts swaying to the first song. Every 30 seconds or so, the techno Britney babble is muted once again by KoKo:

---

[50] Rig Pigs: Pejorative. An oil-patch worker who has more money than brains. Usually are prolific alcoholics and drug abusers. Most Rig Pigs drive Chevy half-tonne pickups, which they pimp out with chrome and mud tires.

239

"HALRIGHT YOU PERVERTS. IF YOU LIKE WHAT YOU SEE SAY HELL YEAH."

A few men coo out, "hell yeah." Most of them are too mesmerized or too drunk, or both.

"She has the body of a 15-year-old," a breathy voice says from across the bar.

The music stops completely. A naked girl without music brings way too much self-awareness to a strip club. The silencing of the beat and the power chords lets your brain process complete thoughts and suddenly you're asking yourself, *Jesus fuck, am I really just standing here naked in front of a bunch of ogres and this is how the world goes round?* But Marissa smiles unflinchingly. She's obviously familiar with the routine that I am witnessing for the first time.

"EH!" The speakers screech. KoKo's voice, in addition to the volume of the sound system, has reached full capacity.

"IF YOU WANNA SEE DIS GIRL DANCE YOU BETTER SHOW 'ER SOME FUCKIN' APPRECIATION. I'LL TAKE 'ER RIGHT OFF STAGE IF I DON'T 'EAR YOU YELL 'HELL YEAH.' HUNDERSTAND?"

The audience is silent. Marissa smiles, standing at attention.

"DO YOU HUNDERSTAND?"

"YES!" scream the obedient ones. Plebeians.

Britney blasts once again through the speakers and Marissa resumes her dance.

Over the music, KoKo yells, "HALRIGHT HEVERYBODY, ON THREE, I WANNA 'EAR A 'HELL YEAH.' ONE, TWO, THREE—"

The men scream a "HELL YEAH" and like magic, Marissa loses her top to reveal a surgically engineered bust on her otherwise prepubescent frame.

I'm whisked away once again before I can bear witness to the grand finale: pussy out, coins flying.

"Excuse me, miss. You're just about the prettiest woman I have ever seen in my entire life. Can we please go for a dance?"

His name is Chuck, and he's got a lot of curiously voluminous grey hair itching to burst out from under his green John Deere trucker hat. I take Chuck by the hand and walk him to the VIP cubby.

"Oh man, I love your man in a boat[51]" Chuck says, licking his lips with a click. He rubs his thighs with his palms as I switch from a forward bend to a leg lift. "Oh, would I ever love to eat your little man in a boat. See," he lifts his fingers to his lips, "I have false teeth … so when I eat pussy, I take 'em out, and every woman I eat says I'm the best she's ever had."

I had thought he was high on blow, but really, he had just needed to head off to the powder room to reapply his Fixodent. I quietly chastise myself for being so quick to judge: *for every hundred Chatty Kathys, there is one Chatty Chuck.*

"Really," Chuck persists, nodding. "The best you'll ever have."

I've heard a lot about toothless women giving good head, so I decide that the toothless men don't get the same good press because PATRIARCHY. People don't brag enough about the virtues of an especially cunning linguist. I reason that it is because it doesn't quite look as eventful on camera. And when it does, it looks ridiculous and not pleasurable at all. If I was into random acts of pussy eating and not totally terrified of herpes, I would really like to take Chuck up on his offer to see if he can walk the walk. Instead, I thank him as he hands me a generous tip and tell him that I'd love to dance for him again sometime.

*

---

[51] Man in a Boat: Canadian informal for vagina. Picture a canoe (the labia), with a man sitting at the stern (the clitoris).

The next day, I eat breakfast in the motel restaurant where the waitress plays *Divorce Court* at an excessively high volume. All of the arguing makes it hard to enjoy my Canadian omelette: bacon bits, tomato, and Velveeta. I opt for the bottomless cup of watery coffee instead.

Last night was a whirlwind of cash. I was so busy dancing in the VIP booths that I didn't even get to dance on stage. But fuck—cursed be any strip club that does not have wall-to-wall carpet. The ache in my knees is something so profound that I worry I'll be needing surgery by the time I'm 26. Carpeting in cheesy night clubs, as decadent as it may seem, is in fact an essential tool used to cushion the impact on the knees, legs, and ankles of the dancers. This important cushioning is also why we wear platforms. The more distance between the balls of our feet and the cement flooring, the longer we last without slipping into our flats and ordering the annoying guy who has been following us around all night to piggyback us back to our hotel.

I will have no such luxury in the coming weeks; I do not want any of those rig pigs knowing where I'm staying.

On an adventure from my room to the vending machine at the end of the hotel hallway, I run into the two chain smokers from last night. Bonnie and Kristi, Hungarian and Russian, respectively. They live in Toronto. This is their last of three weeks at Slick Chicks.

"We come here every two months or so," Bonnie says, lifting an e-cigarette to her chapped lips.

"The men here are disgusting. Disgusting pigs," Kristi chimes in, exhaling vapour and shaking her bangs out of her face. "But don't worry, baby, it's *really* easy money. You'll do fine. Would you like a Sour Patch Kid?"

"Do you want to go for dinner with us before work?" Bonnie asks. "It's just next door. The food sucks, but it's better than staying in this shithole all day."

"Sure, I just need to shave my legs and—"

"Shaving out here? It's a waste of a razor." Bonnie pauses to unstick a Sour Patch Kid from her molar. She swallows. "Baby, they can't even touch you. The rooms are dark, and the men are so drunk they're blind. Your pussy could be sideways and no one would know the difference."

Over chicken caesar salads and soggy shoestring fries, Bonnie and Kristi tell me the pros and cons of working in a city with legalized prostitution: "Toronto is a great place to make money if you're a whore," Bonnie says with a sneer.

"But if you're not selling blow jobs with your lap dance, you may as well be broke," Kristi says. "This is the best place to work nowadays."

The three weeks have been profitable for the girls, but Kristi misses her husband, 10 years her junior, and Bonnie misses her studio, where she paints. "Windows. I miss the windows," she says with a sigh.

"And I miss my babies so much," Kristi says.

"You have kids?" I ask, as you're supposed to when someone tells you about their kids.

Correcting her posture, she smiles: "I breed chinchillas."

***

When I get to the club for night number two, the place is already swarming. Every dude who walks into the bar gives the manager a kiss on the cheek, followed by a round of lemon drop shots. Over half the people who come into Slick Chicks are here to see KoKo. They linger around the bar, run her errands, and hang on her every word, even if the words are most often to the tone of "Come on, you cheap motherfucking rig pig, show some respect and fucking generosity to my girls!"

Weaving through a gap in her fan club, KoKo greets me with a lemon drop before I can manage 'hello.'

"Alright 'oney, get dressed—we got guys who want dances."

I hit the floor running, doing laps from the VIP room to the bar and back.

Dance Number 10:
"Won't you just come home with me?"
"Give me one good reason why I should go home with you."
"Uhhh …"
"Just one."
"Uhhh … oh, I don't know. I guess you're right, eh? Well, can't blame a guy for tryin.' "

Dance Number 29:
"So where are you from?"
"You're so sexy."
"I just got to The Patch. Where can I find some tasty and moderately healthy food in this town?"
"You're so sexy."
"Thank you. And what do you get up to on your days off?"
"You're so sexy."

Dance Number 48:
Guy, a Quebecois dude waiting for his next assignment. He demolishes pipeline, rigs, and old Cold War U.S. military bases that blow highly toxic dust into Nunavut. His job is to take down as many structures as possible before the the entire territory is diagnosed with Cancer. Night after night, he comes in, buys me so many drinks I end up switching to a Blue Lagoon[52] out of sheer boredom, and tries to convince me to give him a pair of my panties to supplant his pine-scented car freshener.

"I tell you, girl, if you sell da panty you make *alodda money*."
Eyes closed, Guy goes for the deep inhale of a dedicated panty sniffer.

Dance Number 102:
The guy clearly has an outbreak of herpes on his face.
"I got a nine-inch cock, you like that?"
"What happened to your lip?"

---

[52] A radioactively blue-looking cocktail made with Blue Curacao. High in sugar content, tasting like a generic brand melted Popsicle. When you choose to drink this, no one over the age of 22 will take you seriously.

"I got … in a fight."

"Right."

"You should see the other guy. But first, you wanna see my cock?"

Two hours of non-stop panty peeling pass before I hear a shout from across the room: "Bebe! I need you on da stage!"

A loonie is valued at one Canadian dollar, and measures about 2.5 centimetres[53] in diameter. It's about twice as heavy as a quarter. Anywhere else in Canada, it is illegal to throw coins at dancers; it's dangerous, it hurts, and some assholes are sick fucks and do things like lick the coins before they throw them, or worse, heat them up with a lighter, sometimes causing permanent scarring. But, in true Albertan[54] fashion, this province has decided against following with the rest of Canada and has turned the loonie toss into a drinking game.

For three songs I dance around on stage, strutting my stuff. Song number one, I am fully dressed (Read: the Daisy Duke get-up). For song number two, the tits come out. Song number three is a slow tease of the panties rolling over my ass and down to my ankles. The crowd is rapt with attention, screaming and hollering on KoKo's cue.

For the fourth song, and sometimes fifth and sixth, I am instructed to take a business-card-sized magnet with a skanky picture of myself on it, lick it, and stick it somewhere on my body. The magnet becomes the target, and the clients start tossing coins at it. The objective is to knock the magnet off my ass, and claim it as their prize.

"Now you motherfuckers," KoKo starts. "Dis is Anna's first time on stage at Slick Chicks! Be GENTLE and be GENEROUS!"

---

[53] 2.5 centimeters: 1 American inch.

[54] Albertan: An Albertan is a Canadian cowboy or cowgirl who loves her truck. When they're not claiming that Canada would be bankrupt without their oil money, Albertans talk a lot of shit about seceding. Some have said Albertans are "Texans who can read."

To avoid having coins fly anywhere near my face or vagina, I strategically lick and stick the magnet to my ass cheek. I'm hot and sweaty from my dance routine, but I can't tell if the quickness of my heartbeat is from my high-octane finale to Marilyn Manson's *The Dope Show*, or from sheer fear-induced adrenaline.

One eager player at a time, a loonie is tossed at my ass. For the most part, it's painless—no burning coins searing my loins. Slingshots have not been unearthed from coverall pockets. The only true, deep-burning pain is the humiliating realization that I am submitting to having one-dollar coins being thrown at me for sport. My biggest challenge is to keep smiling, all the while encouraging them to continue throwing more.

So many men have lined up to play that I am on stage for three additional tipping songs. After the last contestant makes an unsuccessful attempt to win the prize for his mini-fridge, I pick my winnings up with a magnetized wand and dump them into a pitcher.

Before I can make a thorough judgment about this abhorrent cultural practice, I am handed a few hundred dollars by the bartender, who has quickly counted up my loonies and swapped them for a more lightweight denomination. I barely have time to slip the money into my purse before a young, handsome chap waves me over to his perch at the bar. His eyes are red.

"I've just received some bad news," he starts. "My dog ran away. I need some cheering up."

I take a seat on the barstool next to him. I'm prepared to listen, nod, and rest my hand on his shoulder as he bears his grieving soul to me, a semi-clothed rent-a-friend. (In New York, I would have to sit and listen for at least 20 minutes to have this guy warm up to me and pry open his money clip). But before I can get both cheeks onto the vinyl upholstery, this boy rises to his feet and offers, "Let's go for a lap dance." He flops open his wallet, revealing an abundant rainbow stack of blue, purple, green, and red. Glugging the rest of his Molson, he hands me two reds, and walks me back to the booth.

The sobbing boy's name is Matt. I sit him down. I peel off my bra, Daisy Dukes, and g-string while Matt alternates between choking sobs, stories of his 16-month-old yellow lab, and complete silence. In my most sincere effort to lift this grieving man's spirits, I turn around and reach for my ankles, offering up the best view in northern Alberta.

The third song ends. Taking a few short breaths, Matt watches me slip my kit back on, and draws his hands to his face for a pause. He gets up, pumps his fists in front of him, and draws back the curtain to escort me out of the booth.

Before I can close the sale and formally offer Matt my condolences, I am waved over by another rig pig's toothless grin and hairy forearms.

"YA-WOAH!" Matt screams to my next client, pointing to me. "THIS CHICK'S GOT THE BEST COOCH IN THE WHOLE BAR!"

Eat, sleep, hustle, repeat. Eat, sleep, hustle, repeat.

I really wanted to go dog sledding. I've never been this far north in Canada, and the raddest thing I know that exists up here is that people move about with a pack of huskies. But I am here to work, and any other activities I planned are certainly not happening. It's so dark in the hotel room that, unless I set an alarm, I sleep in until 4 in the afternoon. I brought so many books with me, thinking I would plough through them in the diner next door in between hearty bowls of soup and round-the-world stripper gossip. But everyone is too tired to even gossip. All of my books are buried beneath my workout gear in my suitcase (the treadmill in the lobby ended up breaking on the second day I attempted to use it).

When you work 14 days straight, weird things start to happen. Working like a zombie is a great way to make money, and in The Patch, you don't feel bad ignoring loved ones, social events, or general domestic responsibilities that the perma-fried hotel housekeeper takes care of. Unless I'm slumped under a heap of scratchy motel sheets, I'm in a state of perpetual drunkenness, taking shot after shot, night after night. In most cases, I think shots are great for strip clubs because it makes the guys lose their better judgment at a faster pace. Back in New York, a drunk man was wondrously impressionable and significantly more likely to invest in my precious time. But here, the clients are already ready to throw away their money like confetti, so the shots fail to serve their intended purpose. They are entirely frivolous, and saying 'no' is impossible because there aren't any other strippers to whom I can deflect the offering. They are all either stretching their hamstrings for the viewing pleasure of a paying customer, or right beside you, glass raised, ready to swig it back in fellowship. I'm so saturated in booze that I can't even get drunk anymore. I am a fish in water, trying not to get wet. My eyes are bloodshot and I stink like a freshie at an AA meeting.

I look over at KoKo, who is screaming at a 300-hundred pound oaf as he obediently licks the rim of the shot glass. I wonder how she can do this every fucking day. She is not on contract; this is her life. But then I reflect on her 25-plus years in the business, and realize that two weeks are just a drop in a hazy ocean of limoncello. Plus I'm pretty sure that every stripper who ever gets implants has secret drinking superpowers installed within the silicone. There is something deviantly magical about a set of fake tits. At first I hate it, then I admire it, and now I just get fucking horrified. What secrets doth thy fake titty hold?

By the 14th day, Bonnie and Kristi are long gone, while Marissa is off to watch her son at a piano recital. Tonight, I am the sole entertainer at Slick Chicks. Before I can take a deep breath to prepare for my last hurrah, I'm drunk, quite possibly half-asleep, and richer than I ever thought possible.

Man Camp is not really a hustle. It's just the act of existing with a set of tits. Beyond that, in The Oil Patch there isn't really much of a difference between strippers and rig pigs: a rotating roster of lonely men—and a handful of women—all flocking to the tundra to mine their own small fortune. What's so great about it is that you don't have to sell anything 'special' because you're already fucking special, just for showing up.

The Catwalk Club

There's a girl I'm going to marry back in New York, so against my better judgment, I return. I promise myself not to go back to Russian Dolls, even though I don't have much of a plan beyond that.

I set out to be the blondest, bubbliest-looking fembot in existence, and march up to the Club of the Moment:

"Hi!" I beam to the bouncer. He guards a velvet rope with typical New Yorker ambivalent pride: arms crossed, eyes averted.

"ID and Social Security, please."

"Oh!! Uhh … I'm a student!" I lie. "I don't have my Social Security yet … it's … in the mail."

"Well, you can come back when you do."

The crackdown on human-trafficking laws have illegal aliens such as myself out of a job. Turning around, I head back toward the train before a cab slows down to a near halt.

"You need a ride, baby?"

STRIPPER TIP #28: Never get in a cab directly out of a strip club. Those guys are waiting to pick you up, so they can find out where you live. Always walk a block away and pick up a cab on the next street. Walking a block has its shortcomings, too, so there is really no way to win. But this street is well lit, so I opt for taking my chances at getting mugged over having this cabbie discover my address.

In response to the man's cooing, I shake my head. He persists. I keep walking, trying my best to ignore it, but when I look over to his rolled-down window I cannot help but notice something strange about the ad on the cab's roof:

It's an ad for a strip club that *isn't* Russian Dolls.

It says *The Cat Walk Club*.

Doesn't Jerry have a monopoly over all the cabs? How curious! A driver can either advertise for the Broadway show or the *other* Broadway show. Jerry's a clever and powerful asshole, that's for sure. He wants every tourist coming to see the Russian Dolls, and no one else. But the universe is now telling me otherwise.

***

I walk across town to the listed address, walk in, and meet a very flustered and very tiny man. He is the manager, and introduces himself as Wally. I wait patiently in the middle of the foyer as he bellows into a walkie-talkie: "Ricky, ya fat fuck, I told you to stop playing this shitty fuckin' rave-rock shit."

Wally flails his arms at nothing in particular, takes a deep breath, and smiles sweetly. "Come with me, sweetheart."

Weaving through the club, he shows me to the dressing room. Inside is a handful of dancers sitting on the counters, gossipping while taking selfies in the mirror.

"Mina, this is Anna." Every sentence he utters sounds as if it's an exasperated chore. The final word of every phrase drops with a stern exhale. "She would like to audition."

Mina, with thin black hair and grey roots, sits in the corner of the dressing room, surrounded by paperwork and inspiring quotes tacked to the wall.

"Everything happens for a reason, for it is God's will."

"No matter how good or bad you think life is, wake up each day and be thankful for Life. Someone somewhere else is fighting to survive."

Wally looks around the dressing room nervously. I will learn later that he is looking for someone to yell at. "Okay, get dressed and tell Mina when you're ready." And then I witness the ultimate depiction of a showy tough guy's attempt at tenderness: Wally's mouth curls at the sides. Wally hates everyone in the universe, except for his girls.

I set my backpack down as Mina asks me if I've danced before, how old I am, and if I have a 'luong dress.' Wally returns a few moments later, escorting me to a tiny stage in the corner of the club. I dance for 30 seconds before he walks up, offers his hand, and invites me to come down.

"Can you work tonight?"

"Sure!"

Hired.

The Catwalk Club is a velveteen labyrinth of money. Dancers glide around with stacks of Funny Money wrapped in rubber bands strapped to their wrists, ankles, forearms, and thighs. They seem happy and relaxed as a host dashes back and forth with new credit cards in need of swiping. As Wally leads me around the club spewing his orientation speech, a smiling drunk man in business-casual tugs at my wrist. "When you're done, can I see you? You're perfection."

I smile, nod, and finish learning about the DJ and club rules: "We would *prefer* if you wear luong dresses, and keep your hair down. We would also *prefer* if you wore open-toed shoes, and always have a manicure, pedicure, and your makeup done."

Wally can't say that we 'must' to adhere to these rules. That would be illegal. I read in the paper that droves of Brazilian babes and matryoshka dolls are currently in the throes of a class-action lawsuit against Russian Dolls, which, after imposing strict rules on the dancers, is being sued for not paying them adequate wages. Strippers are usually 'freelancers,' which gets the club out of paying them any sort of salary—and allows said club to charge a house fee. If a club wants to impose restrictions on a person operating their own business in their establishment, they are obliged to pay them. Russian Dolls was certainly not doing this. So now this tiny manager with a missing bottom tooth is telling me how the club would 'prefer' that I present myself. Strip club owners know and exercise the law more than any cop I've ever met.

Ricky—the DJ—asks what music I like.

"Uhhh … white-girl music?"

He nods confidently. Wally whisks me away before I can elaborate on which Bjork tracks I prefer.

"Alright, you'll be great." Wally gets on his toes and kisses my cheek. "Would you like a drink?"

"Thanks, Wally, but I think that man back there wants to get me one."

Business Casual beams like a child with a new toy as I swish back over to him.
"Let's go to the back!" he says, smiling even bigger.

"The back?" Recall: my experience with 'the back' or 'Champagne Rooms' and 'private lounges' has always been terrifying and therefore avoided at all costs. "Don't you want a lap dance first?"

"Oh, that's just too much of a tease. Let's go."

Business Casual pays $600 to the host, and signs a waiver saying that he consents to "no sex and no illegal drugs." A small square at the bottom right of the waiver asks for the querent's thumbprint. On the other side of the billfold is an inkpad.

Business Casual obediently presses his thumb into the pad, and onto the paper. They say that this is so he "understands the rules and regulations of the Catwalk Club," but really it's to prove that Business Casual was physically present when he calls AmEx the next day with buyer's remorse and denies that he was there, or that he charged several thousand dollars of Krug and Funny Money on the card.

The host hands me $300 in Funny Money, and draws the curtain closed. Business Casual and I are all alone for the next 30 minutes.

"Would you like a drink?" Business Casual asks, sipping back on the last of his Amstel Light.

"Yes." I'm terrified, and alcohol will buy time, and I'm hoping it might also numb my terror. I hate these rooms. But I'm making 50 percent more money for half the amount of time I would have spent in a Champagne Room at Second Chances, so despite my anxiety I'm starting to warm to The Catwalk Club.

Business Casual pokes his head through the curtain, summoning a waitress.

"This beautiful woman would like a drink!" He smiles again, inspecting my face. "My god, aren't you beautiful?" He turns back to the waitress, raising an empty bottle and placing it neatly on her tray. "And I will have another beer, please."

Business Casual tries to calm my nerves by repressing his boner and telling self-deprecating jokes. It works.

The drinks come, and Business Casual goes on about how terrible he is at golf. My internal monologue goes off about how much I love self-deprecating men.

"Now, really, Anna …" his smile vanishes. "I just want to smell your asshole."

I can see by the look on his face that he is serious. No one has ever told me that they especially loved smelling assholes. Nor has anyone expressed interest in smelling mine in particular. But he's so sweet and charming and funny that it doesn't sound unreasonable. What do I have to lose? Surely he does not me expect to sniff his in return. *If his pursuit of happiness does not infringe on mine, what's wrong with letting this guy smell my ass?*

"Okat, you can smell it. On one condition: I leave my panties on." STRIPPER TIP #29: You can't always please someone, but you can compromise to keep yourself happy and comfortable at the same time. I keep my panties on because I also know that men are pigs, and if they want to smell you that closely, there is no way that they will also have the restraint to not follow up with a lap of the tongue. And since rim jobs, for me, fall under the 'for my private life' category, my panties are not going anywhere.

Business Casual smiles, ecstatic. "That's totally fine! Here, I'll lie down." He shuffles his neck to the edge of the couch, and tilts his head off the end of the armrest. "All you need to do is stand over me! And sit on my face! Only, you know, backward."

I hesitate for a moment before I stand up, smooth out my hair, and shuffle forward into the assigned position. I straddle Business Casual's face—only I'm too tall in my platforms for this to work at all. I bend my knees until I'm practically reverse-cowgirling in a strenuous squat over his keen nose. Business Casual inhales deeply.

"YOU SMELL SO GOOD."

Although I haven't taken a shit since earlier this morning, I'm pretty positive that my butt smells like the shitty asshole that it is. But Business Casual is way into it! I only had to travel halfway around the world to find my scat fetishist!

I'm staring at the curtain, half-terrified that someone is going to walk in on this, half-trying to concentrate on not laughing at Business Casual's long and deep breaths as he presses his finger tips into my thighs. I look around the room, inspecting the red velvet curtains for holes or cum stains, but they must have been to the cleaner's recently. I'm still not good enough at this job to truly meet someone halfway with enthusiasm. I'm happy to oblige, but I'm not ready to order the man to take a deeper breath as I sit my entire weight on his face. But I am determined to rise in these ranks.

 "Oh man, all I can think about right now is burying my tongue in your butthole."

I stand for a minute to regain my balance and composure. Business Casual shuffles into a more comfortable postition, and gently takes my hips, lowering my ass back onto his face. "Like, it's really nice. Your ass. It's a nice smell." The vibrations of his voice on my ass cheeks make me laugh. He laughs. And time's up. A hundred dollar tip and away he goes.

***

It's not too long before I realize that The Catwalk is almost exclusively a 'room club.' You can sell lap dances at 20 bucks a pop, but the real objective is to get them to max out all of their credit cards. Girls sit at the bar, get clients drunk, and then coax them into a room, where there they aim to keep them entertained, wasted, and spending for as long as possible.

I will learn to call this "personalized entertainment," which really just means you have to make them think that, behind closed doors, adult Disney World unfolds where there are 72 slut-virgins eagerly waiting for him. Really, men are just getting duped into pay $1000 an hour to have a dancer's undivided attention. Some girls suck dicks, jerk on limp ones, fuck, offer up their assholes, and blow cocaine up an array of orifices. And some girls just sit there and giggle. Some girls listen to them talk about how unhappy they are, or what they'll do once their kids finally go off to college and they can finally divorce their high-school sweetheart. The answer is usually "buy a boat."

When the girls file into the club to start their 6 p.m. shifts, they wordlessly gather into clumps around the bar. What clump you gather into is determined by your mother tongue. The Spanish girls chatter away in one corner, the Russians in the other. A handful of Brazialians branch off from the Spanish girls if there re enough of them to carry on some fresh gossip in Portuguese. Two Greek girls prattle on about something potentially serious, and the English-speaking girls flip their hair as if they own the joint. Because they sort of do. Or should I say 'we' sort of do.

Because, like everywhere, white privilege is totally a real thing in strip clubs.

A fiercely intimidating woman covered in tattoos sidles up to the bar next to me. Wordlessly, she stares at the TV. She is empirically beautiful; her face is symmetrical and her skin —or at least whatever is not covered in ink drawings of morose men and women, flowers, and pentagrams—is porcelain. Tall, slim, and freshly done up with comic-book-sized breast implants, she glides across the room and scares men into getting dances with her. Her name is Jenna, and she hates everything and everyone but herself.

She is visibly angry, all the time.

"Botox," she says, pointing to her forehead. "It makes me look awake, all the time. Even when I'm falling asleep dancing for these shit-fucks."

I nod in agreement. She does sort of look consistently awake. She mostly looks angry. But something tells me that I should know better than to disagree with her.

A skinny guy with less than a year at Goldman Sachs under his belt walks up to Jenna.
STRIPPER TIP #31: If a man walks up to you in a strip club, you have the upper hand. Strippers are usually the ones who do the circling and peacock-feather-ruffling. If someone approaches you, it means he really wants you. Exploit this.

"Hi," he says, leaning in at arm's length. "Can I buy you a drink?"

Jenna blinks slowly, and lolls her head to turn and face him. "You can buy a dance," she says out of the side of her ruby red mouth.

"Well, let's start with a drink," Goldman Sachs pipes back with a challenging smile of flirtation.

But Jenna is having none of it: "Well, if I take your vodka-Red Bull and dump it on my ConEdison bill, it's not going to make it go away, now is it?"

This girl is so badass it's amazing. She just totally dissed a guy without taking a breath. From my high-school perspective, I officially have a crush on this hot Mean Girl. But she also lost out on an opportunity to make at least $20. The enterprising businesswoman in me—who exercises compassion every once in a while—thinks she's a nasty bitch who doesn't understand the value of a dollar or basic manners.

STRIPPER TIP #32: Be nice to guys who have the balls to walk up to you. You can only be mean if he is mean first, or if it's after 3 a.m. Everyone is an asshole after 3 a.m.

Goldman Sachs turns and walks away, scoffing loudly to conceal his embarrassment. He sidles back up to the bar a few seats down and stares at the TV.

"I don't drink," she says to me with a sneer. "I was a junkie. Been sober for 18 months."

She lifts a bejewelled and inked hand, nails painted black, up to the nape of my neck. She fondles a curl. "I like your hair like this—classic Marilyn waves."

She is so hot and scary at the same time.

Goosebumps.

For the most part, Jenna ignores me. She chitchats with the other English-speaking blonde girls, stares at Instagram, and hustles. The rest of the blonde girls seem to work in a pack. When one goes to a private room with a client, another goes running in after her. Literally RUNNING. Giant strides, twisted ankles, lunging for the door before it clicks closed. All doors in New York seem to operate this way: Once the door is closed, you've missed the gravy train.

At first glance, the idea of getting a man to pay $1000 for an hour of my time is daunting enough. *But paying DOUBLE that for the same shits and giggles? That's ridiculous!* Then I remind myself that men *are* ridiculous in the face of titties. One nip slip and a man starts panting and wagging his tongue. Two fully exposed areolas render him utterly powerless. So when there are

259

TWO hustlers in there with him—that's four nipples—their powers of extortion are exponentially higher.

But this involves working in a group. Being part of a team. Relying on another person to achieve your goal. I hate teams.

In high school, I would beg and plead with my teachers to exempt me from group work. "Please, I just … can't work with others." Trembling with the laminated and colour-coded dividers on my undecorated purple binder, I would summon some remarkably believable tears. As my teacher was gathering her papers to take home over the weekend for grading (C's, mostly) I would start quivering my lower lip. When she wasn't having any of that, I'd block the doorway. It is, after all, totally illegal and punishable by sexual-assault charges to touch a student. "I'll do it all by myself, including the extra credit! Just don't make me rely on the incompetencies of my peers. They're useless!" Patience wearing thin on the thankless job of teaching teenagers the advantages of having good syntax, she eventually gave in. They all did. At any given moment in my over-achieving career as a friendless high-school student, I would have several four-person assignments on the go all at once, all by myself. Not once in my entire high-school career did I engage in group work.

But this is real life. And if I thought grades mattered when I was 15, it sure pales in comparison to the thrill of counting my own cold hard cash.

In order to get another girl in a room with a customer, I need to get said customer to like her. That means approaching him together, or nabbing a whale so rich that when I ask to bring her over he doesn't flinch at the decimal point moving over a digit or two. I look around to the cliques, women huddled in whispers of fast-talking gossip in languages I claim to understand but can only speak after six beers and seven shots. I don't see an easy in. So I go about hustling my own lap dances and private rooms.

Until—

I don't know *HOW* this happens, but a Chinese client is finally bold enough to say yes to a private room. By and large, Asian customers are very bashful when it comes to being alone in a room with a stripper. Old, fat, and rich white American ones are the boldest when it comes to getting bouncy in a private room, in addition to coughing up generous tips.

My client, hailing from Shanghai, has lived in Chicago for 20 years. His name is Billy, and after one vodka soda and some chitchat about my Canadianness, he invites me to the Jungle Room. I don't even have to lay out a fancy sales pitch!

A sales pitch goes something like this:

Dancer: "You know, baby, there are lounges where we can spend some … *leans in* … private time."
Client: "Oh yeah? Tell me about that."
Dancer: "Well, it's a private room, where we can spend some time together. No one can bother us there."
Client: "And how much is it?"
Dancer: "Well, for half an hour it's ____"
Client: "And what do I get for half an hour?"
Dancer: "Well … it's private … and we're alone … and the 'no-touching' rule is a little more … flexible."
Client: "How flexible?"
Dancer: "Well, baby, let me just say that you won't be disappointed."
Client: "Can you tell me how you're going to do this?"

Men just want to hear that you're going to suck their cock. Legally, a stripper can't say that. So regardless of whether I plan on deepthroating or not, I cannot make any announcement of said action. That would be soliciting (a.k.a. illegal). And even if I'm working in a total whorehouse, undercover cops roam the joint all the goddamn time. STRIPPER TIP #30: Be elusive with your words, yet expressive with your lips, tongue and batting lashes.

This back-and-forth will go on forever. At some point he will either say yes, or the dancer will grow frustrated and walk away.

Billy pays for an hour. "Sorry I cannot stay longer; I have to go back to my hotel room for a conference call with my associates in China."

We pop a bottle of champagne that neither of us has any interest in drinking, and I sit on his lap, fiddling with his lapels for the better half of 45 minutes. I dance a little, turning around, and bending over to squeeze in a yawn.

"Can I see?" Billy asks, gesturing to my vagina.

"Sure," I say, "But no touching!"

He nods in agreement and I take a seat opposite him. I unwedge my g-string from my ass crack[55], and slip it to the side to offer up a front-row seat to my haphazardly shaven vulva.

"Woooooaaaaaaaahhhhh," Billy says, fixated on that which is *technically* forbidden in the state of New York when sipping booze in the company of strippers.

"Can I smell?" he asks.

By now I'm used to this, and I, too, know that hot-girl pussy smells pretty fucking great most of the time. But before I became super empowered and relatively dykey, I thought a woman's scent was terrifying. Had I had the courage to buy a douche at the age of 15, I probably would have. But those days are long gone and now I'm selling panty sniffs like hot cakes.

Billy leans in a little closer, inhaling deeply. He looks up to me, with a surprised look on his face like he found a Tiffany ring in a box of Cracker Jack: "Your pussy smells like salmon!"

"SALMON?" I repeat, hoping I misunderstood the statement.

"Salmon!" Billy says, nodding with unprecedented enthusiasm. "It's a good smell!"

I love salmon, I really do. And I love my cunt, I really, really do. But there are a lot of things in life that I love, such as MDMA and family barbecues, and I love them separately because in life

---

[55] IT IS INCREDIBLY DIFFICULT IS TO MAKE THIS LOOK GRACEFUL AND SEXY.

you really can't have everything snazzy all at once; you'd have a brain aneurysm, or maybe offend someone you care about. But Billy loves salmon and pussy on the same plate, and you know what? I'm cool with that.

The hour ends. I slip my kit back on, accept a meagre tip, and go back to work. To my own surprise, I DO NOT run to the bathroom to baby wipe every feminine fold, followed by several spritzes of deodorant and perfume. I just shake my head incredulously, saying to myself, "*salmon*."

The next guy just wants to make out with me.

"Please, Anna."

"No."

"Please?"

"No."

"I'll tip."

"No, baby." STRIPPER TIP #31: Call a man "baby," *especially* when you're denying him. Or call him "pig." When saying no to a powerful man, you have to either coddle or badger him. If you walk the median, you're boring. You're not getting paid to be boring.

We talk about his ex-girlfriends instead. They were all beautiful and sexy, but never got along with his mother. I sit on his lap and nod, riffing off some bullshit about how lucky he is to have a close relationship with his mother. I've already chosen the coddly route with this guy, so I can't tell him to stop letting her do his laundry and learn how to cook a goddamn casserole. I am, after all, expecting a tip at the end of this naked therapy session, kissing or no kissing.

An hour later, off I trot with another nice stack of cash.

WHY DID I NOT UNDERSTAND THAT BULLSHIT IS THE NAME OF THE GAME? WHY DID I NOT UNDERSTAND THAT MEN ARE LIKE BABIES, SO INSTEAD OF

Perhaps I am just generally more confident now that I have a few additional months of stripping under my garter belt. Second Chances and Russian Dolls certainly had different standards for what was expected from girls in the VIP room. But every club runs the gamut of having girls who put out, and those who stealthily manoeuvre around it with smooth-talking sass. And maybe I just wasn't ready to learn all of the New York City strip club secrets in one go. I had to endure two rounds of Purgatory. I mean, 'initiation.'

Strapping an extra rubber band around the increasingly thick wad of Funny Money on my ankle, I see Jenna out of the corner of my eye. Eyeing my fortune, she strides toward me, and I straighten up and reshape an unruly lock of platinum.

"I've got a guy. Come. Let's go." Jenna turns around and walks toward an early-forties man with blond hair and a vacant expression.

"This is my best friend. She's coming with us."

Vacant, like everyone else, knows not to disagree with Jenna. He nods in agreement and off we go.

As soon as we get paid—Jenna has also already negotiated a $300 dollar tip for each of us in advance—Jenna springs to life smiling, screaming, bouncing around Vacant, and giggling like a menace. She is certifiably insane, and Vacant fucking loves it. He kicks off his shoes and jumps onto the couch. I follow suit.

Suddenly Jenna starts screaming about polar bears.
"VACANT YOU LOOK LIKE A POLAR BEAR. IT IS YOUR SPIRIT ANIMAL. CAN YOU ROAR?"

Vacant roars.

"ANNA IS A BUNNY. WATCH HER WIGGLE HER NOSE."

I wiggle my nose.

"I AM AN ALBINO WEASEL. I DON'T KNOW WHAT THEY DO BUT WHO THE HELL CARES." Jenna crawls across the floor, pops up like a gopher, and jumps onto Vacant's back.

I feel it is worth mentioning again that Jenna is completely sober. We did order a bottle of Dom, but she's secretly drinking ginger ale.

We are leaping from couch to couch as if it's a six-year-old's first sleepover party. Vacant is grinning so broadly that his eyes disappear into his receding hairline. I jump up on the back of the couch and profess to the ceiling in my most eloquent speaking voice: "I am a Barbie Dream House: A beautiful waste of space."

We scream as if we're on a ketamine-fueled episode of *Sesame Street*. Money bleeds from his every orifice into our garter belts. It's fun and easy and RIDICULOUS. It's so unsexy that it becomes sexy. Like that time when you fart so loudly for the first time in front of your lover that you start laughing hysterically, which inevitably turns into sex? Perhaps I am alone on that experience. ANYWAY—the point is, you get so comfortable and getting silly is so FREEING that you may as well be getting a blowjob from Siamese twins who are connected at the esophagus because you're getting fucked in this new, supreme way that you never knew could exist.

Vacant is obviously successful and habitually in charge. He probably has to be serious and assertive all the time. Strippers are his escape, and if it's clowning that he wants, clowning he gets. Plus it's fun as fuck. Infinitely more fun than having some dude rub my nipples raw, which totally happens more than I care to admit.

Vacant stays in the back room with Jenna and me for several hours. I make the most money I've ever made in one night. We exchange numbers with Vacant, and vow to have fun together again soon.

Reaching a personal best is better than getting good oral. What is especially exhilarating is that I didn't earn it by conning this guy into thinking he was going to have sex when he wasn't; we earned it because we entertained him. Because that's what we do. We entertain. Entertaining doesn't always mean dry humping.

I count and recount the money. I have enough to buy the Prada bag I wanted when I first moved to New York, but I know better now: money looks better in the bank than it does on your feet or dangling from a wrist. But since I don't have a bank account, I stuff the stacks of hundreds into a battered copy of *Pippi Longstocking* and and slip the book into a drawer.

Stripping at The Catwalk is teaching me that great things can come from teamwork. For the first time in my life I suddenly have faith in my peers. I mean, how could I ever doubt the conviction of a stripper on her path to financial solvency?

That said, there is the occasional drawback to working in groups. You know, like when a guy prefers your tits to another girl's, even though he was really into her tits last week. Every stripper is someone's flavour of the hour.

So when Vacant texts me the next day asking me when he can see me again, I get blindly excited. MORE MONEY!

"I'm working tonight, as a matter of fact," I type with eager thumbs.

"Wonderful, Anna. I'll see you at 8."

I fail to consider the fact that Jenna introduced me to this guy, which technically makes him her customer.

***

I stride into work with the confidence of a stripper who knows she's about to make bank. When a large sum of money is a sure thing, one tends to become arrogant.

"Will you marry me, Anna?"

"Hell, no. You'll end up taking me for all I've got."

266

I kinda want to make a collage of every phone number given to me by a married man. I would need to find a bigger apartment if I wanted to hang it anywhere.

Jenna isn't here. She's off tonight.

I text her.

"Jenna! Vacant is coming back in! Where are you?"

A millisecond passes and my phone vibrates with a reply from Jenna: "He didn't tell me he was coming in. I'm off tonight. I can come in, though!"

A buzz alerts me that Vacant just walked into the club.

I text Jenna back: "He's here! I'll ask him and let you know."

I drop my phone in my locker and prance through the labyrinth to Vacant, who is leaning like Ralph Lauren himself against the barstool, wearing expensive jeans and a healthy tan.

My mouth spreads into a grin of delight, my arms into a welcoming embrace. "Vacant, my darling." I kiss him on the cheek. "I'm so happy to see you. Jenna is just around the corner!" I lean into his chest with a giggle. "Can she hang out with us, too?"

Vacant pulls back, and assesses my eyeliner and freshly dry-shampooed hair. He smiles with a twinkle of the eye. Leaning in close to my ear, he whispers, "Just you." He places his meaty hand on the small of my back, and we walk toward the private room.

I decide not to think about Jenna.

We order a bottle of champagne, "The Pink One!" I plead, tugging on Vacant's capped t-shirt sleeve. STRIPPER TIP #32: Always sound like a dumbass when you order a high-priced item. It makes you look like you don't know any better. I say "the pink one," because Pierrer-Jouet Rose has a pretty hefty

267

price tag, and I want the commission. But you can't act like it's a big deal. They know it's going to be stupidly expensive, so don't draw attention to this. Just act like you're six years old and you want anything and everything that's pink.

The tag-teaming with Jenna at the helm made Vacant so overwhelmed with boobs and screaming and furry play that he hardly had time to paw at our tits and reconsider the next $1500 expenditure. This time, Vacant paws at my tits a bit, but all in all he's nice. I make an attempt at screaming something frivolous, but it feels weird. For whatever reason, three people screaming in a room is significantly easier, less embarrassing, and more fun than two people screaming in a room, which is what I spent my college days learning to call 'sex.' And since Vacant and I are not having sex, the screaming is stopped before I give him the wrong idea.

But it's too late.

"I'd really like to take you to my cabin in the Berkshires," he says, playing with my hair as I sip on the PJ Rose[56] and examine the hand-stitching on his Cole Haan sneakers. Yes, Cole Haan makes sneakers. Expensive ones.

Vacant and I are not bouncing around on couches. We are not screaming. We are chilling the fuck out. It's nice, but not as lucrative or fun as yesterday. I have obviously destroyed the intricate balance that Jenna, Vacant, and myself created last night. Now that it's just Vacant and me, it's significantly less exciting and funny. He's still sweet, generous, and respectful, and I'm happy he's here. He spends a bit of money, but not nearly as much as the night before.
As I walk Vacant to the door, several pairs of laser-cutting eyes follow my stride. Every other bitch in this joint clearly hates me. It's a quiet night and no one is making much of anything besides gossip and I'm walking my prized pig to the door, stacks of laminated currency strapped to my foot for all to see. Heavy lies the sequinned crown.

---

[56] PJ Rose: Pierrer-Jouet Rose.

I go back to the dressing room to freshen up. My phone has a text from Jenna: "I guess he just wanted you. Good for you! You scored a regular."

Relieved at the nonchalant sincerity of her response, I exhale, fanning through my plastic currency and rifling through my makeup bag for touch-ups. I draw a plushy brush from the depths of a bag, and circle a blush compact to pick up whatever's left, splashing it on my cheeks. STRIPPER TIP #33: Blush is the only sort of makeup one should ever bother to 'touch up' throughout the night. It's the easiest to put on, and making parts of your face darker is easier than slovenly dabbing on a second layer of concealer. Plus covering up zits only works in Photoshop. In real life, a three-dimensional goiter on your face can only truly be obscured by distracting a keen eye with an even redder cheek.

Through a gaggle of wigs and lip gloss, I contort my brows and lips into my bitchy mirror face when I realize: Jenna is not being sincere. The only people who text phrases like, 'Good for you!' are grandparents who don't quite understand you and your achievements but love and support you anyway. Jenna does not have a maternal bone in her body.

Jenna and I both understand that our entire existence as fantasy girls is predicated on the fact that we are fair and fleeting. There is a reason all these dudes buy calendars of attractive women and not posters. A new flavour is just a page away at the end of every other pay period! But strippers have feelings too, and when a guy picks someone else over you—and he always does—it stings. And what do most people do when they are feeling hurt and shitty? They project their hurt and general shittiness onto others.

A week passes before I see Jenna or hear from her. I take a few extra days off because, after two sessions with Vacant, I fancy myself a clowning extortionist. I take Kryptonite out for lobster, contemplate buying some very pricey days-of-the-week Real Girl underwear, decide against it, and dick around Williamsburg. No one seems to have a real or regularly scheduled job in Brooklyn, so I have lots of company.

When Jenna rolls in an hour after I arrive the following Monday, she averts her eyes and quickens her pace as she beelines for the dressing room. I've angered The Catwalk's Resident Angry Bitch.

Jenna avoids me for most of the night. When I'm in the dressing room and she pushes through the door, catching sight of me, she turns right back around. Jenna sacrifices her blood-red lipstick reapplication in the name of not-so-stealth avoidance. To avoid sitting next to me along a row of chairs in the hallway that is specifically designated for snacking and Instagram, she instead walks over to the pile of trash bags, standing next to it with a hand on her hip as she refreshes her feed of fellow emo boys and tattoo artists.

This fuck-up is grave.

I'm uncomfortable. Having someone hate you at your workplace is a terrible experience. It puts me on edge. Because she is avoiding me, does that mean I have to avoid her? Is that how enemies or ex-friends work? I've never really had one before. Canadians don't, usually.

An eternity of awkwardness and glancing over my shoulder passes before I see Jenna at the bar, staring up at ESPN.

"Hey," I start, embarrassingly timid. "I'm sorry about last week. He'll be back, though."

In a quick jerk of her shellacked platinum bob, Jenna turns to face me. "Look, you're new at this so you don't really *get it.* But I negotiated that room, and the tip, and the bottles. He was *my* customer. And don't take this the wrong way, but you're very passive and not really good at this. Men like Vacant only respond to you because they think they can take advantage of you."

The words coming out of her mouth don't match the expression on her face. The words are venom. But Jenna's face is unflinching. She is so deadpan that I think for a moment that she's playing with me. Like being fake-mean before she slaps me on the back and says "NAH … just kidding. Luv U betch."

270

The only sort of emotion I can pick up on is a nervous twitch where she utters every sixth word out of the side of her mouth. Beyond that micro-signifier of sheer anxiety, I am completely lost in the apathetic abyss of Botox. It's confusing. It's basically getting needles in your face so that no one will ever be able to relate to you, ever again.

'Passive?' 'New?' 'Not good at this?' I never thought these kinds of words would feel as shitty as they do right now.

Jenna goes on: "And what's really shitty about this is that we were friends."

I don't even know your real name. Were we friends? Is this what it's like to have friends in New York?

Jenna looks back to ESPN. Sports highlights on mute, no subtitles. A lifetime of linebacker mugshots and stats fade in and out of view before she turns back to me.

"Basically, you fucked my boyfriend."

Shocked at this confusing outpouring of how much I suck at stripping, in addition to the fact that Jenna feels that I fucked one of her internet boyfriends, I make like a Canadian: "Jenna, I'm sorry." My throat tightens. "I'm sorry for responding to Vacant without checking in with you first." I feel small. "I really had fun working with you and I hope you can forgive me so we can work together again."

Jenna rolls her eyes—Botox would NEVER revoke *this* privilege—turns on her heel with a hair flip to end all hair flips, and walks away with a swaggery huff.

I feel sad. I feel like I lost a friend. Maybe we were friends. I feel like I did something wrong. Like I should have included her from the get-go, as soon as Vacant contacted me. But wouldn't that make Jenna my pimp? It's just work. It's not personal, so why did she have to get personal and tell me I suck at this? Just when I thought I was getting the hang of it, apparently I have no idea what the fuck I'm doing. And because Jenna's hot and cynical and angry, I take her opinion very seriously[57].

Disheartened, I revert to back to my lone-wolf ways. I weave through the room, looking to transform a $20 dance into a thousand-dollar private room. But it's tricky to sell lap dances at The Catwalk Club. Like a yawn, lap dances are a contagion; all it takes is one guy to nod in agreement while opening his wallet, and the rest will follow. But if no one is getting one, it's a much harder sell, and all the guys just sit in the chairs and stare at the stage for a free show. It looks kind of like church, these plebeians sitting in rows, all silent and worshippy. Strippers should really pass around offering trays as a dancer gyrates on stage. New York City perverts are far too embarrassed and/or apathetically self-involved to show their support for a dancer by actually walking up to her and giving her a tip. Tourists are even worse, because they follow whatever everyone else is doing, which is a whole lot of NOTHING. Tourists are afraid of us. So they stay really still and just stare. Like maybe if they don't move, and sit it the darkest corner, we won't see them. But we see them.

There is nothing worse than a bunch of guys in a strip club *not* getting lap dances, just sitting there, perving out. It a sad phenomenon that can happen at any time, and it's when strippers get nasty:

"Would you like to go for coffee with me sometime?"
"Why? Do I look tired?"

"Your eyes are the same color as my Porsche."
"Would you like a dance?"
"No."
Pointing my perfectly polished index finger in his face, I correct him: "No *THANK YOU*."

---

[57] It's so hard to take angry hot girls with a grain of salt. Think about it: If Angelina Jolie circa *Gia* told you she was going to the grocery store to buy vinegar, you'd think she was reciting blood-thirsty poetry that could potentially end your life.

There are a lot of guys who refuse to pay for dances, excusing themselves by saying, "I don't need to pay a girl to see her naked."

On this particular day, I am dangerously close to getting my period. It's when my boobs are at their fullest and my body reeks of extreme fertility. It's a prime string of days to make money. It is also when I am the very best at being a no-holds-barred B I T C H.

"Buddy, it's 7 p.m. on a Wednesday night and you're alone in a strip club. You paid the $10 cover, and then dished out 12 bucks for a Miller Light. You *are* paying to see girls naked. You are the *worst* kind of asshole."

The Worst Kind of Asshole scoffs. I seek revenge by walking a few paces away and summoning a few colleagues. I make sure we are within earshot of this cheap, smug fuckwit. Gathering the girls into a huddle, I point back in his direction, and laugh. Without questioning my leadership, all of the girls join in on my cackle. The worst thing a woman can do to a man these days is humiliate him publicly. Even if we don't know the wrong he specifically did, when a girl tells me to look over and laugh at someone, I oblige. It's a stripper solidarity thing. It is without fail, the best way to get a guy to leave.

The Worst Kind of Asshole pouts, and crosses his arms. Quietly, he scans left and right to see who is watching. Every stripper, waitress, and bouncer stares at him. The cheap bastard downs the last half of his Miller Light and leaves.

It's nice to feel like you smashed the soul of a douchebag for a minute. But since revenge rarely turns a profit, I get back to work.

A British guy tells me the following: "You're a dirty bitch … In a nice way … I'm a nice person, really." He doesn't want a dance.

A man contemplates the price of a private room after telling me that lap dances are "far too public:" "Now, I could buy my wife a Mulberry bag for that price!"

I walk up to an Egyptian tourist: "So if I think you pretty, I pay you."

Me: "Yes."

Egyptian: "Okay."

FINALLY!

I dance for him. At the end of the song, the Egyptian pays me $17. When I correct him, saying "TWENTY," pantomiming a two and zero with flustered hands, he shrugs. I opt out of the humiliating exercise of getting a bouncer to muscle the last three dollars out of the clueless tourist, so I put my dress back on and move on to my next target.

I sit next to a young and smiling white dude who seems eager to have my attention. Leaning back in my chair, I smile and twirl a platinum tendril with my ring finger. Young White Dude reaches over, and sticks a finger in my navel.

My smile vanishes and my face flushes RED as I swat his wiggling finger from my stomach: "DO NOT FUCKING TOUCH MY FUCKING BELLY BUTTON YOU FUCKING FUCK."

I stand up, but before I walk away, I blow a silent-but-deadly fart in his face. Usually I can't fart on command. I think I'd be better at handling all the sexual-harassment, cat-calling, and generally asshattery if I could.

I walking back over to the bar to regain some composure. Jeanette, the massage girl, looks around in disbelief: "I'd rather take a melatonin and masturbate than be here right now."

I finally get a private room with a neurotic young man who is so boney it hurts to sit on his lap. Wordlessly, I dance for him. He clutches onto my thighs, then reaches for my tits. Before I can say, "Gentle," like I do to every boob-obsessed man-baby who walks into this place, he squeezes my pre-menstrual and already-throbbing breasts.

OWW. Is this what a mammogram feels like?

I squeeze his wrists like you would squeeze the jaw of a dog that won't release your favourite pair of underwear from its slobbery

274

grip. His fingers relax. I stare him in the face: "Excuse me, but my breasts are not stress balls."

He drops his hands by his sides for all of three seconds before he goes for the death grip once again. Thankfully I am familiar enough with his type, and stop him with a stern, "NO" before he reaches his target. He frowns.

I demonstrate by caressing my breasts softly and tenderly—as breasts should always be treated—telling the kid, "You've lost that privilege."

"How do I get that privilege back?"

"I don't know if you will." I flip my hair. "Only time will tell."

"How much time?"

"Oh … an hour."

"How much is an hour?"

"A thousand."

He slumps back into his chair with a pout.

I know he can't afford it, and I don't want him to. Maybe his mother didn't breastfeed him? Or maybe she still does? Whatever it is, there are too many men who have no fucking clue how to appreciate a woman's figure. I used to be mortified whenever the guys I used to date reached up my skirt in search of my clit. It's as if they were trying to press a sticky button on a vending machine. "NO," I would tell them. "*Gently*. Imagine you're touching your eyelid."

I mean. I sort of get it. Whenever I watch a guy jerk off, it's so *aggressive*. The grip they have on their cock looks positively painful. The clit is something like 4000 times more sensitive than a penis, but you know, boys are shitty multitaskers: when they are trying to focus on baseball so they don't cum in five seconds, the whole ratio of clit-to-penis sensitivity goes straight out the goddamn window. If you're a man and you like fucking women and you are reading this, remember: her clit is more sensitive than your eyelid. So thumb down your cock for four fucking seconds, inhale deeply through your mouth, exhale some of that excited tension, and proceed with tenderness.

I check my watch: It's only 10:30. In a stripper's working day, this means that it's not even time to break for lunch. And we don't really even stop for dinner breaks. We snack on cheese balls and lime wedges while the bulk of our diet is an intricate balance of vodka, champagne, whipped cream, and strawberries.

I see two hot guys scanning the room for something to look at. They seem disappointed, yet curious. In spite of the fact that hot guys in strip clubs fucking suck, I walk over to them with an exasperated *what-the-hell*.

"Hi," I say, bored but smiling.

One of the guys' faces lights up with this acknowledgement. "Are you a model?" he asks.

I'm barely 5 foot 7 with a frame that is anything but androgynous and willowy. So when anyone asks me if I'm a model, I'm only flattered because it means you think I'm 18 and stupid.

"No," I reply flatly. I guess I'm acting like a model: bored and emotionless. "Do you want a dance?"

"Yeah, sure!" says one of them. They both look the same in their flannel and denim. I can't tell which of them said yes, as I wasn't really paying attention. *YEAH, SURE?* I'm shocked. "But before you dance for us, will you tell us what type of jeans you prefer?"

"Excuse me?"

"What jeans do you like best?"

"The ones that make my ass look good, duh." I stand up and start swaying.

The second song ends and the Denim Brothers hand me forty dollars in Funny Money wrapped around a coupon for 30 percent off all regular-priced Levi's. Gotta love guys who get to write off their strip club adventures by calling it 'market research.'

The next man I approach is at least 40. He's never in his life had a lap dance. I will be his first. For this special occasion on this otherwise completely shitty and tedious night, I increase my enthusiasm from 6 percent to 50 percent. I want to give this guy a medium-to-okay impression of medium-to-okay strip club entertainment.

At the end of the dance, he furrows his brow in disappointment.

"What's wrong?" I say. "Did you think I was going to cartwheel onto your dick?"

They next guy I prance over to strokes my thigh as we talk about the weather. When I segue our meaningless chatter into asking if he'd like a dance, he assures me that he's "just looking," and pats me on the back.

I rise from my perch on the arm of his chair: "If you're going to window shop, go to Bergdorfs."

I wish I could give lap dances to super hot gay boys who don't try to touch and just tell me that I'm fabulous.

I look back at my watch. It's 10:50.

When nights like this seem hell-bent on beating every optimistic thought out of your greater consciousness, the best thing you can do is get wasted. STRIPPER TIP #34: There is probably a guy who is sitting at the bar, staring at all the girls, but refusing to tip any of them, or get dances. He will, however, buy you a drink. Men think buying you a drink is less pathetic than buying a dance. Try as I might to convince them that if you buy me a drink and then *don't* get a dance this makes you THE SECOND WORST KIND OF ASSHOLE, this mentality never changes. The best way to work with this sort of guy is to bring your girlfriends over and exploit this. One time this guy refused to get a dance or tip, but he bought me at least six drinks and gave me the rest of his Adderall stash. But I'm not always that lucky. In most cases of The Second Worst Kind of Asshole, I have to put up with listening to a lot of bullshit about stocks, ex-wives, and "crazy" trips to Vegas. In this particular free-drink-a-thon, this guy is mansplaining how to ski. He knows how; he took a lesson once. I've elected not to tell him I grew up on a mountain. I order a double.

Suddenly I'm wasted and Ski Expert is stumbling to the men's room. A curly grey-haired man with blue eyes and thick wrists takes his seat.

"Well, hello, there, Sheila."

SHEILA? Oh my god, it's an Aussie. Aussies are usually cheap unless they are obsessed with your American Girl Doll-ness and then they are like ATM machines hooked up to a wind machine. *WHICH WILL IT BE?* I'm too drunk to profit any more from the Ski Expert and this guy approached me so maybe this night won't suck as much after all.

"Why, hellooooo, Blue Eyes!"

He giggles and stares at the floor.

"Welcome to New York! You're a long way from home, lover boy." I know I'm seriously drunk when the pet names just won't stop. STRIPPER TIP #35: Men *love* pet names. I'm just usually laughing too hard to seriously call a man 'Pookie.' But if you can keep a straight face and call a guy 'Pornstar' for an entire night, you're going to be able to retire by next week.

"You know, Baby Blue, I used to live in Australia."

Blue Eyes frowns: "I'm not 'Strayan! I'm from New Zealand!"

"A Kiwi! Oh, how *delicious*," I say with a squeeze of his thigh. Alcohol. It makes enterprising sluts sluttier and therefore even more enterprising.

Blue Eyes wants to go to the Champagne Room.

Sitting on the couch, he reaches into his pocket, and pulls out six crisp one-hundred-dollar bills. With a quick glance to his wallet, it is clear that there is plenty more where they came from. I take

278

three, and the host takes the other three. Just as the host is out of view, a waitress pops her head in the door with a cheerful grin: "Hi, baby! What sort of champagne are we having?"

I am on the brink of chronic hiccups, but if I shoo her away without pressing Blue Eyes to order, I will be bitched at. With a sigh, I say, "Let's order some Dom Perignon for our Kiwi guest." Blue Eyes smiles. I scratch my nails through his hair and he closes his eyes. STRIPPER TIP #36: If you want to sedate your client without the use of narcotics, rub your hands through his hair and scratch his scalp. Blue Eyes says, "Sure." He forks out four crisp Benjamins and hands them to the waitress.

The waitress closes the door behind her as I dim the lights. Sitting back down beside Blue Eyes, I resume scratching his scalp and getting to know him better.

"So what are you doing here in New York?"

"Business. I trivel most weeks outta ivery month."

"And what do you do for fun?"

"Drink, I giss."

I have about 10 minutes to kill before the champagne arrives.

"You seem athletic," I say, giving his shoulders a squeeze. STRIPPER TIP #37: Always say a man looks athletic, muscular, built, whatever. Always. No matter what. Blue Eyes looks to the ground, bashful. Then he flexes a bicep. "I played a lotta footie in school," he says. "But no time inymore. I work too much."

"Well that's why you're here, Baby Blue. You work hard to play hard." I lean into his shoulder. I'm tired. Drunk and tired.

The bottle of champagne arrives, along with a martini glass brimming with whipped cream and strawberries. The waitress pops the bottle of Dom, and we make a toast. I take a sip, and it tastes like work.

Twenty minutes remain to loll around and giggle and try to get Blue Eyes to spend some more. He pulls me onto his lap, and we chat about his travels.

"Can I have your air miles?" I ask, discreetly checking my watch. Five minutes left. I stand up, take my dress off, and start the sexiest lap dance of all time. This is what you reserve all your energy for: The grand finale, to ensure that it will not be the grand finale. I bite my lip, grind my ass into his cock, which is springing to life under his slacks, and convulse on his lap. Blue Eyes is horny and paying attention.

Casually, and with Blue Eyes watching my moves, I glance back to my watch. "Oh no, Blue Eyes! That man with the clipboard is going to come back and tell us our time is up!" Blue Eyes is breathing heavily. "Can we stay?" I ask, batting my lashes.

"Yiss. Let's stay." Blue Eyes reaches into his wallet and hands me $600. Half for me, half to the house. It's just the way it goes. Pimp Tax.

I spend the next half-hour deflecting Blue Eyes' pawing hands, because now he's all turned on and expecting to get his dick wet. I refill his glass of champagne while tipping most of mine back into the bucket. My politics get so grey in this business: I bitch about wasting dish soap, yet I have no qualms dumping nearly an entire bottle of Dom Perignon.

To keep him at least humoured, I give Blue Eyes a haphazard lap dance. My gut feeling is that this won't be an all-night affair, so at this point I'm straining to keep my eyes open and uncrossed. Writhing around on his lap, I smile mischievously to avoid the reality that he is sitting there waiting for me to get off so he can pull his cock out. I continue shimmying about, giggling like a dumbass until we're five minutes from the buzzer.

With three minutes to spare, I take a chance at seeing whether he wants to stay longer. Readjusting my position on his lap, I slip off and onto the couch beside him. Blue Eyes quickly reaches for his fly, and zips it down.

"But baby, we only have a few minutes left!"

Blue Eyes takes my hand and pulls it towards his crotch. "Do your bist."

"Well, sweetheart," I start, pulling my hand out of his expectant grip and resting it on his chest. His heart is beating fast. "The man with the clipboard could come in at any minute!" I look back at my watch. "Oops! Time's up! We even went over time! I hope I don't get into trouble!"

I stand up, reaching for my dress.

"You know," he starts. "It would have been nice to know before I spent $1600 that you wouldn't be sucking my dick."

This is always a very awkward moment. The moment when a client finally realizes he's been had, and you knew it all along. It happens at the end of every private room, and the only thing I can ever fathom doing is to just sit there and act perfectly aloof. They think you're dumb as rocks anyway, so just embody that stereotype to the best of your ability until he leaves. Blinking helps. If I told every man upfront that he wouldn't be getting a blowjob, I'd be straight-up broke.

IF I WASN'T MARRIED, I'D STALK YA!

-Kerr, 47, Scotland

Redneck Vegas

I'm getting good at this hell haze.

It's easier now. I'm more confident. I 'get' it, I'm way more self-assured with my sexuality and ambition; I've also realized that I don't hate men—at least not totally. It's becoming a breeze, making these men open their minds, libidos, and wallets. I'm having fun and feeling sexy as hell.
I don't have the beginner's luck that I used to, but I have the confidence, the know-how, and all that other shit you get good at because TIME.

***

Jameson, Bunny, and I have worked alongside each other at the Catwalk for a while now. It's hard to say how long, given the fact that it's probably been longer than any of us care to admit. We belong to the English-speaking tribe, but each opt for the lone-wolf approach to hustling. We've all been burned by colleagues before and just want to make some drama-free money. So we nod respectfully to one another, and press on with calming the nerves of overworked financiers over glasses of shitty champagne and wrist touches of reassurance and flirtation.

But then one night, Bunny walks up to me and asks, "Anna, do you want to make out with me for a customer?" Bunny is totally hot and a non-smoker, so I say, "Sure," and follow her through the velvet labyrinth to the very last private room at the end of the hall. This room is twice the size of the rest of the rooms. It's where the guys with preferential treatment enjoy the pleasure of our company. It's just as lame as the other rooms, but since it's bigger, it's better. I always feel like the stakes are higher when I'm in this room—and sometimes they are—but mostly they are not, and the client usually just feels more entitled and is therefore less likely to tip. Being the optimist that I am, I hope this makeout with Bunny will result with the former.

With a giggle and tug on my wrist, she introduces me as "her girlfriend" to a guy named Sam. We proceed to earn a ton of money by feeding each other a porterhouse steak with our bare hands. As we use our canines to theatrically tear and gnaw the bloody meat off the bone with a growl, Sam drools in the corner. Reaching for a shrimp, I lift it, heavy and dripping in garlic butter, and slap it against Bunny's cheek before sloppily pushing it into her mouth. Bunny circles her lip with the tip of the shrimp, getting her mouth all garlicky, giving the best face[58] I've ever seen to Sam, who is losing it in the corner. You haven't seen a kid smile in a candy store until you've seen a guy watch a girl give a blowjob to a shrimp. STRIPPER TIP #38: Find whatever you can that looks like a penis, a.k.a. just about anything, and use it to draw attention to your mouth.

Bunny and I label ourselves The Ravenous Blondes and vow to work together again.

Sam the Foodie returns the following week for a repeat performance of shrimp scampi, during which we sensuously discuss farmers markets through bites of strip-club pub grub, pretending it's Michelin-rated fine cuisine.

---

[58] Face: Dick-sucking face/pussy-eating face. If you don't know what this is, go educate yourself right fucking NOW and look at some porn. Then perform it every time you're going down on a worthy subject (ideally, the subject is always worthy).

Drunk and full, Bunny and I emerge from the private room and follow our ears to a sing-song of *Happy Birthday* for Jameson, our super-hot colleague, who is perched at the bar. A cake is placed in front of her while a man in a crisp shirt and a fresh shave refills her glass of Krug. Her bronzed, endless legs fold into a perfectly poised dangle as she smiles like Marilyn Monroe: chin up, eyes down. STRIPPER TIP #39: If you can master the Marilyn smile without looking totally Xanaxed out, use it sparingly. It's extremely powerful, but also very identifiable. Every woman in the fucking world fancies herself a Marilyn. Because we are. But we're also so fucking not, so don't make yourself look like a basic bitch.

But Jameson could never look like an ass. She's mesmerizing. With a quick glance, Bunny and I wordlessly agree that this birthday girl is equal parts intimidating and hot. As we atonally sing the final "youuuuuu," Jameson blows out the candles and plunges her perfectly manicured hand through the haphazardly scrawled 'Jameson,' in shiny red icing. She looks to Bunny and me, and says, "Sometimes you just need to have your hands in the cake."

Jameson winks at me, picking up a fistful of cheesecake. Her sultry smile hardens into a menacing one as she squeezes the cake and watches it ooze through her fingers. I blush.

As it turns out, Jameson is Canadian, which basically just means generally hotter than most people, yet really easy-going. She's an artist, an Aquarius (read: cultured bitch), and an illegal alien (like me!). When she reveals to Bunny and me that she's two years shy of forty, we shit ourselves, then ask what beauty products she uses.

Now we're three besties en route to Redneck Vegas.

***

Las Vegas is Mecca for strippers. The glitz, the glam, the trashiness, and the oxygen pumping into the clubs and casinos has everyone feeling sexy even after losing all their money to a computer and barfing into a trash can for the second time that night. It's where strippers go to live out their girlhood fantasy of being the ultimate Showgirl: Poolside all day, money-making all night. At least once a year, every stripper I know makes the pilgrimage to Sin City to restock on slut apparel and earn a banana chip[59]... or 10.

But to work in Las Vegas, I need a stripper's permit from the Sheriff. To get one of those, I need a green card. I don't have a green card yet[60]. For those of us without green cards, there is Myrtle Beach, South Carolina, also known as Redneck Vegas. It's where men go to golf and women go to entertain them after the 18th hole. If you are not a golfer or a stripper, **do not ever go there.**

Waking at the crack of dawn, we pack our things into Bunny's champagne-coloured Jetta and hop on the I-95. Jameson cuddles in the back seat with Kudo, her gentle-spirited, long-haired chihuahua. They nap for most of the morning, waking only to swap her Celine sunglasses for her Tom Fords. Bunny prattles about the lingerie store she is in the throes of opening.

"This week better be fucking good because I need to put it all toward inventory." Checking her mirrors, she veers into the passing lane and presses her bare foot on the accelerator.

"You didn't get a loan?" I ask, fishing through a bag of candy in search of a pink Starburst.

"Nope, didn't need one thanks to these babies," she says, cupping her boob and giving it an affectionate squeeze.

After 12 hours and three McDonalds breaks, the Jetta cruises down the North Myrtle Beach strip: fast food, obscene mini-golf courses, shitty steakhouses, and discount beachwear stores boasting confederate flag bikinis in the windows. This is The South.

Turning in to the only hotel in town that accepts dogs, Bunny swings around to the front entrance. We can't pull up to the

---

[59] Banana chip: A yellow poker chip valued at $1000.
[60] I asked Kryptonite to marry me and she said yes. Surrounded by our family and friends, we tied the knot at City Hall, fed each other cake, and are waiting on that magic piece of legitimizing laminate.

lobby; the driveway is lined with Harley-Davidsons. Each bike is accompanied by a Bret Michaels doppelganger. They all stare as Bunny makes an attempt at parking amidst the chrome and trailers.

"Welcome to Bike Week, ladies!" screeches one, revving his hog as we step out of the car in our maxi dresses.

"Bike week?" Bunny furrows her brow. She looks over at me with daggers in her crystal-blue eyes: "I thought you said it was *golf season*!"

"It's still golf season …" I look around and see nothing but Harleys. No souped up golf carts or beige Lexus SUVs. "The internet *said* it was golf season."

As Kudo finds a private bush to take his long-awaited shit, Jameson turns to me, lowering her designer shades to the bridge of her perfectly straight nose: "The *internet* told you."

We almost didn't go on this trip; I was the one who begged and pleaded with them to join me. And now I brought them all this way to Bike Week.

My experiences with bikers have gone something like this:

"Hey, baby," smiles a bearded man with leather chaps and weathered skin. "Now aren't you a treat. But tell me, where are your tattoos?" Using his calloused meat hook of a hand, he grabs my hip to turn me around.

"Would you put a bumper sticker on a Ferrari?" I sass.

"Well, I'll tell you what kinda tattoo you need. You need a Christmas tree on your left thigh, and a turkey on your right thigh."

"And why is that?"

"SO THERE IS ALWAYS SOMETHING TO EAT BETWEEN CHRISTMAS AND THANKSGIVING!"

A roar of laughter ensues. Every biker and every stripper has heard this joke a thousand times. The strippers never laugh and the bikers always do. Bikers talk a lot about eating pussy. Old men with facial hair always do. One thing bikers don't do is tip, or get lap dances. I just led these babes into a trap with 300,000 men who want free mustache rides. I am an asshole. I am probably about to lose the only strippers in America I can call 'friends.'

The internet *also* told me the club is a beautifully decorated free-for-all with an ATM built into the ceiling. But I haven't spoken to any girl who has danced here before, so for all I know I may also be leading us into a human-trafficking ring.

Piling several suitcases onto a single bellhop trolley with two functioning wheels, we push our luggage to room 214: our home address for the next 10 days. Scattering kimonos, scarves, shoes, and makeup bags across the room, we deem it 'lived-in,' and flop onto the beds, falling asleep to *Southern Fried Homicide*, which is a really good show on the ID channel[61].

If you're the kind of stripper who rolls in a pack, you have to be wary of your pack's first impression at a new club. If a manager likes one dancer and not the other, he knows better than to cause a rift between the aspiring recruits, and turns them both down. And even if he does like you, he might turn you down anyway because cliques are bitchy and prone to bully other dancers. Cliques fuck shit up. Cliques are terrible for everyone except for the members that comprise it.

So our clique has devised a plan: I'm going to audition first, and Bunny and Jameson will wait for my signal—a 'thumbs-up' emoji via text message—to come in once I've been hired (read: deemed 'hot enough' by a fat old man in a cheap suit).

*** *

---

[61] 'ID' stands for Investigation Discovery. It is Jameson's favourite cable TV channel. Some other shows she really likes are *Who the (Bleep) Did I Marry?*, *Deadly Women*, and *Blood, Lies, and Alibis*.

288

A minivan squeezes past the Harleys and a staunch, balding man in an oversized grey t-shirt steps out from behind the wheel. This is my cab driver.

"Hello, there, baby!"

"Haaaah," I beam back, trying on a Southern belle accent. Before I reach for the handle of the sliding door, he opens the passenger door.

"Hop up front, sweetheart. Ah ain't gone baat you!"

This is not New York. I can't rudely get in the back and look at my phone the whole time while he listens to NPR up front. This is The South. Everybody always be talkin', but not sayin much o' nothin.'

"Will you please take me to Kittens?"

"Yes ma'am!"

"So what do you know about this place?" I ask. Since all of my research has been so poorly conducted and wrong, it's time to ask a local. And cab drivers know everything.

"Well, ah tell you—them girls make a lotta money there. One taaam ah knew a girl, she made twenty faaave G's in a week cuz one o' them PGA[62] guys came in an' spent the whole naate in the Jacuzzi room."

"There's a Jacuzzi room?"

"Yes ma'am! Y'all get all soapy and sudsy with them golfers and you go come back 'n buy me a cheeseburger, y'hear?"

"You mean the girls get *in* the Jacuzzi with the customers … or they just watch … from a distance?" I'm crossing my fingers

---

[62] PGA: The snoozefest known as the Professional Golfer's Association of America

289

that the Jacuzzi room is in this way reminiscent of my Sydney shower show days of yore.

"Well nah apparently they give them guys sum shorts 'er sumthin … but when yer chargin' a thousand dallars an'err do you care if y'gone get a lil wet? Don't worry blondie, they gone love you. What's yer name, sweetheart?"

I pick the blondest, bimbo-next-door name I can think of:

"Holly."

"Holly! Nass ta meetchoo, Holly. Ah'm Dwayne."

Dwayne nods with a smile as he turns into the Kittens parking lot.

"Nah, ah'm gone make you an offer, Miss Holly. You call me every naat you need a lift to an from Kittens. Ah won't run the meter. Ah make it a flat rate o' tin dallars."

I look at the meter, which is running at 16 dollars as Dwayne puts the van in park. "We have a deal, Dwayne."

Dwayne opens my door, takes my bag, and using his free hand, points a finger at me: "Nah ya gotta call me, y'hear?"

***

The Southern pace of things at this club has me wishing I brought *War and Peace* with me to bide my time. After sitting around in a dressing room for several hours waiting to "complete my dancer profile," I finally signal to Bunny and Jameson to make their way over. The actual completing of the 'profile' is so the at-home viewers can learn a little something about us while we are dancing on stage. 'At-home-viewing' is one of the many dollhouse gimmicks[63]: There is a camera on the stage that live-feeds onto the club's splash site. I've been at this too long to care if someone's dad sees me.

Or even my own dad. We're not that close, so it was easy to tell him over a sushi lunch one day:
"I'm a stripper."

"Oh. Well, I'm pretty liberal-minded. That must be lucrative."

It was awkward, but so are most of our visits nowadays. Men who have offspring aren't always Fathers. Sometimes they are just people who gave you some pretty good genes whom you have to forgive for being so profoundly insecure, selfish, and absent. I usually avoid telling men of a certain age that I'm a dancer. It's the demographic I have the hardest time reasoning with unless I'm in character. They just seem old, faraway, and emotionally retarded with no ability or desire to see women as autonomous and empowered by the very box their species put me in. It's almost like this reverse-objectification. I only see men of a certain age and pedigree as Johns.

Nowadays, as I realize that I don't actually hate men as much as I once thought I did, I'm trying to undo this knee-jerk screening process. Yet I still kind of revel in the discomfort it causes among them. I'm a work in progress.

"Usually I just make the stuff up," the house mom says, tapping on a keyboard using only her index fingers. Tall and robust, with flaming red hair, she fills out a questionnaire that asks questions about things such as 'sexual preference' and 'favorite position.' Without asking me for my input, she types "straight," and then "on top." I decide not to correct her; labels have become pretty dated, limited, and confusing since I started doing this, anyway.

She looks me up and down. "Now you look like you could be one o' those animal doctors," she says, and then proceeds to

---

[63] Every strip club has a gimmick: Kittens has a Jacuzzi; The Fish Bowl has massage chairs; Sydney clubs have Shower Shows; New Zealand has hula hoops; The Catwalk offers body sushi; etc., etc.

type in "V-E-T-E-R-I-N-A-R-I-A-N" with the speed of an arthritic manatee.

The dancer profile is complete when I sign a waiver stating that I am a porn star. In America, being filmed while performing on stage and in underwear is considered pornography. Every dancer that will ever work at Kittens is therefore a federally documented porn star. Having never—to my knowledge—made a sex tape, I'm excited for this new feather in my cap!

"Nah, y'all're gone get a cheque in the mail whenever they tip y'all from the ATM, kay? So when that fake money comes blowin' out the machine, don't go pickin' it up. It's worth nothin."

I will understand what the house mom is talking about later. If a guy tips from the comfort of his laptop and box of tissues, the 'ATM' goes buck wild and makes it rain Funny Money onto the stage. Thankfully we are spared the most embarrassing part, which is picking each individual dollar up. We get a cheque in the mail! For being porn stars!

***

Kittens is one of those clubs where you sit around and chain smoke for the first four hours of your shift, and then by the time you're tired and bored and ready to throw the towel in, money is being thrown at you just to stop and smile at someone. For the non-chain-smokers, we spend this time fighting off headaches.

By the time Bunny and Jameson complete their profiles and trot onto the main floor, the club is packed with cigar smoke, bikers, and … golfers! By some grace of the goddess, there are golfers who, like myself, didn't get the Bike Week memo. In their front-pleated khakis and butter-yellow golf shirts, they line the tipping rail and smile politely.

I fucking hate golf as much as these assholes love it, and I love money just as much as these preps love titties, and it's because of this perfect chemistry that places like Kittens are open every single night of the year.

292

I notice a sprinkle of greasy, bandana-clad gear-heads, but not enough to pay them much heed as I ask married man after married man "to hang out with me." "Do you wanna come hang out with me?" is my new euphemism for "Can I take all of your money while I act like I think you're hot and I want your cock in my ass?"

It's so simple and elusive and *it works so flawlessly.* The less you say about a product, the more people want to buy it.

Myrtle Beach is where the American Man goes to escape his Nagging Wife who is probably at home washing his underwear and feeding his children. He can grope, curse, smoke, and drink to his heart's content, all in the name of the great game of tapping a tiny ball around a rolling landscape of pristine green grass.

After an uncharacteristically enthusiastic table dance, I sit down to catch my breath before I slip my dress back on. But my oxygen intake is promptly fucked as I inhale a thick cloud of cigar smoke instead. I purse my lips as my eyes widen. *I think I'm about to vomit.* Clutching my dress and holding my breath, I search left and right for a space that seems free of swirling clouds of cigar and cigarette smoke. But it's midnight—the witching hour when even the non-smokers are chain smoking. I drop my head between my knees. *Maybe there is some clean air under this chair.*

As a self-righteous non-smoker, I find this fucking disgusting. I'm mortified that I am developing cancer as I live and breathe to make another buck. Everyone is smoking, which keeps everyone drinking and no one ever halting your hustle for "a cigarette break." Smoking indoors is great for my business; no one has to leave, ever. Between the short-order cook and the bathroom attendant, a vacationing man's bases are completely covered. All he has to do is keep spending money.

I take the tail of my gown and cover my mouth. Breathing through the Lycra, I try to filter the smoke, but it's no use: my dress already reeks of sweat, perfume and, yes, smoke.

I don't know how, but I manage not to puke. I fetch myself a bottle of water, and cower in a corner to regain my composure.

293

Sixty seconds pass and I get back to work. There are so many more guys who want to 'hang out with me' and I only have four hours to milk them all dry.

Everything stinks. My hair smells like an ashtray. I feel disgusting. Filthy and rich.

Bunny and Jameson, accustomed to the New York straight-talking, big-spender hustle, have a harder time getting adjusted to the wham-bam of lap dance upon lap dance.

"I just don't get it. These Wallets[64] are so … backwards. They call us 'ma'am,' but won't even buy us a drink!" Bunny leans against a wall in a huff while Jameson lights up a cigarette.

"I think these guys really need to be steered," I offer, popping my fourth and fifth Extra-Strength Advil to keep the headaches at bay. "You have to discretely steer the boat from from the stern while handing the Wallet a tiny paddle and letting him think he's navigating from the bow."

Bunny and Jameson politely listen to my theory, but ultimately they're just annoyed.

"And, if you act really dumb while you do it, they won't think you're hustling them. They'll just think you're dumb! There is something men find utterly irresistible about dumb chicks." I look at myself in the mirror. My hot pink lips match my hot pink dress and I look like Bubble Gum Barbie. "When you wear hot pink, no one takes you seriously. DO YOU KNOW HOW LIBERATING THAT IS? It gives you licence to be completely fucking ridiculous."

"But I hate acting dumb," Jameson says, lighting up another cigarette and quickly exhaling. "I'm not an actress. I'm sensual. I'm sensitive. 'Dumb' isn't my game."

"But this job is about entertaining people and giving them what they want," Bunny offers with a nod. "And sometimes you need to act ridiculous; you need to tap into the ridiculous girl in you.

---

[64] Wallet: A client.

We can't appeal to everyone. And if you're not exactly what they're looking for, you can't take it personally."

"But I'm a *person*. So how can I not take it *personally*?"

Jameson is the most sincere of all of us. She is sensitive and kind and the love she gives to the men who walk in here get the best of her. Her kindness is real and comes from a genuine place. This is beautiful, but from where I'm standing, it also looks dangerous.

In many ways I don't know where Jacq ends and Holly-Iris-Chloe-Anna begins, but I do know this: unless you are sincerely an asshole, in the business of smoke and mirrors, there is little room for sincerity. Polite, candid, and nice—fine. But if you walk onto that stage with an open heart, you may as well be facing a firing squad.

Jameson leaves our huddle, pushing her shoulders back, fumbling with her cigarette case.

"I just wish she knew how fucking hot she was," Bunny says. "If I looked like Jameson, I'd be ruling the world—when I wasn't constantly trying to have sex with myself."

We bob our heads in unison and plot to lift Jameson's spirits after work. But before we can adequately plan a drive-thru scavenger hunt of every fast-food joint between Kittens and our hotel, Jameson walks past us again, this time arm in arm with a soft-looking man in a faded black t-shirt and cargo pants. They are going to the Jacuzzi room. For three hours.

There are as many ways to go about the hustle as there are hustlers. And once in a blue moon, a man in cargo pants has a black Amex.

Bunny nabs a guy to take to the back, and I follow suit. A redneck golfer in shower shoes asks me: "How much is it for you an ah to go to the back room now, Miss Holly?"

"It's 400 for half an hour, sweetheart." This club is great because you can charge a client whatever the fuck you want. There is a minimum, but every new guy is a new opportunity to milk him for all that you think he can afford. The minimum charge for a 30-minute room is $350. Given this man's penchant for paying thousands upon thousands of dollars to drive around in a tiny car chasing an even tinier ball, I am thinking I can extract a few extra bucks out of him. But his shower shoes have me completely thrown off.

"400 dollars!?" Shower Shoes' voice cracks. "That's too much."

"It's worth it, baby." I reply, tracing a finger along his collar. "I promise ... you *won't* be disappointed."

The truth is that he will absolutely disappointed. This makes me a liar, and him a fool. Or maybe this just makes me a woman, and him a man. Or me a stripper, and him a client.

"All right, Miss Holly, let's go."

And it's that easy.

STRIPPER TIP #40: If a man is complaining about the the price from the get-go, he's probably not going to tip or pay for a subsequent half-hour of your resplendently undivided attention. Most strip clubs' private-room payment policies are the same: pay upfront, no refunds. This means you can basically do the Roger Rabbit[65] or talk about *General Hospital* for 30 minutes. But judging by the fap noise I hear coming from the next room, not all dancers understand this.

"Just relax, darling." I sit Shower Shoes on the couch, taking his probing hand into mine and giving it a gentle squeeze.

"Relax? Fer 400 dallars, Imma put my penis in you one way or another!"

After 3- minutes of a sporadic lap dance, chitchat, and time-wasting sips of shitty complimentary bubbly, I slip back into my dress. Shower Shoes gets up, hastily stares down at his half-

---

[65] The Roger Rabbit: A nineties dance move that is like running man in reverse. It's a dope-ass dance move. One thing it is not is 'sexy.'

chub, and says to me with his arms out to his sides, palms raised to the heavens: "Now that was the worst 400 dallars I e'er spent!"

As we leave the room, Shower Shoes returns to his posse of similarly dressed buddies and I make for Bunny, who sits by the bar, counting her money and sipping on a pink cocktail.

"Oh my god Anna—Jacq—fuck … *HOLLY*—I just had the most annoying room ever. FIRST he wanted to pay only a hundred for 15 minutes, and then as soon as we got in there he's kicking his shoes off and pulling at my panties, literally trying to *rip them off.* I was like, 'Oh no, sweetheart, I can't take my panties off!' and he responds with, 'Well, then how am I supposed to fuck you?' and with his shoes still off, he frowns, asking me, '*You are gonna fuck me, right*?' "

Bunny purses her powder-pink lips around her bendy straw, and takes a long drag while rolling her eyes. "I mean, if *he* thinks he gets to fuck *me* for a hundred dollars, these rednecks are even dumber than I thought." She flips her hair, stands up, and bounces off toward her next customer.

Strippers get all sorts of propositions regarding sex and will they take part in it for a small or large (usually small) fee, offering, donation, or exchange. One guy offered to buy me a laptop, while another tried to bribe me with "room service at The Ritz in White Plains."[66] I don't really get offended by the propositioning anymore. I don't really know that I ever did; if anything, it's just curious. It's curious to me because I wonder how much they believe 'sex' to be worth.
 I know their dicks want to fuck me—that's why they walked into the joint. What is curious, though, is how much they think it should cost. Every individual is different, depending on the city, the country, their religious beliefs, salary, age, etc. Younger guys seem eager to ask, but never willing to pay. Maybe they are just as curious as I am. Hot guys never want to pay, while the less-attractive ones tend to be sheepish in the query. Some

---

[66] White Plains is where you never go unless you live in Westchester. The Ritz in White Plains is for the residents of Westchester who are desperately trying to spice things up with their spouse of 28 years.

just want affirmation of their belief that I'm a whore, that all women are whores, that their mothers were terrible, and that all women are evil, scheming hussies.

Where prostitution is illegal, the numbers fluctuate in a different way, taking on a whole new meaning. Someone somewhere down the line told me that the rule of thumb in sex work is never to fuck for less than your rent. Living in New York, Sydney, and Melbourne, where my rent always pushes a grand, I always liked the sound of that. But the scope of sex work would look a lot different if every prostitute actually paid off his or her rent with an hour's work. All I know is that it's not simple. Plus, I don't know the cost of rent down here.

South Carolina is bible-thumping territory, with a relatively low cost of living and a seriously retrograde idea of sex positivity (I think Yanks call it 'slut-shamey,' 'hateful,' and 'misogynist;' Southerners call it 'traditional'). Wouldn't that make sex more expensive since it's so taboo? But it doesn't. It makes sex cheaper.

And yet Myrtle Beach is the alleged 'Redneck Vegas …' Sin City of the South—yeehaw! So what does all this mean for the value of a fuck? I can't answer that, because I'm not going to fuck this guy; I just don't want to, and I don't need to, either. And if I were to explicitly ask, point blank, *what would you pay to put your dick in me?*, I could get busted for prostitution, which would in turn get me deported.

Sex is a commodity, but like all the best commodities (cocaine, organs, moonshine), it's illegal.
The most I've ever been offered to have sex with someone was $20,000. That was back in Melbourne—where anyone can go to a brothel and pick from a line-up of happy hookers in a safe space.

The least I've been offered is, well, nothing. And it's always by some young banker-type guy who thinks his penis is magic. But then again, I'm pretty sure all men think their dicks are magic. Generally, men a) have the memory span of a goldfish or b) are pathologically optimistic about the possibility that a stripper—or any woman, really—will have sex with them.

The high monetary offers can be tempting. Money is sexy. If a man is handing me a lot of money, I get totally, panty-soppingly turned on. I find this frustrating and SO ANNOYING because I'm like *YES I WANT THIS MONEY AND YOU ARE ATTRACTIVE BECAUSE YOU ARE POWERFUL AND I WANT A PIECE OF YOUR POWER PIE.* But if I give in, I think I might feel shitty afterward. Because it wasn't my idea. I signed up to sell a fantasy. I established these boundaries, and I feel empowered when I work within them.

But sometimes we get into sticky situations, like the time I get the closest I will ever get to sleeping with a john in a club—I jerk a guy off.

Hand jobs are boring. They have always been boring. I know that any attempt I make at a hand job will be a thousand times shittier, less aggressive, and more tedious than the one the dick owner can give himself. So with this knowledge, why even bother?

But it's the end of a painfully slow night, and I finally nab a private room with some boring dude and Chrissie, a silver-tongued stripping veteran who loves Harley-Davidsons and cocaine. The coke makes her sometimes annoying, but mostly just really funny. She is always making other dancers laugh. She also always wears bright green contact lenses. This is my first time teaming up with her in a private room.

The door closes, and after a few pleasantries Chrissie dims the lights so low it's nearly pitch dark. Then she zips down the guy's pants.

Gripping his flaccid penis, she gives the shaft a gentle squeeze. Small and weevily, Penis bounces with a twitch. Chrissie smiles while Penis—who made no mention of wanting this sort of (is it second base?) action—looks down in excited disbelief.

At this point I'm thinking, *Damn, if I'm going to push the envelope with what I'm comfortable doing in this job, can it at least be with a guy who's cool, maybe kind of attractive, with a nice-looking dick?* Fact: of all the boners I've sat on in strip clubs (hundreds … possibly thousands), the average strip-club patron's penis is … smaller than the average penises of my

299

college days. Or maybe it's just because I'm all grown up now. Like how your childhood bedroom, when you revisit it, always seems so much *smaller* than you remember it. The more dicks I am in charge of, the smaller they appear.

But today I don't feel in charge. Chrissie is in charge, and every dancer works differently. Yanking on this guy's dick, Chrissie flips her waist-length wig over a shoulder, and stares me into compliance with her radioactive eyes: *Get your hand on his dick, you deadweight.*

I shift a bit closer to Chrissie and the Penis. *Ugh.* I put my hand around hers. Immediately, I feel depressed and gross: *If I want to step out of my comfort zone, can't I do it because I'm turned on and into it rather than feeling pressured and desperate?*

Tugging away, Chrissie asks Penis, "So, baby … if we take you to the finish line … do we get a tip?"

"Yeah, sure," Penis nods, as men always nod when they're hard and want a woman to shut the fuck up.

Together, we jerk him off. Penis unbuttons the bottom few buttons on his shirt just in time to cum on his belly. He gets up, refastens his belt, and tucks his shirt back in. He hands us each $40 and leaves. No thank you, no goodbye—just two lap dances' worth of a tip. I feel like I used to when I was 19 and my much-older boyfriend would wake me up with his dick in me: undervalued, used and sad.

It's a learning experience. STRIPPER TIP #41: Getting out of the sad funk is easy: become a lesbian, and don't give any more handjobs unless a) you want to, or b) get paid upfront for the amount you feel you deserve.

***

As the smoke finally starts to settle at Kittens around 3:30 a.m., I squint my weary and watering eyes in search of Jameson and Bunny. Dancers and clients are stumbling, avoiding direct eye contact—*mustn't let anyone notice that I am indeed too drunk to*

300

drive—as they feel for the exit. I circle the periphery of the main room twice before deciding to give up, and wait for them upstairs in the dressing room.

Clutching the railing, my legs are so spent that I use whatever upper body strength I have to pull myself up the stairs. Weaving though girls peeling off eyelashes and stepping into flip flops, I see a mop of blonde highlights slumped over the vanity in the farthest corner of the room.

"BUNNY?" I place a hand on her shoulder. "ARE YOU OKAY?"

Bunny lifts her head. A huge line streaks across her forehead from the corner of the counter. The purply depth of the indentation tells me she's been here a while.

"How long have you been up here?"

"Oh … I don't know." She blinks slowly.

"What's wrong? Do you need some water?"

"Oh, I'm just so tired. I WISH I were drunk! I'm just not used to all this … *running* around …" She flops her head back down on the vanity. *Thank fuck.* When a fellow dancer is passed out, I always assume the worst: date-rape drugs, theft, tears, misogynist bullies. But it's Bunny's first time dancing outside The Catwalk Club. The Cardiovascular Shit Show takes a certain getting used to. The Catwalk is a pretty relaxing place to work. The money is trickier to earn, but a skillful girl can turn quite a profit. If The Catwalk is like chess, or hunting in the woods, Kittens is like fishing with dynamite.

"You'll find your stride, Bunn." I brush her golden hair from her face and pull her Real Girl clothes out of our locker. "Let's go home." I step out of my platforms. I can hear my feet crack, but I can't feel anything. Handing Bunny her sweatshirt and yoga pants, I ask, "Have you seen Jameson?"

"Nope."

As I smear a baby wipe across my face, Jameson turns the corner, arms outstretched. "I've been looking *everywhere* for you guys!"

Eyes still closed, Bunny raises her eyebrows in acknowledgement.

Fingers curling around a thick stack of cash, Jameson glides toward us like Gloria Swanson, if Gloria Swanson was a raver. "When you introduce yourself as Jameson, there is no hope in hell of ever staying sober." She smiles deliriously and leans against the locker. "I just had the most … exhilarating night."

"With Cargo Pants?"

"Yessss." Jameson traces a blood-red fingernail from her chin down to her cleavage. "He dominated me. It was … fucking … *amazing*." Innocently giddy, she shakes her shoulders and fans through her winnings. "I've never been submissive before." She stares me square in my eyes: "It was fucking HOT."

STRIPPER TIP #42: Stripping isn't just about catering to other people's desires. It's also about discovering the extent of yours. If you are presented with an opportunity (especially a new and exciting one) to enjoy yourself, enjoy yourself!

Jameson and I each take a Bunny arm and lead her down the stairs and out into the parking lot, where Dwayne is waiting for us.

"Nah how y'all pretty ladies doin'?" Dwayne slides our doors closed with a heave-ho and climbs into the driver's seat.

"We're GREAT," Jameson says with a sincere enthusiasm no one else could possibly muster at 4 in the morning.

"Well lemma tell y'all mah naaat was CRAZY. Terrible! It's Friday an one o' my friends who ah drive all over the place calls me an' he TELLS me, 'Hey Dwayne I need a favour.' So he's my friend, an ah ask him 'What y'all need?' An' he's like "Ah need you to go pick me up some pickles fer mah waaf.' An' ahm like FIRST OF ALL: Pickles? Ah don't even EAT pickles so IF ah DID go to the store, ah wouldn't even know what

302

AISLE to git' em in. SECOND OF ALL: IT'S FRIDAY NAAT an ah got shit ta do. THIRD OF ALL: Where's your waaf?' An he's laake 'She's on'er way home!' An' he's askin' ME for PICKLES on a FRIDAY NAAT."

"Can you get us weed?" Jameson asks.

Dwayne raises his eyebrows, checking us both in his rearview mirror.

"Well," he starts.

Suddenly Bunny is wide awake: "Oh please, can you get us some weed?"

"Alraat darlings, 'All see what ah can do."

We hand Dwayne 20 one-dollar bills, and slump back to our room, where we are greeted by a very excited Kudo. His tail wags so much it shakes his entire body. Bunny falls asleep in her clothes on top of the covers while Jameson takes Kudo out to piss on the shiniest Harley he can find.

***

'Mornings'—1 p.m. on Standard Stripper Time—start with a routine trip to Walmart[67] to buy mixed greens and cheese balls, which we eat by the motel pool as the clock strikes 2.

"You know, since we came all this way," Jameson starts, eyeing the peeling yellow paint covering the motel (it looks like a long-abandoned school bus), "We might as well drive to Miami so we can at least experience some sort of *culture* between shifts."

"I would love to go to Miami! Then at least I wouldn't feel so out of place wearing this bikini," says Bunny, who turns over to show her practically bare ass: she prefers the g-string tan-line look.

---

[67] Tragically, Walmart is the only establishment in Myrtle Beach where one can buy fresh produce.

"Yeah, there's a Dali exhibit there that I'd love to see," Jameson adds.

"Dolly?" My ears perk up. "Dolly Parton? I LOVE HER."

"No ... *Salvador* Dali." Jameson says, deadpan.

"Oh." I turn my head back to optimal even-tanned position. "That's cool, too."

"The guys would be so much hotter in Miami," Bunny says, spritzing tanning oil on her ass. "I mean, I'm pretty sure any man anywhere else is hotter than the guys here. The only thing that some of these golfers have going for them is that they are Southern gentlemen. But my mother always told me that 'a gentleman is just a patient wolf,' so fuck that." She lies back down, glistening. "I really hope Dwayne finds us that weed."

"Me too." Jameson reaches for the oil.

"Yeah," I agree, lifting a cheese ball to my mouth. Wiping orange dust on the white motel towel, I squeeze some SPF 80 into my hand, and smear it over my prickly shins. "You know ... for all this time I've been stripping, not once have I ever properly, thoroughly shaved my legs."

"I just tell them, 'go with the grain,' " Jameson says. "It's not like they come in with a fresh shave for us."

Bunny giggles mischievously: "Sometimes guys feel my leg stubble and I say, 'Ooh, that felt so good, you gave me goosebumps!" STRIPPER TIP #43: No matter what a customer says, you have to "Yes AND" him. Example: A man no younger than 65 once told me, while sitting dollarlessly up front in Pervert Row, "You look like you enjoy anal sex." To which I replied, "It's my favourite. It's how I like to start every time. No preamble with the pussy, no lube. Just dry, hard, painful ANAL. It helps loosen my bowels when I'm constipated!" He ended up getting a dance after my set. Another time a guy asked me, "Why aren't you an actress or a comedian?" To which I replied: "1. I am both, but 2. I'd rather not be perpetually unemployed.

Stripping is basically the highest-paid improv acting gig you can find."

As soon as we turn over to bronze our bellies, it's time to wash the stink out of our hair and head back to the club for another night of smokey mayem. It's probably best that we're not in Miami, as working back-to-back shifts leaves hardly any time for exploring any of the thousand miniature golf courses dotting the strip between our school-bus squat and Kittens.

When Dwayne drops us off the sun is still blaring, high in the sky. "Nah ladies, ahm gone FIND you that weed, come heller haah water, y'hear?"

Staring at the blue door, it feels like we just left. Because we did. Being the new girls means we have to show up for the happy-hour shift. Management welcomes dancers to the all-night challenge. To make it through to peak hour on our fourth consecutive night, I've brought with me some over-the-counter Adderall derivative I picked up in Mexico a few months back[68].

As we pass through the doors, Jameson lights up a bitch stick. Bunny and I pop Advils.

Adderall is the ultimate enabler. It lasts for about eight hours, and in those eight hours I am the most efficient and productive human being to ever exist. Adderall is also fun to take recreationally. But here's the thing: at work, I use drugs with purpose, not for play. I don't like to be wasteful with my drugs *or* my brain cells. So before I take anything, I need to *know* that it will be useful. But how do I know if I'm going to need drugs when it comes time to take them? It's not like coke, where you do a bump and an hour later you kind of hate yourself but at least you're not high any more—when you pop Adderall, you're committing to eight hours of focus and unbridled ambition. This one time I popped a Dexedrine[69] thinking it would be a really

---

[68] I went to Mexico to hang out with some fellow drifters and try my hand at LSD. It didn't go so well.

[69] Dexedrine: like Adderall but even more cracky. No fucking idea re: its initial use.

busy night and NO ONE showed up for some reason I can't remember because I was too busy licking my teeth. What an embarrassing waste THAT was.

So I have this Mexican speed and I don't know whether to take it or not. Will I even need it? It IS day number four, it IS Saturday, and I refuse to not make money because of exhaustion and sleep deprivation. As the clock strikes 8, I down the little pill.

***

Prance, wiggle, shimmy, and grind.

"You're good for breeding,"

"Why thank you, baby! I've got a mind for business and a body for sin. Let's go for a dance!"

"You almost gave me a heart attack! That was AWESOME!"

Twenties, fifties, hundreds. A grope, a profit, repeat. Having my ass grabbed for 20 bucks feels better than being cat-called for free. Money makes me feel more powerful than pretending it's not happening and continuing on with my daily errands. I acknowledge that my feminism is getting pretty convoluted and fucked up, but I feel like it's the most honest and true feminism I've ever known and felt; I scour for my next twenty. Twenty dollars doesn't seem like a lot of money, but it is when you multiply it by every man of legal age in the South.

The Mexican speed hit me like the dose of motivation I felt at 15 in AP history class: I'm unstoppable. The focus I felt on my first day of getting naked has returned to me, only now I have the wherewithal to know how to use it. For the next eight hours I am the most efficient hustler I've ever known myself to be.

I blink, and it's 4:30 in the morning.

I'm striding ahead but my wrist yanks in the other direction: "Holly!" Jameson pulls me to the side as a parade of wilted dancers file to the dressing room. "It's time to go, babe. Only the creepers wanting to pay with quarters are still standing."

306

"Quarters are great for the laundromat!"

Jameson laughs, my wrist still in her hand. Her hand on my shoulder, we fall in line, climb the stairs, pick up Bunny— asleep, again, in the dressing room—and make for the parking lot.

Dwayne spills out of his van like bag of Skittles. "Nah how did Seeterday naat treat y'all?"

"Good," we all chime, entertained, but tired. The Mexican speed is finally wearing off.

Rounding the minivan, Dwayne opens each of our doors. Climbing in last, his eyebrows dance as he confesses: "Ah got a surprise fer y'all!"

In one fell swoop, Dwayne slams his door closed and throws a crumpled dollar bill over his shoulder and into Jameson's lap.

"IS THAT WEED?" Bunny asks from the back seat.

"IT'S A ROCK!" Dwayne screams, pumping his fist. "An lemme tell you it wuddn't easy gettin' over here! There were some cops an dogs roamin' up an' down the Hooters parkin' lot where all the baahkers're hangin an lemme tell you, ah was shittin' Twinkies!"

Carefully opening the bill, Jameson silently mouths "WHAT THE FUCK," as she unearths what looks like a twelve-sided sugar cube.

Bunny peeks between our two captain seats, and under her breath, says, "How could this possibly serve as a stand-in for marijuana?"

"Nah, y'all, it's hard ta faaahnd weed in these parts. We already slow enough daaahn saaahhth. But I KNOW Y'ALL CAN 'PRECIATE A GOOD ROCK WHEN YA SEE ONE! Ah mean, it ain't Tiffanys but … it's a helluva lot more fun now, ain't it!" Dwayne cranks the late-night country station, and plays some rendition of *Chopsticks* on the steering wheel. "Man, am I ever feelin' like takin' a dip in a Jacuzzi!"

Bunny is visibly disappointed and mortified. Bunny is the Stoner Princess of Long Island, and not the Cocaine Queen of Manhattan (that's Jameson). I guess that makes me the MDMA Witch of Williamsburg? But enough with the nicknames: Dwayne just dumped a chunk of mysterious contraband into our laps. We all know there is no such thing as a free lunch. When men give you drugs they usually want something in return.

Jameson flips her hair assertively. Under her breath, she assures us, "He's just trying to impress us." Bunny flops back in the seat, and Jameson smiles at me with a shrug. "Thank you, Dwayne, sweetheart. You're a *true* Southern gentleman. It's so charming to us city girls."

Like the polite houseguests that we are, Jameson and I scratch off some of the rock onto the ditch of our thumbs and do some of Dwayne's drugs. Bunny stares in disbelief, and shakes her head when we pass it to her.

Snorting my nostril to the back of my hand, I feel a sting-burn of what I can only imagine to be freeze-dried Windex. My eyes water and widen. I look over to Jameson, who is holding back a sneer of hilarious disgust.

"Nah y'all ladies have a good naat!" Dwayne brushes his nose with his index finger, and smiles. "All see ya'll tahmarrah."

Dwayne peels off into the night as Jameson and I stand in the parking lot, stunned. Bunny is already halfway down the hallway.

"That was not cocaine. That was not even *close* to cocaine," I say to Jameson as Kudo circles the Jetta in search of a place to shit in peace. I grind my teeth and stare at my phone. It buzzes. Dwayne has sent us a photo of his balding head peeking out of the froth of a Jacuzzi.

"He looks like a steaming hot dog!" Jameson cackles. "These drugs are fucked up. I am way too cracked out for my own well-being."

308

And as if there were a level of acceptable cracked-outness, we smooth out the one-dollar bill, and flush the sugar cube's remains. An intense conversation about something riveting that I will never remember ensues. Eventually, we fall asleep.

***

Our last night at Kittens begins with the three of us dragging our feet through the blue door, up the stairs and slumping into the corner of the club we have adopted as ours. It's the homestretch of the Redneck Vegas leg of our tour as international babes of mystery, and we're beat.

I strain to keep my eyes open, but refuse to pop another one of my Mexican enabler pills. A gaggle of *Duck Dynasty* plebeians crowd around a table next to ours.

When a group of pigs come in, common practice is for dancers to scatter—in such crises, every woman must fend for herself. Bunny dodges left while Jameson beelines toward the bathroom. Swinging my arms to gain momentum so that I can reach the opposite end of the room, I notice a broad-shouldered man with a brush cut and red t-shirt. He is alone in a dark corner by the service bar, smiling. Men who sit in corners at strip clubs usually have some sort of connection to management (read: they want freebies all the time STRIPPER TIP #44: Any man who says he knows the owner is not going to pay you shit. Always be polit, and always, ALWAYS walk away).

"You look way too happy to work here," I say, slowing down my stride.

"Oh. I don't work here … I just like to be out o' the ruckus." He smiles broader, and this odd aura of sincerity beams back at me. I take a seat next to him. "Name's Keith," he says, offering out his sturdy hand.

"Holly," I say, meeting a firm and friendly shake.

"May I offer you a drink?"

"You may!"

"Anything you want."

LIFE TIP: EVERYONE LOVES TO HEAR THESE THREE WORDS MORE THAN THE OTHER THREE WORDS

By the time we finally get the attention of one of the waitresses, I ask for "a vodka soda, please." I flip my fair. "Make it a double."

"A double?" Keith asks.

You know you're a veteran stripper when your first drink of the night is a double.

"How long did it take you to get that Bud Light?"

"Too long," Keith says with a nod.

"Exactly. I'm not waiting another 20 minutes for a watered-down beverage, and if I started worrying what you'll think of me now, then I wouldn't be cut out for this type of job, would I?"

Keith makes a valiant effort at keeping my doubles topped as we huddle in the dark corner, avoiding the clouds of smoke and throngs of drunk bikers who seem particularly hell-bent on talking shit to each girl who deigns to approach them.

"Those guys are somethin' else," Keith says with a headshake of disdain. "See, I like comin' to these places, but you don't have to be a dick."

Keith's words are simple yet somehow profound.

"I just like it. I dunno. I just like it. And I got a daughter, y'know. She's 12 now."

Keith is one of those Hank Moody types who is in love with his ex-wife but is too much of a shit (or something) to actually be with her. He loves women and doesn't seem afraid of them.

"You must have a lot of sisters," I smack.

310

"Six."

"I could swing a bloody tampon around and you'd tell me to aim it at your belly button, wouldn't you?"

"I'd paint a target on a white t-shirt just for you, darlin'."

WHY ARE MEN WHO ARE UNFAZED BY MENSES SO ATTRACTIVE?

Keith is fun and feminist and he smiles a lot. I see these types a lot, who are fun to be around, but they either don't have the money or they see me as too disarmingly 'real' to feel like they could support my business. So when I invite Keith to a private room for 600 big ones, I'm flabbergasted when he says, "Well, I'd love that, Holly."

STRIPPER TIP #45: YOU NEVER FUCKING KNOW. As Sophie put it, "every fucking cool opportunity either LANDS IN YOUR LAP or requires seven degrees and 8000 blowjobs to obtain."

Of course I can't act flabbergasted. I have to maintain sweet, smooth and coy. Because even if I feel natural, comfortable and connected to someone, I'm still working.

"Now tell me, what are you doing here?" Keith asks as I peel off my dress and straddle his lap. I lean in close and grind my hips.

"Because this is as close as I can get to Vegas."

"I mean all the way from Alberta, Canada, and now here—at the Shoe Show[70]?"

Flipping around, I sit on his lap, leaning my back into his chest. "This question is condescending, Keith."

---

[70] The Shoe Show: Girls parading around in shoes, and nothing else. A code name men use when referring to strip clubs. Another popular code name is "The Ballet."

"I can see how that could be true," he says, reaching for his Bud Light.

"It's also trite and annoying." I bounce on his lap with a witchy cackle as I feel his cock get harder under my thigh. I take his beer out of his hand, and place it on the side table. I rise to my feet. "If you enjoy this place so much, Keith, why can't I?" Balancing on my left foot, I raise my right leg and slowly press a knee into his panting chest. "Men are always going to be buying into the beaver show,[71]" I add, pressing harder and biting my lip. "I'm just figuring out how to participate while coming out on top."

I straddle Keith's lap once more, clawing my nails down his chest toward his belt. Keith lets out a faint whisper: "You seem … pretty happy about that."

With a slow smile, I nod: "I just really like dry-humping people for money."

I do, it's true. I try not to think about retirement from this completely fucked-up and wondrous career I've been enjoying for the past four years. I'm terrified. I've never been so dedicated to any job than this one. I don't know what's next, or how I'm going to channel my penchant for dress-up, sex, manipulation, and secrets into a viable career for the 30-plus crowd, but goddammit, I'm going to manifest one. It might not pay as well, and I might not be encouraged to get drunk all the time, and I just might even have to start paying taxes. But not today.

Hours pass in what feels like minutes and it's time to call it a night. Keith smiles bashfully, handing me a very generous tip. "This was the best visit to the Shoe Show I've had in a long while."

"I really had a nice time with you, too." I say honestly.

---

[71] "Porn is like McDonald's. It's gonna be here, whether you love it or hate it." - Sasha Grey.

"See you in Vegas?"

"See you in Vegas."

" PLEASE HIGH-FIVE YOUR PARENTS FOR GETTING TOGETHER."

– Pouya, 26, Queens

Acknowledgments

Thank you to every stripper everywhere – you inspire me every day to be myself, to keep going, and to never back away from an unpaid debt. I love you all so much. Thank you to every client for investing in the finest of fleshy entertainment in titty bars everywhere. Thank you John Waters, Jane Fonda, Virginie Despentes, Anna Nicole Smith, Elizabeth Berkley, Jennifer Beals, and all the characters in The L Word. To my mother, Karryn Karrys, for always living life on your own terms. Thank you to Fern Massar for your friendship, sharp eyes and unrelenting ability to know what I mean even when I don't. To Anna Maxymiw for your keen focus and making me feel like this might finally be ready to share with the world. To Chris Urquhart for being so radiantly weird and always believing in me. Thank you Emily Ames for bringing the rebel out in me, and to Mallory Bey for always (and I mean *always*) egging me on. And most of all, thank you to Danielle Rafanan: you are the fire in my heart and under my ass. None of this would exist without your unyielding love, support, patience and perseverance. I love you.

About the Author

Jacqueline Frances is a Canadian writer, stripper, illustrator and comedian. She lives in Brooklyn with her wife and plants.